John W. Bear

The Life and Travels

John W. Bear

The Life and Travels

ISBN/EAN: 9783337315252

Printed in Europe, USA, Canada, Australia, Japan

Cover: Foto ©Andreas Hilbeck / pixelio.de

More available books at **www.hansebooks.com**

THE

LIFE AND TRAVELS

OF

JOHN W. BEAR,

"THE BUCKEYE BLACKSMITH."

WRITTEN BY HIMSELF.

BALTIMORE:
D. BINSWANGER & CO., BOOK AND JOB PRINTERS.

1873.

CHAPTER I.

I WAS born in the year 1800, in Frederick County, Maryland, near New Market, of poor but respectable parents, and was the eldest son. At the early age of ten years I was put out to service with an old gentleman by the name of Hagan, who kept a tavern and had several grown sons and a number of slaves; so I was at once deprived of all moral influence. It would be folly for me to describe a country tavern in those days; suffice to say that all the old bloats of the neighborhood would gather there on Saturday and Public days to run horses, fight chickens, drink bad whisky and black each others eyes. Many were the knock downs and bloody noses I saw in the three or four years I lived there. You can well imagine that my moral training was very poor, as I was only a lacky boy for any who chose to avail themselves of my services, and many was the sound flogging I got for not coming up to time.

In the fall of the year when election time came on it was the habit of wealthy politicians to get all the poor white voters they could a day or two before election and furnish them rooms in the upper part of their houses and supply them with plenty of the best the market could afford, and plenty of whisky, and cards to play with, and keep them there until the morning of the election, (this they called cooping,) and then

men and measures they knew nothing about, that I
made up my mind that if ever I became a man that I
would do my own thinking and voting, so I determined
to take Mr. Clay's advice and go to a free country where
I could improve my mind and as he said become a
man. I said nothing about the matter to any person,
but intended the following summer when the weather
got warm to bid farewell to my native land. So one
cold Sunday in March 1 went home to see my mother,
when she gave me a new pair of stockings that she had
knit for herself but were too small for her, and she also
gave me a nice apple. I went home to Hagan's and
hid my apple in the barn intending to give it to a young
girl of my acquaintance the next day, but on Monday
morning before day one of the young Hagans went
with me to the barn to see that I fed the horses right,
when I showed him the apple; he took it away from me
and began to eat it. I commenced fighting him for it
when he slapped me in the mouth until the blood started
when I saw the blood, it at once kindled the fire of in-
dignation in my bosom and I determined to have revenge, so I seized a flail (an article used for thrashing
out grain) and swinging it around at him struck him
on the head just above the ear, and laid him out, as I
thought dead; at any rate he stopped eating my apple.
I felt of his face and found him laying quite still; supposing him dead I thought now is the time for me to
leave, so I went quietly to the house, got my new stockings and a shirt that I had and left by the back door,
as I supposed never to return. This was my first experience in pugilistic affairs. I had often been told that
if a person committed any crime and run away from
his master and could avoid detection for a year and a
day he would de declared free. Now the question
with me was how could I get away, for I had but seventeen cents to travel on, and it was cold weather. I had
many fears that I should freeze or be caught, but go I
must and go I did. There was a stream of water close

by, it was frozen over but not sufficient to bear me—I waded through, cold as it was and made for the Sugar Loaf Mountains. It was a fearful undertaking for a boy not fifteen years old, to undertake such a hazardous journey all alone, without money, education or friends to protect me; but here I was in a cold mountain at daylight in the morning, probably a murderer, and I so young. One thought consoled me, he had struck me first, and I had a right though poor boy as I was to take my own part. I had no knowledge of the country, or where to find freedom, which was a great drawback to me. I had never read a newspaper or book and only knew what little I had gleaned from the conversation of those who had occasionally conversed in my presence. I knew where the Potomac river was, so I made for it, and when I got there the trouble was to cross; it was frozen over, but would the ice bear me; if I fell through I should be drowned. But as luck had it there was no current at that place in the river, so the ice was strong enough to bear me, so after great anxiety and caution, with the aid of a small rail to hold me up if I fell through the ice, I succeeded in safely making my way across.

I must now take a look back at home and see what is going on there. As soon as matters became known at the hotel that there had been a fight between me and young Hagan and that I was missing, they sent a messenger to my mother. After hearing the story that we had been fighting and that the barn floor was pretty well smeared with blood, and I was not to be found she became very much alarmed and at once caused a thorough search to be made; they dragged every spot in the creek where the ice was broken and also searched several old wells in the neighborhood and in fact every place where a person could be concealed, supposing of course that Hagan had murdered and concealed me. Finally when all hope of ever finding me was gone they gave me up as lost. They even went a long distance to consult a fortune teller about me; she told them that I was dead, and they believed her, (what an old liar she was.) Almost every person through the whole country thought that young Hagan had made way with me. Hagan's mother however always said that I would sometime turn up all right, which the reader already knows I did.

We will now return to the South side of the Potomac river. I was now in Virginia, I knew that but it was not a free country and to a free country I was determined to make my way. Mr. Clay had said that I ought to go west, this seemed to impress itself on my mind, so I concluded to take the first road runing west and keep as much out of public roads as I could, and to go to no white peoples house if I could help it. I knew the negroes were like myself, they could not read and I did not fear any detection from them. The Hagans had always told me that if I ran away from them and they caught me that they could sell me the same as if I were a negro. So I had great fear of detection on that account in addition to the fears of being caught as I feared for killing Hagan.

The first idea that struck me when I started, was what name I should go by and what I should tell the people when questioned. I finally concluded to tell the colored people that I had ran away from a hard master and was trying to get to a free country, and promise them when I got there, and became a man, I would help them to get free too, and in this I have been very successful. I also concluded to never tell white people anything, and never give them the same name nor the same place of destination. I had been so badly treated by the Hagans that I had lost all confidence in white people. The only friend I had while at Hagans was an old black woman. She often hid away a cake or piece of pie for me, so I had all confidence in the colored people.

When I left the Potomac river I took the Winchester

road and traveled all day without eating anything and at night stopped at a negro quarter and asked an old woman to give me something to eat and let me stay all night; I told her and her husband all about my affairs, they pitied me very much and I heard them talking after they thought me asleep. They agreed to give me something to take with me to eat, and start me early in the morning a safer road. "The poor little fellow" the old woman said "I will give him all the money I have got to help him along." So before day in the morning they gave me the best they had to eat and some to take with me and a few pennies in money; the old man took me across the country a mile or more, and put me on an old unfrequented road that led to Romney, a small town in the mountains bordering the south branch of the Potomac river. Nothing occurred during the day to mar my progress. I had plenty to eat with me, but when night came the trouble was to find a place to stay. I saw a small house some distance from the road, supposing it was occupied by negroes, I went there but found it occupied by white people. The man was drunk, well this was nothing for me to see, so I asked him if I could stay all night. He said certainly I could, and said, you d——d little rascal I expect that you have run away from some place—well I dont care if you have. Can you sing? I love to hear a good song. I said I could sing Blackeyed Susan, like a bird. Says he that is the exact thing, my wife's name is Susan and she is the best old gal living. Well I was a pretty good singer, and knew several good Irish ditties and other songs, so I amused him for a long time by singing for him; he had plenty of whisky but no meat in the house, but he had a pretty fat pig in a pen. So next morning he concluded that I must stay with him that day and butcher his pig for him. I done so and we had plenty to eat. Next morning when I was ready to start they filled my little bundle with plenty of bread and pork to last me two days; so I went away full of spirits. But I had not traveled more than two hours when a young man on horseback overtook me and called out to me, where are you going you young rascal? I believe you are a run away.

Well, that was an insult I felt bound to resent. So I told him it was none of his business. He up with his horse whip and struck me two or three times across the shoulders; that was too much for me to take from any man, for I began to consider myself some on the muscle since my encounter with Hagan. So I dropped my bundle and up with a good sized stone and hurled at him with such good aim that he began to retreat, and it was well for him he did, for I could throw a stone equal to any man in the country. Now the trouble was he was going the same road that I would probably go, get help, and arrest and put me in jail and that would be the end of me. I finally concluded to die game, so I went ahead and in a few miles came to a store and tavern. I saw his horse tied there and when I came up opposite the tavern he and several young men came out and commenced to laugh. As soon as they did so I stooped and began to gather up several stones and told them to come on, when several of them said that's right my lad, take your own part, and if you can't do it with your fist, do it with stones. They seemed to greatly enjoy my pluck, as did also the fellow who I had stoned.

Nothing of interest occurred for several days. I traveled slowly and whenever I could, staid all night with colored people. At one place I stayed with the owner of a mill. The miller's wife treated me very well but asked me more questions than I cared to answer; I told her at last that I was running away to overtake a young girl to marry her—her parents had sent her away to her uncle to keep her out of my way. This was a choker for her. I told her I was in disguise —that my people were rich. She at last gave me some credit for my perseverance, and at that we parted, never to meet again, though I promised to write to her when I got married, and let her know how I managed to get her. Well, she has had a long time to wait, as I have never overtook the girl yet.

I continued on my journey for several weeks getting along pretty well, the farther I went the less fears I had of being detected; I passed up through Romney, Clarksburgh, and then turned towards Kentucky. I thought that would be a good place for me; I cared but little which way I went, so that I kept out of towns and got to a free country. I went by the Kanawha salt works and from them to the nearest point in Kentucky, but when I got there I found it was a slave state. I stayed several days with a very nice family, it being weather not fit to travel; I found these people very kind to me and wanted me to stay with them, and to do a good part by me, but I was bound to go to a free country and told them what Mr. Clay had said to me about it; they then advised me to go to Indiana. So after a good rest I started and traveled through the interior of Kentucky until I reached the Ohio river, twenty miles below Louisville, where I found some trouble in getting across. I began to think that although in sight of the 'Promised Land' I was never to reach it.

There was a man by the name of Duncan, who had a boat but refused to put me over; he said I was a runaway and he would be put to trouble if it was known that he sent me out of the State. He concluded to have me arrested and kept confined for a time and advertise me as a stray boy. He kept me all night and in the morning while he went to see a Squire, his wife pitied me and a neighbor calling they concluded for the man to take the boat and set me across the river and let me go; she said she would tell her husband that I had got away. When I stepped my foot on Indiana soil the man who put me over the river said to me that I was now on free land and was safe from arrests; he gave me a shilling and wished me good luck and hurried back before Duncan's return. I never heard what he said when he did return, neither do I care, and if I had ever come across him in a free State, I would have learned him how to advertise a runaway boy.

As soon as I got into Indiana I felt comparatively safe and began to think about finding a home; at that early period there were very few people in Indiana.— I very shortly found a place for a few days, and while resting myself I learned that there was a good settlement on the White river, near where Indianapolis now stands, and there being a young man going there I concluded to go with him. When I arrived in the White river settlement I soon found a home with a widow by the name of Miller, who had a son somewhat older than myself and one younger. She was a very kind lady and treated me as a mother. She said she would give me two dollars a month to help her sons clear up land, so I went to work with a will; at the end of two months a neighbor of her's offered me four dollars a month, for I could almost do a man's work. I told her what I had been offered and she agreed to give me the same, as also some old clothes of her sons. I had told her that I had run away from home and wanted to take my money back to help get my mother and father and family to a free country, for which she gave me great credit as also did the neighbors. I remained with her until November, when I concluded to make my way to the east part of Ohio, where I have an Uncle; there was a young man in the neighborhood who seemed to be acquainted with the people around there, who said he was going on to Ohio, and I prepared to accompany him when he went. I had sixteen dollars in silver and gold and Mrs. Miller made me a little belt to carry it in, and in this way I carried it around my body for five or six months, without any person knowing it but Mrs. Miller. Well, this man, I have forgotten his name, and myself started on foot through a wilderness country, for there was only a small settlement every few miles; we had plenty to eat with us the first and part of the second day. The second day at night we came to a small river called Whitewater; it was very much swollen by recent heavy rains, there was no bridge and the question was how shall we cross. This man said he knew where there was a boat a short distance below, and we would go down there and cross and then stay all night with a friend of his. I had some fears that all was not right, but went with him; I could do nothing better, for there were no houses on that side of the river. Well, we traveled several miles, and at last come to the boat; it was a small affair and I was afraid to get in it, for I could not swim, but he coaxed me into it, and when we got into the middle he turned down stream, saying he knew the owner of the boat and it was all right. I was frightened almost out of my senses, I expected to be drowned every moment, but he only laughed at me. We passed over a small mill dam but the water being so high it was nearly smooth over the dam. At last we saw several fires burning in a field, there we landed and tied up the boat, and went to the nearest fire, when he told me to stay there until he went to the house and got something for us to eat. I sat down by the burning log heap and commenced to think matters over. Here I was in a strange land, with a doubtful companion. Just think of it young men, me a boy but fifteen years old, seven hundred miles from home, sitting all alone in the dead hour of night for it was at least two o'clock, not knowing what moment my companion might return and murder me. He might know that I had money, and had therefore coaxed me this lonesome route. I sat there in an awful suspense, until tired nature gave way and I fell asleep. How long I slept I do not know, I only awakened when he called me to get up and get something to eat. How or where he got it I never knew. He said the people on that farm were his friends; but when I asked

him why he did'nt stay there till morning, he said he
wanted to get to Eaton, Ohio, that day. Well we eat
some bread and meat and turnips we found in the field
and pushed on and arrived in Eaton, Ohio about two
o'clock that afternoon. When we got there we found
a number of men playing ball against the Court House.
The Court house was not finished the walls only being
up. I very soon saw several men eyeing us very closely
so much so that I felt somewhat alarmed. At last one
of the men who I learned afterwards was the high
sheriff of the county commenced talking with me and
asking me questions about this man, where I first
got acquainted with him and how long I had known
him. Well I came to the conclusion that my impress-
ions of the night before were correct that I had a sus-
picious companion. So I told this gentleman all I
knew about him, he told me that he should arrest him
on suspicion, which he did. They all had a conversation with me afterwards and came to the conclusion
that I was only a boy and was innocent of any connection with him in his crimes, therefore they let me
go free. A gentleman (a carpenter) took me home
with him and treated me very kindly, and gave me
much good advice which I did not soon forget. During that night some officers of an adjoining county,
came there and found this man in prison arrested and
took him away

The next morning I told some gentleman that I was
trying to get to my uncle's in the eastern part of the
state, and they gave me a little money, and got a gentleman who lived in Dayton, who was going home that
day in a little wagon, to take me that far with him.
When I got to Dayton, this gentleman took me to a
Mr. Hoffman's house, who, he said wanted a boy. I
stayed all night with him, he was a merchant and kept
a dry goods store and was rich. He owned a farm ten
miles up Mad river and wanted me to work with his
hired farmer, and agreed to give me four dollars a

month. I stayed a few days with him until his farmer came down, and then went home with him to go to work till Spring; but when supper was ready I found that I was to eat in the kitchen by myself, his wife being too important to eat with a hired boy, although her husband was a hired man himself. She was a Virginia lady, one of those poor devils that have more hair on their head than brains in it. So next morning I took Scotch leave of that place, and made another start for the East. I stopped all night with a farmer, by the name of Maddox, who took a notion that I must stay with him. I stayed a few days but found a chance to go East with a drove of cattle, the gentleman offering me twenty cents a day and board I started and went as far as Mt. Pleasant in Jefferson county, Ohio, when I heard from my uncle, who lived but a few miles north of there. So I concluded to leave the drove, and go to my uncle's, which I did, and found them very much surprised to see me, so much so that I found it necessary to tell them all.

I would state that here at my uncle's was the first place that I had ever told my real name; I had a different name every place I stopped and intended to do so until the year and a day was out; but by the time I reached my uncle's I had learned considerable of the manners and customs, as well as laws of the country, and was not half so superstitious as I was when I started. I stayed at my uncle's until the middle of March and engaged myself very much with my cousin, a young girl near my age, who took me to every party in the country and there were plenty of them. I became quite a beau among the younger girls and many was the boy that was jealous of me, and was glad when I went away; but the girls were all sorry, even the older ones, for I had become quite a gay boy, and could sing like a nightinggale, which, I suppose, made me popular. But the time arrived for me to start; my uncle sent me to the Ohio river on horseback, I crossed and started on foot for Washington, Pennsylvania, and reached a small town called Hickory, where I stayed all night with a farmer who lived on the edge of the town. He wanted me to stay with him and break flax for him, which I agreed to do at twenty-five cents a day, provided he would find me an old suit of clothes to work in, as I had a new suit I earned while at my uncle's. He had a young daughter who was foolish enough to fall in love with me the first week I was there and the result was that he discharged me to get us apart. Here I was again on the road all alone, making a fresh start for home; the year was now out and I was bound to go home and face the music.

When I left Hickory I went to Washington, Pa., and struck the turnpike road that led East, there I expected to fall in with a wagon going to Baltimore or some place East so that I could have company.— I had great fears of falling in with traveling footmen since the only one I had traveled with proved a dangerous companion for a boy. While I was looking around for a chance a drove of horses came up to the hotel where I was going to stay all-night; I at once made a bargain with the owner to go with him for my board to Frederick, Maryland, where I would be near my home. We started next morning and in three days were in Cumberland, Md., where the owner sold out his horses to a stage company. Here I was again adrift alone in the world, in a strange land, but I had got used to disappointments and vexations, so it had but little effect on me, for I was only a little over a hundred miles from home and I could soon get there. I was standing talking with boys when a man came up and said he wanted two hands to go to Georgetown, D. C., on a boat loaded with flour, for which he would give fifty cents a day with board, there and back. I told him that I wanted to go there and would go for fifty cents a day without being paid for my time coming back, but that I had never worked on a boat but could learn. He said he would take me, for any person could help pull an oar; so the next morning found me a boatman on the Potomac.

The first day out we had a fine time at it. I soon learned to pull an oar, but the second day just before dark we got on a rock and had to stay there all-night without anything to eat, for we had no place for fire, to cook with, and we all expected to be drowned before we got through with the scrape we were in; but as luck had it, next day the water raised and we got off; we went ashore and built a fire, cooked and eat until we were filled. When we made a second start we went on smoothly until we got within four or five miles of Georgetown when we brought ourselves up on another rock; here we were in for another nights peril, but we managed some how next morning, about ten o'clock, to get off, and in one hour more we were safely landed at the wharf; we had eat but little for twenty-four hours, so we went to a tavern kept for boatmen, and such a breakfast I never eat before or since as I eat there. We had slept but little, so we all went to bed and got a good sleep; the next morning the Captain paid me off and I started for home which was about thirty-three miles. I started full of hopes and fears, for I had never heard a word from home since I left, which was then some fourteen months, but go I must and go I did. When I got within four miles of my mothers house I stayed all-night, for I wanted to hear the news and get home in the morning. The family I stayed with knew me and told me all about the affairs at home and was glad to see me alive. I waited the next morning until after breakfast and then started for home. I avoided the neighbours as much as I could, as I had a desire for my mother to be the first to know that I was still alive, and I think the longest mile I ever traveled was the mile that brought me home. I went to the house the back way and when there walked around to the front door and there stood my mother washing her breakfast dishes; I shall never forget the scene that then occurred; she gave one loud scream and then caught me in her arms and fell on her knees and thanked God for my safe deliverance to her. She could scarcely believe her own eyes, I had grown considerably and been gone so long that she thought it almost impossible that I was the same. Poor mother! although near fifty years have rolled around since then, and more than forty years have passed since you were called to that land where sighing and sorrow never comes, your image is still impressed indelibly on my mind, and I never will forget the many blessings you heaped upon my head the day I returned home when you thought me dead.

Young reader, remember this, that every sigh and every pain you give your mother will only return to torment you when she is gone. Oh! what a pleasing thought, when you are about to take the last look in this world at your mother, to think that you never caused her one sigh or tear by your disobedience to her.

My father and younger sisters and brothers soon gathered around me and we had a grand rejoicing; my oldest sister was sent for (she living out a sewing) and she too, at first, refused to believe that I was really her brother. In a few days we all became ourselves again. My mother and father were highly pleased with the money I had brought them and had made up their minds from what I told them to remove to the West. So it was agreed that I should go up the Monocacy Valley and work through hay-making and harvest and earn all I could and then in the Fall all go to Ohio. I went and mowed, hauled hay, cut grain and oats, and helped gather all the harvest crops which kept me two months; I made a man's wages the whole time. When I was done I had a nice little pile of money, for I had not spent a cent. I then left for home, I came to Frederick, bought myself a nice suit of clothes and had twenty dollars left for my mother. Upon my arrival home we immediately made preparations for going West, and by the first of October we were all on the road with an old horse and cart to seek our fortune in Ohio, where we arrived safely in about three weeks.

I felt very proud to think that I had been able to earn enough money to take my father and mother, sisters and brothers to a free country and that, too, before I was sixteen years old, for I was only sixteen a few days after we arrived in Ohio. I make this statement to show young men and boys what perseverance will do. After our arrival in Ohio we all went to work to fix for the winter; we settled in a small village called Flushing, in Belmont county, about twenty miles north-west of Wheeling, Va., where some of the family still reside. It was soon agreed upon that the family could very well do without my services, as everything was cheap and a great demand for all kind of labor, so I concluded to learn the blacksmith trade. I went to work the first of the year with a Mr. Jones who was a fine workman; I had a natural talent for that business and by Spring could do almost any kind of work. My boss declared that I had been at the trade before I came to him; he said no person could learn as much as I knew in so short a time; he gave me four dollars a month for the next six months commencing the first of April. I stayed with him until Fall and gave all I earned to my mother for she took care of my clothes.

It was during this year that I first began to shape my political course. That region of Ohio was settled by people from all parts of the East, consequently there was a mixed population, which led me to take the course in politics I did. It was this: whenever I met with boys or girls of my own age that came from Maryland or Virginia, I found them uneducated and ignorant, as much so as myself and family, (it was true I had learned considerable in my travels,) but when I met with boys and girls from Pennsylvania or any of the Eastern States they were well educated and sharp. I looked at this, I studied the matter over, I thought nature had done as much for one as the other. Then what was the cause of the difference?— There was a difference; if any of us wanted a letter written we had to go to a Northern family to get it done, (none of us could write a word.) Well, after long and patient investigation of the subject, I saw the cause : it was slavery. In the North it was the policy of the leaders to educate the masses so as to fit every man for usefulness. In the South, it was the policy of the slave holder to keep the masses of the poor whites in ignorance, in order that they could the better use them to sustain their own peculiar institutions. If you educate the poor white man, he, laboring and being in daily intercourse with the slave, will educate him, and as soon as the negro is educated he will no longer be a slave ; further, if you educate the poor white man you thereby teach him that he has rights, and therefore you can no longer coop him up and vote him as you have been doing, so the only plan was to keep them uneducated, which has ever been the policy of the South, until this day. After I had fully made up my mind on this point I was determined that no vote of mine should ever be given to any man or party that would sanction the perpetuation of this system, and as time rolled on and I became a man and voter I discovered that the democratic party was the apologist of the slave power, and as such could never get a vote from me, and how well I have kept my resolution you will see when I tell you that in fifty years voting I have never voted for a democrat.

I will now return to my former subject. I stayed with Jones until October when I concluded that I would travel a year and work under instructions with different bosses thinking it the better plan. I had a great idea that Pennsylvania was the greatest country in the world, so I concluded to finish my trade there. About this time there was a man from Pennsylvania buying cattle through our country and I made a bargain to go with him east; he gave me fifty cents a day with no return money and advanced my mother ten dollars. So I left home again, this time with my mothers consent to be gone a year; by this time I considered myself a man, and was a pretty good workman at some things. I could shoe a horse with the best of them.

Nothing unusual occurred during our long and tedious journey. We arrived at last at a place called Doe Run, Chester Co., Pennsylvania, where, in the course of a week, my boss sold out his cattle, paid me a small balance due, and I started to hunt work. I went back to the Susquehanna river to a small town called Highspire and went to work with a man under instructions to learn edge tool making. This was a branch of the business much needed in the West, and I knew but little about it. A few days after my arrival there the young people got up what they called a Strouse dance, a thing which I had never seen, of course every man had a right to go and take a girl with him if he bought a ticket; I being an entire stranger, had no girl, but went by myself to see the fun.

When I arrived the tickets were all sold but one, and I bought that one. They were waiting to sell the last ticket so as to begin the dance. A Strouse dance is nothing more nor less than this: The manager buys the materials for a full suit for a lady, (dress, bonnet, shoes, stockings, &c.,) spreads them on a pine bush as a prize; they then place a candle in a dark lantern, tie a string around it, pass the string through the lantern and fasten a small key to it on the outside,

*2

light the candle and commence dancing a regular step around the room. The manager, when the dancing begins, hands the head of the column a small stick; he carries it around the room, hands it to his partner, if he has one, if not, he carries it twice around and then hands it to the next, and he to his partner, she to the next, and so on, until at the end of several hours the candle burns down to the string, burns it off and the key falls; whoever has the stick when the key falls, wins the strouse. If it is a gentleman he gives it to his partner, if a lady it is hers. Well, I had the luck to win the strouse which caused no little jealousy among the young men, and all the girls wondered who would get it, as I had no partner. After the strouse is over they turn it into a general hoe-down dance; I having no partner got my eye on a pretty good looking girl and asked her partner to allow her to dance with me but he at once refused, telling me to get a partner for myself. I felt very indignant at such an insult, but concluded, as I was a stranger, not to resent it there but settle the matter with him some other time. I was very stout, and but few men could handle me but withal was very quiet, preferring fun to fighting, but never intended to take an insult without resenting it to the best of my ability. I therefore walked away without saying anything; the whole party seemed to enjoy his insult to me. The young girl immediately walked up to me and said for his insulting language she would dance with me. I took her by the hand, walked out on the floor, paid the fiddler to play a tune and danced a set with her. When we got through the dance I led her to a seat and sat down by her. As soon as we were seated her partner came up and said he could thrash any man that would take another's partner from him. I raised from my seat and told him that I had not taken his partner from him but she had left him of her own accord, and so far as thrashing was concerned that he could not whip one side of me, and whenever he thought he could, to just pitch in. This caused considerable commotion among the crowd; he started at me in a menacing manner, when I simply dealt him a blow above his eye that laid him flat on the floor; I gave him a few kicks when he cried out take him off. I had not been scratched. I found several of them preparing for a fight, when one of them said: you can't do that with me. I said come out in the street, I can thrash you all. Out they all rushed, pulling off their coats as they went; I followed and in laying down my coat on a pile of stones I picked up a good sized one, held it in my hand and made at the man who was to fight me and dealt him a blow that laid him out as they thought for dead; no one knew that I struck him with a stone nor did they ever know. The whole crowd immediately made a rush on me with clubs, and one with an axe knocked me down, and if it had not been for several strong teamsters that were working among their horses across the street at a tavern, they would no doubt have killed me. My employer and several others came and took me home, and the first thing I knew was the next day, when I found myself in my room pretty badly beat and cut about the head. The young girl and her mother were sitting by me taking care of me.— The girl had not left me one moment since I had got home. She had my prize all safe and had sent for her mother; of course I gave her the prize and in a few days was all right again. I visited her several times after I got able to go about. One Sunday a few weeks after my fight I walked down the river a mile or so to a tavern kept on the river bank, when I met one of the fellows who helped to beat me. He asked me to drink, when I took a tumbler of whisky and threw tumbler, whisky and all into his face, knocked him down and paid him well for his share in beating me. I knew that I could not stay in that place any longer and I went home, settled with my boss, visited my girl and left. I never saw her after that, but heard several years after, that she had married well and was considered one of the first women in the country.

After crossing the river I went to York and got work with an excellent man by the name of Elefritz, where I stayed until harvest. During the Spring there was a regimental muster in York when all the country people of course came to town; during the evening I saw a young man mistreating a young girl; I thought this a proper time for me to show my manhood, to protect a female, so I stepped up and asked what was wrong. The girl said he wanted to go home with her and because she refused him he had insulted her; I told him to leave or I should make him do so. The crowd raised a great laugh when I said I will go with you my little duck and she took my arm and away we went amid the shouts of the crowd of old and young. He followed to have revenge as he said; well, he got it in the shape of being knocked down and kicked two or three times, but I went home with the girl and stayed until next day, and so ended this affair.

At the beginning of harvest I went back to Maryland to work on the Monocacy with my old employers at harvesting. I earned a nice little sum this time also. I then left for Hancock, a town on the road to Cumberland, Md.,) to shoe horses for Reeside & Co., stage proprietors. I worked there several months, when my boss ran away and I lost all my wages, he having drawn all the money and kept it—his name was Pool.

I packed my kit and started for new quarters, and had not travelled far before I fell in with a man going west; when we came to the foot of a mountain he said he knew a short path across the mountain that would save several miles walk, so we went that way and when we had got to the top of the mountain we sat down to take a drink of whisky, for we had a bottle full with us; we had just taken a drink when he was seized with a fit, and continued to rave and froth at the mouth for a long time. Just think of it, here I was on the top of a high mountain two miles from a living being, all alone, with as I thought a dying man ; what to do I did not know. I began to pour whisky into him when at last he became sensible and able to walk ; I managed to get him down the hill to a tavern on the road, and there I left him and never heard of him since.

I found work at Bevan's tavern at the foot of Twin mountains, with a man by the name of Knight, to shoe horses for the stage company; he was a poor, drunken sot and I soon found that he was not the man for me, but not until I had got myself in a scrape about him. One night he got into a fuss with one of the stage drivers who I saw choking him severely ; when I went to his assistance the man let go of him and with a stable fork struck me across the head and gave me a mark that I shall carry to my grave. I was not able to thrash him, for he was very stout, so from shear necessity I had to let the matter rest there, and as soon as I was able I started for Cumberland, Md.

I had not received a cent for more than four months work and began to think that I had better go home, but got work with a very good man who gave me good wages and paid me honestly, his name was Riser who I believe is still living. But while I was at Cumberland I became acquainted with L. W. Stockton, who run a line of stages to Wheeling, Va. He took a liking to me and offered me a shop and tools to shoe horses for him twelve miles east of Uniontown, Pa., so I packed up and left for my new field of labor. I got along finely, the drivers all liked my shoeing and I had plenty of time to do considerable other work. Soon after I went to this place there was a wood chopping and quilting in the neighbourhood and all the mountain girls and boys were invited, I among the rest. I went and was finely dressed, which took the eye of the girls as you all know it will do, so it was little wood that I chopped; I had plenty to do to talk to the girls. This of course caused some jealousy among the mountaineers, so when night came and dancing began, I went to the kitchen and commenced singing; being a good singer, I soon had the whole flock of girls around me; none wanted to dance while I would sing; this stirred up a fuss, one fellow said to his girl, if she refused to go to the other room and dance with him there would be a bear skinned before morning. My name being Bear, I knew he alluded to me—this was an insult which I resented at once, by saying that he nor any of his friends could skin me. I had but one friend there as I knew of and he but a small pattern, but I always found that a game chicken generally fared the best, so I showed pluck to the last. No sooner had I said what I did than he and others began to strip for a fight; I always found that the first lick was an advantage so I hauled away at him and laid him out and was not long settling matters with him, when another fellow began to say something, I up with my fist and laid him out. At this moment a large, powerful looking man was pulling off his coat as I supposed to attack me, but to my supprise he stepped out and swore that I could lick any man in the mountains, and if I could not, he could, and slapped me on the shoulder and called me by my first name and said he knew me from childhood, although I did'nt know him; "Say what you please and I will back you." Well in less than ten minutes we had cleaned the house and had the field to ourselves; they went for my girl's father, he came to take her home but we out-witted the old man and got out of his way.

The next Sunday I went with her to a woods meeting two or three miles from there, where this whole party saw us, as I expected they would and so prepared myself; I borrowed a pair of fine pistols from the landlord I boarded with and went without fear. When we started home the two that I had licked and another followed us; I told the girl not to be frightened, neither was she, as I soon found out. When we had got a short distance from the meeting they came up to us and said "we will now settle our old scrape." Agreed boys, said I and hauled out both pistols and held them all cocked and ready to fire right at them and said, leave you villains or I will blow your brains out. Well you never saw three such scared men in your life; I said run or I'll fire. They began to back out, I following up and the girl saying shoot them, shoot them. Just at this time I saw my large friend with one or two others, coming on the run, for they had missed us and supposed that they had followed us; when they saw my friends coming they took to their heels and ran like wild turkeys down through the woods; I fired one shot after them, only to scare them, and it was the last I saw of them, as I never had the pleasure of meeting them again.

I stayed at that place several months, until my mother desired me so earnestly to come home (for I had sent her regular letters as also a little money) that I concluded to go home, which I did and arrived home in the Fall, about the same time I had left two years before. I was now a grown man and made up my mind that I would quit travelling and settle down to work, as I was now nineteen years old and tired of travelling.

My friends were all glad to see me and I to see them. I rested a week or two and then got work seven miles from home, but went home every Saturday night.

My mother and father were getting along very well at this time, with what little I helped them. So in order to keep me from travelling away from home my mother advised me to get married although I was so young, which on the 6th of the following month I did. With this narrative of my early history and travels I shall drop the curtain over my early life. Hoping that all young men and boys who read this chapter may find means and opportunity to improve upon the course that I pursued, as many might have done worse than I did, with the start in life that I had. In all my short comings I never forgot my mother, nor did I ever forget that one great idea, that honesty is the best policy. If I had not pursued that course, I never should have gotten through as well as I did.

CHAPTER II.
MY START IN POLITICAL LIFE.

THE first thing after my marriage, was to get a shop and commence business for myself, although I could neither read or write, I thought that I could get along very well, as my wife was a good scholar, and in place of trying to get an education, I would study the human character, and politics. I had seen so much of the deception of men, both in and out of politics, that I thought it was of vital importance to a successful career in life, to thoroughly understand the human character, and in this I think I was pretty successful.

Nothing occurred until the year 1824 to divide the people in politics in our section of country, until Gen. Jackson was nominated for the Presidency as was also Henry Clay, John Q. Adams and Wm. Wirt.

I very soon found that Gen. Jackson was not the man for me. Every man in our county who was opposed to free schools, free labor, or protection to American industry, was a Jackson man. At that time most of our people were ignorant of these subjects, which were new to them, and consequently did not meet their approbation. I differed with the most of them, believing that the only hope of laboring men was in free education and protection to their industry, against the cheap labor of the old world.

In addition to the above I had learned to read a little, and had got hold of the history of England and found that as far back as 1447 Edward III. had said that no nation could ever become independent, that depended upon any other country for supplies. I had fully investigated the matter, and came to the conclusion that so long as we, as a nation, purchased more from other countries than we sold to them we thereby brought the balance of trade against us, and had to pay in cash the difference between what we bought and sold. In this way we were continually draining our country of our gold and silver. I believed and do yet, that in order to become prosperous as a nation, we must sell more than we buy, thereby bringing the balance of trade in our favor. Of this I was convinced and so I argued, and on this point I took my stand against Gen. Jackson.

As soon as it was known that Gen. Jackson had been defeated by the people, I took a decided stand for Mr. Adams, as Mr. Clay was not in the field, and at once became a warm supporter of the Tariff that passed the following winter, known as the Tariff of 1824. I then commenced looking at parties as they stood in our own state, and soon found that the Jackson Party were the men to pass negro laws and oppose free schools and every other measure calculated to elevate labor and the cause of freedom.

Every four weeks there came a colored itinerant

Preacher along and I invited him to preach for us in a small Methodist church near by, — the society gave their consent, and turned out in a body to hear him, when they all agreed he could out preach any man they had heard for a long time, but no person would invite him to his home. Although I was not a Methodist I would not see the man after kindly preaching for us such a good sermon turned out of doors, so I invited him to stay with me, which he did. As soon as it was known that I had "harboured," as they called it, a negro, several of my customers took their work from me, and I was so much persecuted for that act, that I moved to another place. This act only confirmed me more fully, that the Democratic party was the apologist for slavery and were opposed to freedom and the elevation of the poor man. Further I found that almost every good Christain man of broad progressive views, was a Whig. The reader will thus see the reason I had for my opposition to the Democratic party.

As soon as Mr. Adams took his seat and appointed Mr. Clay his Secretary of State, the whole Jackson party began a howl about bargain and sale; a more villainous and black-hearted falsehood was never hatched out of Hell than that charge, as all readers know. Mr. Clay was a Senator at the time and had no vote on the question; the Lower House of Congress alone electing the President by States, Mr. Clay simply using his influence as a Senator, with the delegation from his state in Congress for Mr. Adams, as he had a right to do the same as any other citizen. I have no doubt but that charge of bargain and sale had much to do in the defeat of Mr. Clay in 1832, as many of the old Democrats believed the story. Some of them the ignorant ones especially, believe it to this day; and I do not wonder when I look at the complexion of the present Democratic Party. During the interval between the elections of 1824 and 1828, I gathered all the information I could from the best men of our country, on the great questions that were then agitating the public mind, such as the Tariff, and National Bank, and many were the debates and disputes I had with the friends of Jackson on the subject. Our disputes often run very high, and many were the black eyes and bloody noses I gave them for their abuse of Mr. Adams and his principles. The Democratic party was then, as it is now, composed of the roughs and ignorant portion of the country. In nine cases out of ten, at that period, as well as at the present time, whenever you found a man whose skull was too thick for one sensible idea to penetrate it, that man was a Democrat. In my young and wild days I concluded, that if I could not talk "common sense" into their heads, I would beat it in them. So whenever they began to abuse Mr. Adams or Mr. Clay, in my presence, I generally paid them for it with a bloody nose.

I was in the habit of speaking at small meetings about the country, in those days, and on one occasion the Democrats said that no Whig should speak at a school house in the upper end of the county. I thought this was a chance for me to show my pluck, so I went to the school directors and rented the school-house for a certain Saturday afternoon, and drew up a regular lease for it, paying twenty five cents for rent; so that afternoon the property was mine; I then got a man by the name of Sills, in an adjoining county, who was a great fighter, to go with me. We took our rifles with us, and at the appointed time we were on the spot. I told the people that I had come to speak, and that I was on my own property and did not intend to be interrupted. Many of them knew Sills as well as they knew me, and concluded that the better way for them was to keep quiet. I made as strong a speech as I could. After I closed I invited them to reply, when one of them stepped froward and commenced to deny some of my charges against his party; but I floored

him in that, by producing a Democratic speech in Congress, portions of which I had just quoted, and thereby raised the laugh on him by his own friends. When the meeting was over, Sills and myself mounted our horses bidding them good-bye and asked them if they had any more school-houses at which Whigs dare not speak, if they had to let us know it. With this we rode off singing
"The star spangled banner in triumph shall wave.
O'er the land of the free and the home of the brave."

Just before the election in 1828, I removed some distance West to Muskingum County, where I was not known, and being a stranger, said but little on politics, as nearly all my neighbours were Democrats, therefore but few knew my politics until the day of election. There were but five votes polled for Mr. Adams, in our election district, and one of them was mine. The Jackson men knew of but four Adams men in the district, and when they found five votes for him, they offered a gallon of whisky, (for whisky was then as it is now, their staple commodity) for any one to show them the fifth man. I stepped up and said "I don't want your whisky gentlemen, but I am the man you are looking for, what do you want with me?" when something was said about licking the man that did it. I said gentlemen, I heard something said about licking the man that did it. I voted for Adams, and I can thrash any Jackson man in the county, and whenever you are ready bring on your best man for to begin with. They immediately in a most cowardly manner crowded around me, and all that could get a chance to strike me fell on me and beat me nearly dead. The poor cowardly devils then left me to be taken home by one of my neighbours. Well I paid two of them well for it afterwards. One or two of the leaders left the neighborhood and I never met them again.

Jackson was elected, and things as they usually do, after the election is over, settled down quietly and all bitter feeling mostly subsided. Things went on pretty smoothly until the summer of 1832, when my great friend and favorite, Henry Clay, of Kentucky, was nominated for the Presidency by the Whig party.— I was determined to make use of every available means to secure his election, and spent much of my time in my county, riding around among the people, holding friendly talks with them, showing them that Jackson's course in removing the deposits from the State banks, and his opposition to the protective policy of the Whig party, would work detrimental to the best interest of the country. In this way I got the greater part of the people to thinking, and examining the subject for themselves. So strongly did I agitate the subject, that when the election came off, the same district that gave Adams but five votes four years before, gave Mr. Clay fifty-six majority. But with all of Jackson's arbitrary acts staring him in the face, the people had not become enlightened enough to defeat him, and he was re-elected in preference to that great and good man, Henry Clay.

I shall now drop the curtain for a short time as nothing occurred of any note, until 1834, when our county had become pretty evenly divided in politics.— The Democrats began to have some fears that they would loose the county, as there was an election to take place that winter, as a Supreme Judge was to be elected by the Legislature, and our county was entitled to two members of the Lower House, and one Senator. So both parties went to work with a will.— There were some public improvements going on in our end of the county, which employed about a hundred Irish laborers, the most of them were not entitled to vote, but the Democrats, as usual, were determined to vote them; and in order to carry out their villainous plan, they got all their tickets printed on blue paper in order that if any man undertook to vote a white ticket, that was not entitled to vote, they would challenge his vote. I found this out a day or so before the election, and went to town and got the same kind of tickets printed, headed Democratic ticket, with all Whig names for offices. The night before the election I went to the Irish shanties, and gave them the tickets, charging them not to show the tickets to any person, for the Whig's would find it out and counterfeit them. So the next day, when the Irish saw all the Democratic tickets were blue, they, of course, thought it all right, and the most of them voted our ticket. No person knew anything about it until it was too late, and we thereby elected our whole ticket. The Democrats never forgave me for that trick while I lived in that county. Had the Irish have gotten hold of me that night after the election was over, they would have treated me pretty roughly; but I had glory enough over our victory in the election of our whole ticket without stopping to consult the feelings of my worthy Irish friends, who so blindly voted our ticket.

Time passed on, when in 1836 Gen. Harrison was the nominee of the Whig party for the Presidency.— I again went to work in my own county, using all my ability to secure his election. Then was the time to have run Mr. Clay! Van Buren was a very weak man, having nothing to recommend him to public favor, except the popularity of Gen. Jackson. This, I always thought, Mr. Clay could have overcome.— Harrison was poor and not very well known; Jackson took advantage of this, and by recommending Van Buren to his friends and bringing the patronage of the Government to bear in his favor, succeeded in electing him.

There was one incident that occurred in that Campaign that I wish to relate in order to show, to what length the Democrats would go to carry a point, when hard pushed. I had been a thorn in their side in that county for a year or two back, and they were determined to have some revenge upon me. So the morning of the election in 1836 they got one of their tools to swear out a warrant for me for selling whisky without license when I had never sold a drop of whisky in my life, with or without license. They had me arrested and taken twelve miles to the county town, thinking to hold me until too late to vote, but in this they failed; I gave security and got back in good time, not only to vote, but to thrash two of their dupes who had undertaken to do the dirty work for them, and in a few days my trial came off and I was honorably acquitted.

The night of election I carried the vote of our district to town. We had beat them pretty badly in our district as well as through the county, which raised their dander to such a pitch, that their candidate for Congress, finding how matters stood, rallied a lot of his rowdy friends to thrash us Whigs who were rejoicing over our victory, among them one Casey, a gambler, and a loafer, who said he could lick any Whig in the town, and bantered me out to fight, but as I did not feel inclined to dirty my hands with such a character as he was, I just picked up a good sized stone, and hurled it at his head, which settled him for that night. We then rallied, drove the whole herd from the field, and went to this Casey's gambling hell and smashed in every window in it, and thus had our revenge for the insult they gave us. Casey was glad to get off as well as he did, and their candidate for Congress hid himself or he would have fared badly, as did several of their leaders. After the election was over all our bitter feelings soon died away, and all went on right again.

As all my youthful days had been spent in wandering about the world, I had little inclination to remain in one place long, so in the Spring of 1837 I heard of a good place for my business in South Bloomfield, Pickaway county, on the Scioto river a few miles South of Columbus. To this place I removed and went to work.

The little village I moved to as well as the township in which it was the only village, was composed of Whigs. We could beat them five to one, this suited me, as I could now say and do almost as I pleased.—Sometimes some hard-shell Democrat would come to town and imbibe a little too freely in democratic argument (whisky) when some of the boys would put him on a small hand cart they called a rolling machine and give him a good ride around, to shake his democratic principles out of him. Whenever any of these fellows got too much for the boys we men would come to their rescue.

I soon became very popular with the people in that place, for I was considered the best posted man on politics in the county, as I had thoroughly studied every question of that day. Whenever I could not fully understand a question, in place of remaining in ignorance, I always went to some well posted man and got the information I needed. In this way I had learned much of what I knew.

Here allow me to remark, that thousands of young men and old ones too, remain all their lives in ignorance of very much valuable information because of a very foolish conceited notion, that no person is able to learn them anything. I have often talked with men, who were entirely ignorant of the subject they were talking about, and could have learned them much that would have been valuable to them but they were conceited and refused to be enlightened. This is, in a great measure, the cause of so much ignorance in the world. I have seen men so ignorant on the subject of politics, that they charged the Declaration of Independance with being a Whig lie, because a young Whig lawyer read it at a Fourth of July celebration. Had a Democrat have read it he would have called it the best thing he ever heard. One Democrat in the mountains of Virginia refused to go and hear me make a Tariff speech, because he thought it was a disease among cattle and that I was going to tell them that I knew a cure. He said that all I would tell them was a lie, for it could not be cured, that he knew of three cows that had died of the disease only a few days ago up the country a few miles from him. Of such men as he we find plenty in the Democratic ranks. They are the men they want, as such men can be more easily controlled than men of sense and information. Just tell such a fellow that it is all a damned Whig lie and he goes away fully satisfied, without investigating the subject for himself. Of such men we could never make Whigs or Republicans. To be a Whig or a Republican, a man must be possessed of thought and action, of enterprise and progress, not willing to stand still and remain where our fathers left us, but to press forward, and open wide the gates, that lead to the prosperity and to the elevation of every living being.

During the Summer and Fall of 1839 there was much speculation about who would be the Whig candidate for the Presidency at its next National Convention that was to meet at Harrisburg, Pa., in December of that year. Finally when they met they nominated Gen. Harrison, this time with a fair prospect of electing him. The Whigs of Ohio immediately made arrangements to hold a grand ratification meeting the 22d of the following February, and accordingly sent invitations to all the neighbouring States to join them; they expected to make (as they did) a grand affair of it. So by the 20th the people began to come to Columbus by thousands, from all parts of the country, so much so that by the 21st there was no place to put them, every house had to be turned into a hotel. They came in all possible ways, had all kinds of banners and devices and were dressed in all kinds of costumes, representing every trade and country that could be thought of, hauling on their wagons steamboats, forts, log cabins, coons tied on long poles, barrels of cider and every other conceivable thing, as a burlesque on what the Democrats had said of Gen. Harrison, they having called him the log cabin, hard cider and coon skin candidate when a candidate in 1836.

On the morning of the 21st I too concluded to go in my blacksmith clothes, leather apron and all. So I started with my leather apron on and my face all black just as I came out of the shop, and arrived in Columbus just as they commenced speaking at the main stand and by twelve o'clock they were speaking at several stands.

It was a miserable day, wet and cold, but none of us cared for the weather, we were too much elated by the great demonstration around us. The Convention adjourned about 2 o'clock to enable the various committees to prepare shelter for the great multitude of people; I was standing by the main-stand, talking with some friends, when Col. Cochran, a customer of mine, who had often heard me talk at our Primary meetings in our town, stepped up and said: "Get on the stand Bear and give us a speech, you can do it as well as the best of them." "No sir," said I, "that would be too much for me," when he called out, "Bear, a speech from Bear—gentlemen he is a first-rate speaker." The crowd rushed on me, and before I had time to think about it, had hoisted me on the stand. Well, here I was with at least twenty thousand people around me, yelling at the top of their voices, "He's a blacksmith, he's a blacksmith, go on, go on, I know that you can speak." Here I was, a plain, humble mechanic, that had never made a speech in all my life, to more than a few dozen people and they my acquaintances.— What was I to do with thousands of well educated men around? If I said nothing they would think I was a fool; if I made a speech I could only make a fool of myself, so I concluded to pitch in, and pitch in I did.

As luck would have it, I saw before me Sam. Medary, the editor of the leading Democratic paper in Ohio.

This Medary had been State printer, a few years before, and had used the outside quires of the paper belonging to the State without giving any account of it, which amounted to several hundred dollars, which the Whigs made him pay for when they got the control of the State a few years after. This circumstance gave Sam. the name of the "Outside Quires," and every man in the State knew him by that name. So I concluded to pitch into him to begin with by telling a dream I had made up on him. I said:

GENTLEMEN—"I see before me my old and worthy friend Sam. Medary. I am glad to see you Sam. for I had a very singular dream about you last night. I dreamed that I was coming to this Convention, and met the devil who said to me "where are you going Bear," said I to Columbus, to the Whig Convention.— Why, said he, "I thought the Whig's were all divided, some for Harrison, some for Clay, and some for John McLean and so on," said I "they were divided before the National Convention, but they are all united now. He said : "This will never do," and calling a dozen or two of his little imps that were around him, said : "boys I want you to go through Ohio, divide the Whig's, separate them if possible, if you can't do it any other way, lie them out of it." They started and he turned to me and said : "bye the bye, when did you see my old and worthy friend Sam. Medary," said I "a few days ago." "Well, what is Sam. doing now-adays," "he is editing the *Ohio Statesman* said I." "What!" said he in surprise, "is Sam. Medary at the head of that paper," and turning around said at the top of his voice, "come back boys, come back, if Sam. Medary is at the head of the *Ohio Statesman*, and can't lie the Whig's out of it, all the devils in hell can't do it, so it is no use of your going."

This raised a shout among the crowd, when Sam. looked up and said : "that's a lie." I took hold of my coat and said : "say that again Sam. and I'll take off the outside quires for you;" this was too much for the crowd, they all understood it, I thought they would tear up the earth on which they stood, with their long continued shouts, and before they subsided, Sam. had to leave, it became too hot for him, so I had the field all to myself, when I pitched into Van Buren's weakest points and made the best of it that I could.

When I concluded my speech and came from the stand, my friends and many of the crowd gathered around me, so much so, that I had fears that they would crush me to death in their eagerness to shake hands with me, and congratulate me upon my success as a speaker. Col. Cochran, as soon as he could, got me away from the crowd, when thousands of them followed me with the wildest enthusiasm, determined to shake me by the hand, as they said, they had never seen such a blacksmith. At length he got me in a house of one of his acquaintances, where he had a chance to talk to me. He told me that I had that day made a man of myself, that I had immortalized my name, and that he felt proud of me as a citizen of his town.

Col. Cochran was a worthy citizen of our town, and I felt proud of his good opinion of me. After some time spent with him I left and went to the lower part of town and stayed all night with a friend of mine (a blacksmith.) During that night I heard nothing more about the blacksmith, but by daylight the Whig committee of Columbus had found me, when to my surprise I was surrounded by a body of the leading men of the State, enquiring who and what I was. They said the whole town had been in the wildest excitement all night about me, and that Sam. Medary had devoted the half of his paper in abusing me, and they said that I must be of some account or Sam. would not have devoted so much time and space to me.

"Well, gentlemen," said I, "you see me as I am, a plain mechanic, with but little education, and all that I know I have learned of such men as you; as regards my speaking, I never made a speech in my life until yesterday, unless it was at a school-house meeting, and I suppose that my popularity grows out of the fact, that I am a plain working man." They at once said, that I must be announced as one of the speakers from the main stand, so that the most of the people could hear me. After considerable talk I very reluctantly agreed to the arrangement, and by ten o'clock, the hour the convention met, I was placarded all over town, as the Pickaway Blacksmith, to speak as the second speaker at the main stand. (I was a citizen of Pickaway county, hence the above title.)

But Prentiss of the *Louisville Journal,* soon after that, gave me the title of the Buckeye Blacksmith, in honor of Ohio, which was called the Buckeye-state, and which name I have always borne since.

At the appointed hour the convention met; I had prepared a boy with a blacksmith's tongs, and a basin of water, some soap and a towel. When it was my turn to speak, I stepped forward, with leather apron on, sleeves rolled up, and tongs in hand, ready for business, amid the shouts of the multitude. When order was restored, I said, "Gentlemen of the convention, I have a very dirty job to do, so I have my tongs with me, as you see." Medary's paper was lying on the stand, I lifted it up with the tongs, read a short paragraph from it, and then let it fall, and wiped my feet on it, then called for soap and water, washed the tongs and sent them to their owner, as I said, without defiling them with such a dirty thing as Sam. Medary's paper. This caused the wildest excitement I ever saw; I repeated much that I had said the day before, but the people were too much excited to notice it.

I would here state, that I have no doubt but that my little spat with Medary the day before, and his severe attack on me in his paper that morning had very much to do in giving me the great notoriety that has since followed me as a speaker. Had not Medary attacked me as he did, the Whigs would never have found me, and I should have gone home as others did, went to work and never have been known out of my own county, but his unmanly attack put the Whigs to investigating me, which resulted in my being placed before the public as one of their speakers, a position I have occupied ever since. Therefore whatever popularity I have ever attained, I owe it all to Sam. Medary.

When I came from the stand that day I was overwhelmed with congratulations by the leading Whigs of Ohio, as also of other States. That night meetings were held at various places about town, and I spoke at two of them, one at the Buckeye House, and the other at the Market House. It was at this last meeting I first met our present distinguished soldier and statesman, General Schenck.

After the meetings were over myself and company left for home, where we arrived about sunrise next morning. It was no sooner known, that I had gotten home, than all my neighbours without regard to party or sex flocked around me to congratulate me upon my great success (as they said) at Columbus the last two days. Col. Cochran was spokesman and made a little speech of welcome to which I had to reply. This was the hardest job of my life, to reply to the eulogies of my near neighbors, but I did it. They said, just right; at anyrate I did the best I could, when they all left, highly elated.

It was Saturday, the 23d of February that I arrived at home, and by two o'clock three committees were after me to go with them to speak; one of them was from Lancaster, one from Chillicothe, and one from Portsmouth. They would take no denial, go I must. I fixed up, put a man in my shop, and went with the Lancaster committee to speak for them that night—with a promise to speak at Chillicothe on Monday and

Portsmouth on Tuesday, and then return home and go to work, but alas! in this I was much mistaken, as I did not return until the day of election, the second of November, just in time to vote.

The Democrats of Lancaster had prepared a quack doctor to speak against me, so on the way over, the committee who had me in charge, posted me on this fellow. He knew but little, and did not know that I was in possession of every act of his life. So when he pitched into me, I got up in turn and gave a full history of his life, which was not a very creditable one, amid the shouts and laughter of the whole crowd.— When the place became too hot for him, he left, swearing that we were all a set of d——d blackguards. This caused another roar of laughter. I then had the field to myself, when I asked if they had any other doctor for me to desect, if they had to bring him on, while my knife was sharp, and my hand was in; when all was over, my friends gathered around me, congratulating me on my success in driving this doctor from the field. The Democrats were ashamed of him, and said they hoped he would never attempt to speak again.

Before day on Monday morning they started me in a carriage to Chillicothe, where I arrived by noon, amidst the shouts of the people that were gathered at the hotel where I was to stay. By two o'clock there was a large crowd at the Court House where I was to speak, all anxious to hear and see the blacksmith, for my fame had got there before me. The Democrats denied that I was the blacksmith the Whigs said I was, and had got a stage driver who knew me to confront me, when I would begin to speak; well the stage driver came forward and looked at me, then turned to his friends and said "be damned if he aint the same man," when the leading ones of the party began to drop their heads and sneak away. When I was made acquainted with their game, I said to the driver "walk upon the stand my friend, if you please, I wish to see you a moment." He came forward when I said "I presume that you are a Democrat, but that don't matter. Is this true," showing him a short article in a paper of that place, printed that morning, charging me with being a drunken loafer. He looked at it and promptly said, "No sir, its a lie, if our own paper does say it." "Thank you sir," I said, "I knew you were an honest man if you are a Democrat, did you ever see or hear any thing against me as a man." He said he never did. Then said I, "Gentlemen out of their own mouth have I convicted them, why is it that they have attacked me in the manner they have. Is it because said I, they are opposed to a working man thinking and acting for himself.

I left Chillicothe next morning and arrived at Portsmouth that afternoon, where I found other committees awaiting to take me to Kentucky. There was a large meeting that night and I so stirred up the Democracy, that several of them wanted to ask questions at a time. I was so well posted on all great questions of the day, that they found it up-hill business to begin with me. The leading Whigs of every place I went, posted me upon every Democrat in their town, so that I had the advantage of them, for they knew nothing against me, and I knew all about them, therefore whenever any of them said anything regarding myself, I would pitch into them on private matters, that would generally floor them.

I had intended to go home from there, and go to work again, but that was no go, the Kentuckians were determined to take me to Maysville, and had a steamboat with them for that purpose. So my friends in Portsmouth made up some cash to send home, and I concluded to go with the Kentuckians. We had a gay time going down the river, and I began to think I was some pumpkins. I had been so carressed and flattered for the past week, that I had become quite conceited. At any rate I feared none of them on the stump. At

Maysville we had a fine meeting, but here I found a strong opposition as well as the most bitter set of Democrats I had ever met. On returning from the meeting that night three of their rowdies attacked me striking at me with a club, I warded off the blow, drew a pistol (for I had two of them) and pulled away at them, and struck one of them in the hand, when they took to their heels and run away, and had me arrested, but I was discharged at once.

The next day I was taken to a large meeting of the old soldiers that had served under Harrison in the war, which was held some miles from Maysville, in the interior of the state, at a place called Washington. At this meeting I first met Geo. D. Prentiss, and it was at that meeting I first got the name of the Buckeye Blacksmith, which I ever bear. Here I met a large number of Harrison's old soldiers, as well as many of the distinguished men of Kentucky, to whom I related some of the incidents of my early life, particularly those that referred to Mr. Clay. This alone made me very popular with them.

At this meeting I met a Committee from Cincinnati, who took me with them to that city, to speak at their ratification meeting that was to take place on the following Tuesday. Here I had a day or two to rest, which I very much needed. The meeting was a great success; the papers had extolled me, as it were, to the top of the ladder, until public curiosity was at its pitch, to see and hear me. After the meeting I attended a reception at Judge Burnets. This was my first introduction into high life, and it made me feel very awkward at first, but I soon got acquainted with their manners and customs. I here met a young lady by the name of Churber, who had heard me speak that night, and had carefully noted down all my grammatical errors; she politely pointed them out to me, and gave me the proper words to use, which I never after forgot. Gen. Harrison was there, as well as most of the distinguished men of Cincinnati; they gave me much information. They formed themselves into a Committee, and said from what they had seen and heard of me, that I would be a valuable speaker in that campaign, and that I must not think of going home, but continue speaking until the election, which I consented to do. So in a day or two they had provided me with all the documents they could, and I left for Kentucky, to speak a few times there until meetings could be got ready for me in different large towns in Ohio, where I was to stay until the first of May, and then go to Virginia and Pennsylvania. They dressed me up pretty nicely before I started, and gave me a letter addressed to the Whigs of Louisville, to which place I went, where I met a most cordial welcome. It was very laughable to see the Democrats peeping into the parlor or around the corners at me, then going away, saying, "all but a blacksmith," why that fellow is a gentleman. I never saw so much peeping in all my life; even when I would be walking the streets, they would come running from every direction, just to get a look at me. Many of them went away swearing that I was a lawyer in disguise. Some said: "he's a member of Congress!" and others said I was a minister. All this speculation was owing to my new suit of clothes, that my friends had given me. When night came, they all made a rush for the meeting; when I was introduced to them, I told them, that I was a plain man, with a very limited education, and they, therefore, must not expect a very flowery speech from me.

Prentiss, with all the leading men of the city, had been closeted with me pretty much all day, posting me on all the leading questions, that they wished me to speak upon, as well as upon all the leading Democrats of the place. I had an excellent memory, that enabled me to follow out their plans, so that when I got through with my speech, many of the people were astonished at the manner in which I had handled both, the question, as well as the thrashing I had given the leading Democrats.

Mr. Van Buren had two very weak points—his Sub-Treasury scheme, and his Army Bill—and on these points I made my attack; and in all cases fastened my Sam. Medary's dream on the leading Democratic paper of every place where I spoke.

When I left Louisville, I visited Frankford, the Capital of the State, where I met with a warm reception and was lionized by all the dignatary's, both male and female in the place. I spoke to a large meeting in the State house and was much applauded by the ladies for my complimentary remarks on female influence. I left there with the good wishes of all my friends and the curses of my enemies (the Democrats).

I then went to Lexington, the home of Mr. Clay, where I received one of the warmest receptions, except two or three, that I have ever met in my travels. All the people appeared to try to outdo each other in kindness to me, even the Democrats seemed unwilling to let the Whigs outdo them in courtesy.

Mr. Clay was at Washington city at the time, and therefore I did not see him, but visited his family and was treated very kindly by them. Mrs. Clay, was one of the finest ladies that I ever met. My meeting there was a grand success, for at this meeting I related the little incidents connected with Mr. Clay and myself in early life, and gave him the credit of making me all that I was or ever expected to be. This alone, made me a Lion instead of a Bear. I left Lexington and spoke at one or two other places on my route to Ohio. I arrived back in Cincinnati about ten days after leaving there, ready to fill a series of appointments at the principle towns along the Miama river. At Dayton I fell in with a shoemaker, who bantered me to discuss the questions of the day with him. I accepted the banter, but when I had learned that he was an infidel in his religious views, I said that I would not hold a discussion with a man that did not hold himself responsible to God for his words and actions. They then brought out another fellow, that had but little brains; I soon floored him, and that night, as I was going to my hotel, from a friends house, at a late hour, I met two of the Democratic rowdies, who insulted me as I passed them. I turned on them, and told them that I generally thrashed men in my country for talking to me in that way. They laughed at me, when I hauled away at one of them and laid him out, the other took the best course that he could, for he took to his heels and ran off.

From Dayton I visited all the large sized towns in the interior of Ohio. Every place I went I met a most hearty welcome from the Whigs, who took great pains in instructing me on all the topics of the day. During all this time Medary was pouring his abuse on me, which only served to make me the more popular with all right minded men.

I would here state, that if ever I lose my self-respect, or confidence in my own integrity, it will be when Democratic papers speak well of me. One thing that made them hate me worse than all others, was that I never charged anything on them or their party, that I was not prepared to prove by authentic documents. This is a rule that I have always adhered to, for many times have I came in contact with their speakers, when they would make wholesale attacks on me and my party, and when called on for the proofs, they could not produce them, and I would floor them on that point. The Whig leaders had furnished me with every document that was necessary to a successful campaign; I had half a cart load of them. By constant practice and the instructions I received daily from the leading Whigs in Ohio, and members of Congress who were furnishing me with the documents, I had so improved in speaking that I had no fears of any man, and was no longer timid before the great men of the country.

I was at length through with my Ohio appointments, for the present, and was preparing to make my way to Virginia. On my arrival in Wheeling, Virginia, I found them making great preparation to receive me, for my fame had by this time spread through the entire country. Everybody wanted to see and hear the blacksmith, (Barnum in his palmiest days was not half so much sought after.) They had a large stand put up and seats for the ladies; they too, were anxious to see and hear me. Well, when I came on the stage, a servant with me to help carry my books and documents, the whole of the people raised a shout, and some swore that I was a book-pedler, in place of a blacksmith. One fellow sung out to me, "Can you shoe a horse?" "Yes," says I "as well as any man in your State." This raised another shout and waving of handkerchiefs. "We'll try you when you are done speaking," said he, "all right," said I." "For I can not only shoe horses, but can shoe mules, so you had better be there if you wish to be shod by a master workman." I have never seen or heard of that fellow since.

I went from there to Wellsville, some miles up the river, next day, and had a meeting and got along finely; and from Wellsville I took a boat for Pittsburg, Pa., arriving there in the evening. I put up at a hotel, enquired of the landlord where I could find some of the active Whigs of the place, as I was not announced for a meeting, yet I thought I would see them that night. He told me that there was a meeting at Liberty Hall that evening, if I would go there I would see them all. He directed me where to find the Hall, and when I arrived they had already organized and were waiting for a speaker. No person knew that I was in the city. Just as I worked my way to the stand, the President asked if some person would please make a few remarks until the speakers came. I thought this a good opportunity to make myself known, so I stepped on the stand, and said, that I would entertain the audience until their speakers came. Tell me sir, when they come and I will stop. I commenced by pitching into a dirty little paper of that city, that had been abusing me for a week or two back, and then commenced to desect Van Buren. After speaking a half hour or more, I said: "tell me when your speakers come, if you please," but the crowd whom I had kept in a roar of laughter all the time, cried out, "go on, go on!" until I started again and spoke altogether over an hour, when I closed amid the wildest excitement.

The moment I closed the speakers, who had heard the most of my speech, and a number of the leading Whigs of the city, came forward, and said: "We wish, sir, to congratulate you upon your success tonight, and to ask if you are not the blacksmith from Ohio." I told them that I thanked them for their congratulations, and that I was the blacksmith they spoke of. The President at once announced to the meeting that I was the genuine Ohio Blacksmith that they had been reading about for the past few weeks, when all hands, speakers and all, cried out for another speech, and I had to step on the stand and make them another short speech, when we adjourned to meet the next night in a grand mass meeting in the Diamond Market Square. The next morning this little dirty Democratic sheet gave me a column of extracts from Sam. Medary's paper, for which I paid him that night at Market Square to his hearts content. Our meeting was a fine one and all seemed satisfied. I left in a day or two for the East, with a promise to go through the county later in the campaign which I did. I was to open the campaign the 21st of June, in Philadelphia, and remain in Pennsylvania until the October election, so I concluded to make my way to Maryland, and spend a few days in my native place.

I left Pittsburg by the way of Washington, Brownsville and Uniontown, speaking at each place to large crowds. Nothing unusual occurred until I got to Brownsville, where I had a fuss with a drover, who pretended he knew me, and that he knew something about me, but refused to say what it was; I took him by the throat, shook him a little, until he was frightened half out of his wits, and he let me alone after that.

When I got to Uniontown I met Andrew Stewart, whom I had known before, as also L. W. Stockton whom I had once worked for when quite young. He at once recognized me and made a great ado over me. He could hardly believe his own eyes, he said he could never have believed that I was the boy who had worked for him. When I went to the Court House to speak, the Sheriff, who was a Democrat, refused to let me in the house, because he said that I carried pistols, when I told him that I not only carried them but that I would use them if he, or any of his crew interfered with me. Messrs. Stewart and Stockton influenced the County Commisioners to give us the Court House, where I made the first regular Tariff speech that I had attempted to make during the campaign; my usual course was to tear down Van Buren, and build up Harrison, by attacking Van Buren's weak points, and building up Harrison's strong ones. This I found had the best effect.

I left Uniontown with flying colors and spoke at Smithfield and Frostburg, Md., on my road to Cumberland, where they had made great preparation to receive me, in my native State. Here I was met by Committees from Hagerstown and Frederick, inviting me to speak for them. I made appointments with them for a few meetings, and when I left Cumberland, I went to the Berkeley Springs, in Virginia, to rest a few days until my Maryland meetings were ready.— While at the Springs I was met by the Philadelphia Committee who were determined to take me home with them, in order to have me there by the 21st of June, which was some two weeks ahead. After hearing my arrangements in Maryland, they concluded to travel with me. So we went to Hagerstown, where we had a gay time. The Philadelphia boys had plenty of money, and spent it freely, and they became very popular with the people of Maryland. The next day we all went to a mass meeting at Sharpsburg, a town that has since been made historical by the late rebellion. At this meeting I met a brother that I had not seen for many years, who was a Democrat, and had come twenty miles to see if I was his brother. He no sooner saw me, than he came upon the stand, took me by the hand, and said: "brother John how are you," I hope you will forgive me for being heretofore a Democrat, for since you have been so much abused by my party as you have been, I will never vote another Democratic ticket while I live." I said "amen," and turning to the Democratic part of the audience said: "go ahead Democrats for every lie you tell on me you will drive some of my relations or other honest men from your ranks," and I knew of no better way to make Harrison votes than to distribute Democratic documents among the people, for I have always contended that the mass of the people, without regard to their religious or political views were honest, and would vote right if correctly informed. I told them that the Democratic party were afraid of the truth, they reminded me of an Irishman that was brought into Court for some offense that he had committed, when he began to cry; his lawyer being a humane man, as lawyers generally are, told him not to cry, he hoped to have justice done him, when the Irishman cried out, "be me souel Justice is what I'm afraid of." So it is with the Democratic party, they fear the truth, hence their lies. This raised a shout among the crowd, while many of the leading Democrats went away swearing vengeance on me.

The same night I spoke at Boonsboro, a few miles from there. Spoke at a large meeting, and the next day visited my brother and spoke at Middletown, near where he lived; I had also an uncle there, whom I had not seen since my boyhood days. Here I had a fine time, as most of the people in Middletown and in that vicinity were Whigs, and are Republicans to this day. I was to speak in Frederick the next night, and concluded to go there in disguise, therefore I sent my Philadelphia friends ahead and I walked, arriving there just at dark, and stopped at a small tavern at the edge of town and asked for supper, when I was told that it would be ready in a few minutes. The landlord remarked to me that they were going to have a great time in town that night, for the great Whig Blacksmith, of Ohio, was to speak there, and that the Whigs were making preparations for a grand display. "Ah!" said I, "is that so, have you ever seen this Blacksmith." "No," said he, "I never have, but intend to not only see but hear him to-night, if I am a Democrat." The supper bell rang about this time, when we all, (some twenty in number,) took our seats at the table. Soon after we were seated, a gentleman at my side, asked me if ever I had seen this blacksmith, I told him that I had often seen him. "Well, what sort of a man is he?" the papers tell some pretty hard things on him; are they true or not." Well, sir, that is more than I can say, I suppose that he is like the most of us, has his good and bad traits of character. The landlord here spoke up and said, my rule is never to condemn a man until I know something about him myself; I am told that he is a Frederick county man, and has respectable connections, therefore I wish to see and hear for myself. "That's right," said I, when several others said, "they never believed all they read in political papers. "Nor I either," said I. Just then a fellow on the opposite side of the table said, "gentlemen, if you knew as much about him as I, you would not have a very good opinion of him, I know him well, I only live a short distance from him. "Ah!" said I, "then you know whether these stories they tell on him are true or not." "They are all true, and the half has not been told, he is not a blacksmith at all but a miserable drunken lawyer that would plead a case for fifty cents to get whisky with." "Is it possible," I said, "I suppose you have often seen him." "Oh! yes, nearly every day," said he, (oh how I wished to maul him, but concluded to carry on the joke.) "Well," said I, "the most of those stories are generally gotten up for political effect, for if they were true, parties would not countenance such imposters." "That is true" said several of those present, but he insisted that these stories were all true to his knowledge. By this time supper was over, and I paid my bill and left. When I arrived at the meeting it was already organized and the Chairman was telling the people that I would soon be there, it was early yet. I told a gentleman by my side to tell him that I was in the crowd, when he invited me on the stand, and introduced me to the great mass of men and women that had congregated to see and hear me. I took off my coat and began to roll up my sleeves, when an old fellow sung out, "I'll bet fifty dollars he's a blacksmith by the way he rolls up his sleeves." When order was restored I turned to the audience, and to my surprise I saw the whole party that I had met at the tavern, standing right in front of me. The landlord and a few of the others were smiling, but my Ohio friend looked as if he could crawl out of the little end of a tin horn. I commenced by making an apology to the audience for keeping them waiting so long, by telling them that I had been so agreeably entertained at the hotel, where I had taken my supper, by a pretended acquaintance of mine from Ohio, that the time had passed unnoticed, and I am proud to see him as well as the other guests of the hotel now here. I then related all the conversation as it occurred at the supper-table, amid the wildest shouts of laughter, the guests as well as the landlord enjoyed the joke as well as the rest of the crowd, for I had spoken well of them. I told the people that this fellow was there, and, therefore, they had better look well to their pocket-books, and lock their stables and hen coops when they went home. This was too much for my Ohio friend. He was soon missing and I never had the pleasure of meeting him after that night.

I made my speech and was warmly congratulated by the elite of the city. I would here state that I had often heard it said, "that a prophet is not without honor save in his own country," this was not the case on this occasion, for the first families of Maryland, such as the Pitts, McPherson's and Schleys, all took me by the hand and bid me a hearty welcome back to my native land. This was the grandest reception I ever met with during all my travels in life, and I feel proud of it to this day.

Next morning I made a horse-shoe at an old Democrats shop, in the presence of a large crowd, he was offered ten dollars for the shoe, but he said if he was a Democrat he would never part with that shoe. I agreed to visit the county again later in the Campaign, which I did, and the next morning left with my Philadelphia friends for Harrisburg on their route home, where we arrived safely the second day after.

CHAPTER III.

MY CAMPAIGN IN PENNSYLVANIA.

AFTER my arrival in Philadelphia I had a day or two to rest prior to our great meeting that was to come off on the 21st of June. The committee gave me quarters at the Madison House in Second street, in order to have me in a quiet place, where none but the leading men knew where to find me, until the day of the meeting. All the leading politicians of that day, in the city, visited me during those few days and posted me on all the various topics they wished me to talk upon; among them were the great E. Joy Morris, Charles Nailor, Jas. R. Chandler, J. P. Wethered and many others whose names do not occur to me at this distant day.

I had become pretty well posted on all questions that were connected with general politics, but needed some posting in the affairs of Pennsylvania, so as to be able to meet the questions that were peculiarly adapted to that section of the country. This they gave me, so by the time that the meeting came off the people were astonished to find me, a poor uneducated mechanic, from a distant State, so well posted on all the affairs of that country. Many of them came to me after I had spoken to know where or how I had gotten hold of so much information concerning the affairs of Pennsylvania. I generally told them that we blacksmiths in the West were all the time prying into other peoples business. Many a laugh we had over the way I got so much information on the affairs of the old Keystone State.

The day of the great meeting arrived and at the appointed hour Independance Square was packed with people, they had come from all quarters of the State as well as from New Jersey and Delaware, to see and hear the blacksmith. There were but few blacksmiths in all that region of the country that were not there, as well as other mechanics; it was a new thing to them. I suppose, that I was among the first that ever took such an active part in politics.

The first speaker that day was Mr. Alford of Georgia, he said, "I am not a blacksmith myself, but my father was one, so you see I understand a little about the business, at any rate I think I am able to act as helper or striker for the boss; which you know is necessary in doing a good job of work. So I will blow the bellows and heat the iron for him and then let him finish the job himself." He then went on and gave a short history of me, and finished with an appeal to the working men to stand by me, for I was their best friend. He said "this man will show you that labor should own capital, and not capital own labor, as is too much the case all over our country, as well as through the entire old world. He will show you that you ought to be protected in your industry against the pauper labor of the old world, which the Democrats deny to you in and out of Congress, and still have the hardihood to ask you for your votes," with this he closed.

I was then introduced amid the wildest shouts and huzzas I ever heard. I took off my coat, rolled up my sleeves, and commenced by saying, that in appearing before them to-day, that I labored under many disadvantages, for I was a stranger to them all, and only a plain, unassuming mechanic, with a very limited education, and therefore could not give them a very flowery speech. I only know a half dozen of those big words that most speakers use, and I hardly ever undertake to climb up very high to get at them, for fear that I might have some trouble in getting down again, so I generally let them alone. This raised a great shout; I told them I would give them a plain talk, that I would put the questions fairly and plainly before them, and in doing so I should speak the plain, unvarnished truth, and nothing else. With one voice they seemed to call out " that's just what we want to hear." I then began by showing up Van Buren's Army-Bill and when I finished that point, asked them " do you want that, gentlemen?" "No! no!" was the cry. I read his message to prove my point.

I then took up his Sub-Treasury scheme, showed that up and said, "do you want this, gentlemen?" "No! to h——l mid him," shouted an Irishman in the crowd. Well this is what Mr. Van Buren offers you, and here is his message to prove it, although the Democrats of Pennsylvania deny it, do they not? — "Yes, they do," said a thousand voices in the crowd. Well, said I, they dare not meet me and deny that Mr. Van Buren wrote this message, and recommended to Congress to pass the Bills that I have just read. I shall stay in the City a few days, at the Madison House, where they can find me at any time they wish. They must not wait until I leave the City and say that it was all a Whig lie, or I will come back and punch some of their heads for them. At this I had to wait five minutes for the crowd to get through with their laugh, some were shouting up to me, saying, "that's right, I like a man that has pluck."

I then took the subject of Protection to American

Industry, showing them that it was the laboring man who needed it; the rich could live without, but the poor could not. I told them that the poor man loved his wife and children as well as the rich man loved his, and was as fond of seeing his family well fed and well clothed as the rich man. How is he to feed and clothe his family unless he is paid a fair price for his labor; he never can. "No never," said many of them. Do you men of family, wish to work for the wages that is paid to the slaves and serfs of foreign countries? if not, vote for protection to your own labor, vote for the party that will give it to you, throw aside your politics when the interests of yourself and family are at stake. A man must be a fool that gives his vote against his best interests, dont you think so, fellow workingmen? There was one shout of "yes! yes!" If you are opposed to free trade and low wages you must vote for Harrison, for Mr. Van Buren will never give you anything else.

I went on in this strain of argument for near three hours when my voice failed me and I had to close.

When I was through I had to be taken away in a hack to keep my friends from shaking my arm off.— The whole crowd seemed to be crazy with excitement, and hundreds followed me to my hotel in order to shake me by the hand, and I have no doubt but that I shook hands during that day and evening with five thousand men. The next day I spent my time in making arrangements with the committee to open the campaign through the state, commencing at Philadelphia. On the fourth of July I was to speak in Washington city, Baltimore, and a few other places in Maryland in the interval, so as to give time to get up a meeting in Pennsylvania.

Several members of Congress were present at my meeting in Philadelphia and took me to Washington with them, where I had a monster meeting at the City Hall steps. Mr. Van Buren heard me speak at this meeting, and was very much amused at some of my

anecdotes that I told on him, and said to Mr. Crittenden that he never heard a man speak, that could carry the people away with him, better than I could; he said that with a few such men as I was in the free States, the Whigs could beat any man the Democrats could get up at this time, for it was a new thing for a working man to speak at public meetings, and would take a powerful hold upon men of that class, and of such men the Democratic party is chiefly composed.—
"Just see how they flock around him, he has got them all in a roar of laughter at me, this is the way to beat an opponent, get the people to laughing at him, and you have him whipped, this that blacksmith can do."

The next day Mr. Crittenden told me all that Van Buren had said, which I tried to improve on after that, through the whole campaign.

After I concluded my speech I was taken in charge by the Ohio delegation in Congress, and feasted and flattered for a day or two, when I was invited to a grand party, given by Ex-President Adams at his residence in Washington, where I met many of the leading men of the nation, who enjoyed my answers to the questions propounded to me by Mr. Adams and others that chose to put them to me. Mr. Adams said, "Mr. Bear I wish to ask you what induced you, a poor mechanic, to take such a stand in this campaign as you have taken." Said I, "the same reason sir, I suppose, that prompted you and all other great men in the country that ever took an active part in politics; it was to distinguish myself, I know of no other reason sir."

This raised a roar of laughter at Mr. Adams expense. Some of those present, said "what do you think of the blacksmith now?" to Mr. Adams, when he said "it is a good answer, better than I expected," then turning to me, he said, "I think that you are able to hold your own with any of us. The party soon after that separated and went home.

The next day every member of the Senate or House

that I met at the Capitol, had something to say about the way that I answered Mr. Adams the night before, for it had spread all over both Houses before twelve o'clock next day. Many a laugh we had about it when I would meet some member at my meetings during the campaign.

From Washington I came to Baltimore, and spoke at Monument Square, to one of the largest meetings that was ever held there. I was well received by the leading Whigs of the city, many of whom are dead, among those that are living who treated me in the kindest manner, was the Hon. Reverdy Johnson, who I am sorry to say some years after that, left our party and is acting with the Democratic party, but was a true Union man through the war.

After my meeting in the Square, I returned to my hotel (the Exchange) now the Custom House; about eleven o'clock, three gentlemanly looking men called on me, and said they were a committee to invite me to a friend's house for a short time. I at first refused to go owing to the lateness of the hour, but finally concluded to go, as they said it was only a short square, just around the corner; we started but when we got in the street, they turned the wrong way to go to Baltimore street, when I began to conclude that all was not right, and said gentlemen, I don't intend to go with you down that street, for that is not the course you told me your friend lived, when they said "its all right, so come along, you put us to the trouble to come after you, and you must not back out now." I said, "gentlemen you see that I do not want to go, now if you are my friends you ought not ask me to go, and if you are not my friends, I ought not go with you. At which one of them took hold of my arm, and said you must go, and began to pull me, when I pulled loose from him and drew a pistol and said "stand back or I'll shoot you," and then turned back into the hotel. When they had run away, none of the persons appeared to know them that were in the hotel. We at once made search for them but they could not be found. The street they wished me to go, led directly to a dock that was but a few yards off. I have never had a doubt but that they intended to throw me in the dock and drown me, for no person could ever be found that would acknowledge that they were the committee.

The next day I went to Ellicotts Mills to speak and about the time that I got fairly under way, a parcel of Democrats tried to break up our meeting, and when they found they could do it in no other way, they got a locomotive and run it up and down by our stand blew the whistle so as to prevent the people hearing me, and finally we had to adjourn. They then bantered me to meet one of their speakers the next day, in a joint discussion, but not until they found that I was to speak at Elkton, fifty miles from there on that day. This was a small game they often tried to play on me but sometimes when I had to speak at a small meeting I posponed it and met them, but in such cases they would mostly back out, by saying their speaker could not get ready in time, and would set a day ten days ahead when I would be many miles away at some other meeting.

I left Baltimore the night of the day I spoke at Ellicotts Mills and went to Elkton, and spoke there to a very good and orderly meeting, and was well received by the Whigs of that place. This was on the second day of July and I was to speak at Wilmington on the third, ready to be in Philadelphia by the fourth. I had made an arrangement with some gentlemen of Wilmington on the twentieth of June to be there that day, so as to give them time to prepare for a grand affair. When I arrived there I found great preparations being made for the meeting, and a grand affair it was, more so than it would have been, if it had not been for the reason that I will now state.

The Democrats as soon as they found that I was to

be there, (which they did, the day I promised the committee that I would come,) started a man by the name of Orr, post-haste to Ohio to the town that I lived in to get all the testimony against me that he could, (for they believed all that they had read in their papers) and when I would come and begin to speak, he was to come and confront me with the testimony of my neighbours, (this man Orr was a good speaker.) Neither I or my friends knew anything about this arrangement. The Democrats had kept it very quiet, but had boasted that when I came there to speak they would have a man ready to floor me. This I heard talked around all the morning before the hour of meeting. Several low-priced Democrats gathered around where I was talking to some friends, and would say loud enough for me and my friends to hear, " has he got back yet?" " Where did he go?" " I heard that he went to Bloomfield, Ohio." " Yes, that's the place," said another.— " Oh," said one, " he will be here in time, I'll bet you, it will be glorious sport, wont it?"

When the hour arrived for the meeting to commence the Democrats were there in a body, as well as the Whigs. I was introduced and made a long speech, and as soon as I closed, this man Orr stepped on the stand and asked to make a statement. Permission was given him to do so, when he made a full disclosure of all their plans, as well as his trip to Ohio in order to obtain the necessary proofs of my guilt and unworthiness as a man, to enable him to follow me wherever I went, and expose me to the world. He said he was an honest Democrat and felt determined, if what he had read about me was true, that the world should know it. " Well, gentlemen," said he, " I have just returned from Ohio this morning," and turning to me said, " I have just returned from a visit to your neighbours, in South Bloomfield, Ohio, sir. I went there an honest man, to find out your character, and I have come back an honest man, with your full history."—

Here the Democrats raised a shout, expecting of course that I would be fully exposed; but oh, ye Gods, when he turned to the audience and in a loud voice declared that he was not able to find a Democrat, let alone a Whig, in the town that would say or could say anything against me, the worst word he had heard against me was from an old Democrat, who said he wished I would stop running around and come home to my shop for he wanted his horses shod. At this stage of affairs the Whigs raised a shout, when some of the leading Democrats began to hunt a milder climate to cool off.

Mr. Orr then said, "gentlemen, if this is the course my party intends to pursue, in order to elect Mr. Van Buren, whenever unable to meet an opponent to attack and destroy his private character, simply because he may be a plain, unassuming mechanic, it is high time that all honest laboring men should leave the party, and from this day I shall devote all the ability or talent that I may possess, to the election of General Harrison and the defeat of this sham Democracy," and from that day to the day of election he remained a firm friend of the Whig party.

The Democrats as soon as they heard what Orr had to say, swore that the Whigs had bought him over, and at once began to traduce his character by saying all manner of hard things about him; this they did as well against him, as they did against me, in order to destroy what ever influence we might have as working men, with that class of voters in their party. They were not able to meet the great issue of that day with either of us, hence they had no other course to pursue, than to attack our private character, but that course acted then, as it always does, to the injury of those that attempt it.

The Democratic party was then, as it now is, a negative party, never originating any plan or idea of its own, but always opposing the ideas and plans of the opposite party. All Democrats can tell you what they are opposed to, but very few can tell you what they are in favor of, unless they go to the county town and ask their leader, when he will tell them equal rights to all men, and an honest administration of public affairs which is every word false, as I have shown you by the manner in which they tried to distroy me. Had I not a right to speak my sentiments as well as they had? Then why destroy me, if they are in favor of equal rights to all men? Are they in favor of an honest administration of public affairs? Look, I pray you, to day, at the two great cities of New York and Baltimore and then answer me that question. But I shall speak more fully upon this subject hereafter. The meeting at Wilmington was a grand success for the Whig party, and I think it will be a long time before the Democrats of Wilmington will pay another man's expenses to go to Ohio to hunt up my character, for fear they may catch another tarter like Orr proved to be.

On the fourth I went to Philadelphia, where I was to speak five times during that day and evening, at different localities in the city and suburbs. The first place I spoke was in Vance's yard up Second street, at 10 o'clock, A. M. Here they had a blacksmith's forge, bellows, anvil and tools, all arranged on a large platform out in the open air, where the multitude could see for themselves that I was a blacksmith, for this as the Democrats said could be proved that I was not. They said they had a man that knew me well and would confront me on the stand that day, and would prove that I was a fraud, hence the Whigs had fixed up this forge and tools to prove that the Democrats lied. Accordingly when the meeting was organized, I took off my coat, rolled up my sleeves, put on a leather apron, and was introduced to the great meeting numbering not less than twenty-five thousand people. I said, "my friends and fellow countrymen, I am proud to see so many honest men and women as now stand before me, to the nailing of another lie to the Democratic party. I am ready to work, as you see, what kind of a job do you wish me to do first? "make us a good horse shoe nail," said an old blacksmith present, "certainly sir, I will," said I and commenced and made a first rate one. What next gentlemen, for I want to be at work? "Make us a good horse shoe," said another; at it I went and very soon had one made as good as any other man in the country could make. I held it up in my tongs, and said aloud "I would like to nail it on the Jackass that said I was not a blacksmith. This raised the greatest shout of applause I ever heard. When order was finally restored I laid down my tools and spoke on the leading issues of the day, for about an hour, and then left for another meeting in West Philadelphia, and from there to one in the South-eastern part of the city, and then out near Fairmount Water Works, and then winding up with a monster meeting on Smith's Island between Philadelphia and Camden, New Jersey. At this meeting I drank the first Champaign wine I ever drank; they told me that it was Jersey cider and would not hurt me, so I drank it as free as water, but by the time I got to my hotel I found that my head was beginning to feel pretty light, so I went to bed without my supper and laid there two days before I got over it. This was my first indulgence in drinking to excess since I had been in the campaign, and I made up my mind that it would be the last, and it was during that campaign, for I have always thought if anything on earth looked ridiculous it was a public speaker drunk on the stand, trying to address a meeting, which none but Democrats often do.

My next meeting was at Bristol, a few miles from Philadelphia, in Buck's county, where I had to speak to a Democratic audience, and the only way that I could get along there, was to get them to fighting among themselves; this I did by praising Jackson and the working men, and denouncing the leaders in that town, as soon as any of them would interrupt me. I would say there is one of the leaders; he is afraid for you honest men to hear a workman speak; this only made the leaders more anxious to interrupt me, and poor men more anxious to hear me; at last I got them to fighting, when I left, believing that every one that got whipped would vote the Whig ticket to spite the man that licked him, which I afterwards heard they did.

I then visited Chestnut Hill, in Philadelphia county, a place almost entirely Democratic; they had said that I should not speak there, and if I came there they would thrash me, but I went, and had about fifty of the best picked men in the city to back me. When we arrived there our few friends had a stand fixed up in good order, and I commenced by saying, gentlemen, I have come here to make a speech to you, and I understand that you are all good Jackson men and if you are you may well feel proud of it, for he was a great and good man in his day. He fought our battles and won our victories for us, for which we should all honor him, and I propose, in view of what he has done for his country and for us as a people, that we give him three hearty cheers without respect to party feelings, when all hands raised their hats and gave three thundering cheers for Jackson. I said, gentlemen, we have another great General who, if he has not won as many and as great victories as General Jackson, he has still done great service for his country, and I propose, as we all joined in giving three cheers for Jackson, we all join in giving three more for Gen. Harrison; when to my surprise they all with one accord joined in and gave three just as hearty cheers for Harrison. I then commenced by saying that I was a plain workingman, and as such wished to address myself to the working portion of my audience. It was the labor of the country and the laboring man's interest that I felt a desire of seeing promoted; and it was this, and this alone that had brought me here, that if I felt certain that the success of the Democratic party would result in promoting these objects, I would now stop and go home, and let politics alone, but having with me to-night Mr. Van Buren's views in his own party papers, that cannot be denied, which fully satisfies me that if he is re-elected and carries out, as he most certainly will, those views, that it will prove most ruinous to the workingman's interest. I therefore feel it my duty to lay these things before you and let you judge for yourselves. I then went on to show and explain my documents until I had finished. The leading men saw plainly that I had made some impression upon the party and began to accuse me of saying many things that I did not say, when some of their own men contradicted them, which brought on a general fight among themselves, in the midst of which myself and party stepped into our omnibusses and left, giving cheer after cheer for Harrison. This fight did our cause much good, as many of them came out boldly for Harrison after that night.

I next went to Doylestown, Buck's county, where we had a great meeting in a grove near the town, at which place I pitched into the editor of the Democratic paper which had been abusing me from week to week, since I had first come to the State. He was pointed out to me at the meeting, when I went to him and told him that if he did not leave before I was done speaking that I would certainly thrash him, which he took good care to do. We had a gay time that night at my hotel, laughing over the manner in which we made him leave, and as long as he lived the people would laugh at him for letting me back him out. I had many difficulties to encounter in my travels at that day, that would not have to be encountered now. Then the Democratic party was made up mostly of the working class of the country. Nearly all the learned men of the country were Whigs, and it was seldom you saw a working man that was not a poor Whig. I being a plain working man, and Whig speaker, the leading men of the Democratic party feared that I would be able to make an impression on their party, that a professional or rich man would not be able to do. Hence their persecutions of me, for they generally poured out all their venom on my devoted head; they often had me insulted in hotels and every other place where opportunity afforded, and on one occasion I was surrounded at a railroad station on the Sabbath day, by a lawless mob of laboring men attached to the road, and had to get out of the cars with a pistol in each hand to defend myself from the men I was trying to elevate. But such was the ignorance and prejudice of the Democratic party at that day that it was not much trouble to raise a mob to do anything you wished, with a little Democratic argument (whisky) for that has always been a powerful lever in moving the Democratic car; for whenever you take whisky and the "damned nigger" away from the Democrat, there is nothing left of him, at least this has been my experience for more than fifty years.

When I left Doylestown, I went to Easton, a fine flourishing town on the Delaware river, in the north part of the State, where we were to have a great meeting; this was a great Democratic place, and I expected to have some trouble there. I had my wife and daughter (who had been in the East all Summer) with me, as also Hon. Charles Nailor, wife and daughter. We arrived early in the day and found the town alive with people, who had come from all parts of the country to see and hear me. I was to be presented with a silver cup by the Whig ladies of the place, as a token of their appreciation of my labors in the Whig cause, which was generally known, hence the great crowd of people.

The Democrats of course were determined to neutralize any influence that I might have in that manufacturing town among the working men. They had
*4

prepared a circular with twelve men's sworn testimony, from my county in Ohio, that I had a wife and six children suffering for bread at home, and that I had also been charged with stealing some years before. This they had already to throw among the people (by boys) as soon as the meeting would organize, and before I was introduced to the meeting hundreds of these circulars were picked up and were being read. One was handed to me, when I had read it I was introduced to the meeting and began by saying that I held in my hand a Democratic document, which if true, would render me an unfit person to stand before such an audience as was now before me; this document appears to have been sworn to by twelve highly respectable men who know me in my own county, with the broad seal of the county in which I live. Well ladies and gentlemen let us see how far this document is true. I see a gentleman of your town, who knew me and my family in Ohio, standing now before me, you all know him, he is I believe much of a gentleman, if he is a Democrat. I will ask you sir to please step on the stand for a moment. He did so; I asked him to be so kind as to say if he had ever known me and my family; he said he had and at once recognized my wife and daughter who were on the stand at the time, and turning to the audience he said, these are all the family that Mr. Bear has, and at once took a seat with them on the stand where he remained during the meeting. When order was restored, I turned to the audience and said "ladies and gentlemen you have seen my suffering family, what do you think of them, do they look like they were starving; what do you think brother working men of a party that stoops so low to carry a point? Who do you think got up this lie? I can tell you and you will see a poor miserable looking wretch, who looks as if he had just come out of a hen's roost at midnight, after an unsuccessful raid among the chickens; you can tell him from all other men, by his sneaking looks, I see him now, and will bet fifty dollars that I can point him out, and if I owned a dog that would bark at such a creature as he, I would shoot him. This raised a shout and all eyes were turned on the editor of the Democratic paper of that place.

You see that the first charge is false, now let us look at the other, which charges me with stealing, (let me see) they say it was in the fall of 1832 that I was charged with stealing; well I have a Democratic paper here, that was printed about that time (let me here state that in 1832 I had by some mistake of the Democratic County Committee, been appointed a delegate to the Democratic State Convention, to nominate a candidate for Governor, and my name was published as such in the Democratic organ of the county ; I not being one of the party of course paid no attention to it, but had kept the paper more by accident than otherwise; (this paper I had with me that day) and you will see by that paper (holding it up,) that I was a Democrat then, and if I did steal, I was only walking in the footsteps of the Democratic party, for stealing and drinking bad whisky has ever been two of the cardinal principles of that party, but since I have been a Whig, in respectable company I believe they have had no charge against me. This complete refutation of this libelious attack on me, created the wildest applause from the mass of people that were around me, so much so, that the place became too hot for the editor, the author of the circular above alluded to. He had to leave as well as some of his backers, or the people in their excitement would no doubt have handled him roughly.

I made my speech and was presented with a beautiful Silver cup by the ladies; and at night spoke again, in front of the hotel where I was staying, to a large meeting and was very much annoyed by the only arguments the Democrats could use with any success against me, and that was throwing stones into our crowd from dark corners at a distance, the poor devils could use no better argument than that.

My dear reader you can only imagine what I suffered, the many insults and privations I had to endure the narrow escapes I had to pass through in order to defend my party and principles; did you know what I suffered, you would wonder how I ever made my way through it, with the poor start I had in life. My party never has, nor never will, fully realize what I have done and sacrifised for them, in the last fifty years; I often wonder myself how I ever got along as well as I did, I had but one great stimulant to urge me on, and that was I knew I was right. I was working to advance the interest of the laboring man, and the freedom of the world, and felt confident in the fulness of time, that right would overcome error, and the principles that I was advocating would triumph, and this alone bore me up.

Nothing occured at Bethleham a place where there is a large female school, where I spoke after leaving Easton; the most of the inhabitants are very religious and as a consequence were Whigs, for pious men don't make very good Democrats. I was well treated there and stayed a day or two until my appointment was ready at Allentown in Lehigh County, at which place the Democrats got a drunken showman to get up a meeting on the opposite corner to draw their friends away from hearing me, but it was no go, he had too much whisky in him to effect any thing, and then they kicked up a fight among themselves, but finding they could not stop our speaking, they undertook to raise a row at our meeting, and in this they failed, and after several of them got their eyes blacked and noses pretty well smashed up, they concluded to leave and let us have our meeting go on quietly.

I was to speak at Reading the next day, and was met at Rutzstown, a small place on the road in Berks county, the hardest place this side of purgatory, by a large committee from Reading, among them several of the Philadelphia Whigs. They had called a meeting there for me to make a short speech while dinner would be getting ready. Just as I had begun to speak, the Democrats had prepared a stuffed paddy with a red petticoat, to represent Gen. Harrison as an old woman, and had it setting on a two wheeled sulky drawn by a big negro, who pulled it right up in front of where I was speaking. As soon as the Whigs saw it, they commenced to beat the negro over the head with clubs, when the white Democrats interfered and a general fight commenced. I being very stout, jumped down and pitched into a bull headed dutchman and in less than two minutes we cleaned the ground of every Democrat that was there. I guess some of them and the old negro if living, have never forgotten the day the Buckeye Blacksmith took dinner at their town.

We left Rutzstown at twelve o'clock, and were met on the road by another delegation which were all mechanics and by the time we had reached Reading, we had over a hundred vehicles in our procession. We had a great meeting that afternoon and my speech had the effect of bringing down all the Democratic papers and leaders on me; they manufactured a new set of lies on me, for which I had two of them arrested. The Court being in session, the cases were at once sent before the Grand Jury, and to the everlasting disgrace of the Democracy of Berks county, twenty three Grand Jurymen under their solemn oaths surrounded me in the Grand Jury room, and like a pack of hyeanes attempted to mob me, refusing to let me or any other witness testify before them, and not only ignored the two bills without hearing any testimony, but actually held me a prisoner until the cost was paid. I have no doubt, if it had not been that I expected a row, and went prepared for them, that they would have maltreated me right in the Grand Jury room, they said that I ought to be hung for coming there to speak against the Democrats. I confess that I would rather have been in some other place just then, than locked up in a room with twenty-three ignorant copperheads in a county where no Whig had any show for justice in their courts, but I faced the music as best I could, and finally got clear of them by paying thirteen dollars and fifty cents cost. This was the first case that I ever knew the Grand Jury to commit a man and hold him a prisoner for cost, that is generally done by the courts. All this persecution was brought to bear against me, to destroy my influence among the mass of the working men that were every where flocking to hear a working man speak, and to the credit of many of the mechanics of Reading of that early day, they boldly came out and condemned the course of their leaders, and many forever after that treatment of me by the Grand Jury, left the party and never after acted with them, so that they lost more than they gained by their persecution of me.

My next appointment was Pottsville; here I had a gay old time, they wanted to fight me, I agreed to fight the whole party one at a time, with the understanding that every Democrat that I licked should vote for Harrison, under a penalty of one thousand dollars, and I would furnish a Whig to vote for Van Buren for every one that licked me, under the same bond. I told them that I could make votes faster that way than by talking, but that argument would not suit them, so that matter was settled by my having to knock one fellow down for calling me a liar. I had experienced great difficulty during my travels to get letters through the mails, as all the post masters as well as the department at Washington was Democratic. I had to get my letters sent to me under an assumed name and then when the post master recognised me he would refuse to give me my letters; this was the case at Pottsville, where I had two letters one with a lottery ticket in it that drew a small prize, and the other simply the drawing of the lottery; these letters I never received. I was told that they were sent to the dead letter office at Washington. I wrote to the manager of the lottery and stopped payment of the prize, and this was the last I ever heard of it, and the last ticket I wrote for also.

There was one very interesting incident that occurred at my meeting at this place, that I shall never forget, it was this, a certain young man in a small village near Pottsville was courting a young lady, who was a good Whig girl, and had refused to marry him unless he would vote the Whig ticket; this he would not consent to do, but when I came along, she invited him to take her to hear me, thinking that possibly I might make some impression on him, I being a mechanic; he came with her, and during my remarks upon the tariff question, I seemed to satisfy him that it was to the interest of all working men to stand by the party who favored protection to American labor, in order to protect themselves. So at the close of the speech he promptly informed her that he was convinced that it was to his interest to vote the Whig ticket, and shall therefore go for Harrison; then said she I shall go for you, and at once went to the hotel, sent for a minister and in the presence of myself and a large number of ladies and gentlemen of their acquaintance were married.

At this place I found a large number of miners mostly foreigners, many of them very intelligent men, particularly the Scotch and Welch. These people had never been in the habit of going to political meetings, they seemed to take but little interest in politics, but when I came along, being a working man, they turned out to a man, to hear me, and many of them became my warmest friends. The Irish generally went against me. The Democrats soon found out that I was in their road in that region of the State, and tried all manner of means to put me down. But notwithstanding all their abuse and insults, I remained a week or more in that county, visiting the mines and speaking at small meetings every day. It was not safe to speak after night at those small places, they would mob us, so the only plan was to speak in the day time, this they did not like, the darker the night, the better it was for them, they could then answer our arguments with stones, without being seen.

I next visited Danville Montour county, where I had some fun with an ex-member of Congress, who was Judge of the Court, and had adjourned Court two hours to give me time to speak; this Judge had been in Congress four years and had never said a word while there, except now and then to rise in his seat and say Mr. Speaker I object; he had become known to every person in the country, by the name of I object Mr. Speaker; he had been pointed out to me as the Judge, when I had spoken near my two hours, I turned to the president and said is my time most out, I fear if I speak much longer the Honorable Court might object, this brought the house down with a tremendous burst of applause, when the Judge sprang to his feet and said in a very angry manner, "Mr. President, I did not adjourn this Court to be insulted, by you nor any other man you may choose to bring here, I was born in this country, and pay taxes here, and do not intend to be insulted in this Court room." Mr. President, said I, "you will please keep order, for to this interruption I do most positively object," this brought the house down again worse than ever, when the Judge called out, "I demand of you sir, your author of this slanderous stuff." "To give you my author sir, I must surely object," this raised the wildest shouts of laughter I ever witnessed. There was no more speaking, but my friends flocked around me and shook me by the hands until they nearly pulled my arms off; among the crowd that gathered around me, were a number of moderate Democrats, who enjoyed the fun as well as the Whigs did.

After the meeting was over I went to a blacksmith shop, made a set of horse shoes and nails, and shod a horse for one of the leading Democrats of the place, who seemed to enjoy the fun as well as any of the rest.

From Danville I made a tour up the north branch of the Susquehanna river, and spoke in all the towns of any size through the northern part of the State. At almost every place I went I had to encounter new difficulties with the Democrats, they seemed to forget every other question that was agitating the public mind, and devoted all their ingenuity and talent in trying to break me down; they even went so far, as to send all the way to Ohio and buy a small note on me, that was unpaid when I left home, and had me arrested while I was speaking, on a *capias* as a non-resident and on various occasions, they would wait until a very late hour in the evening until the most of my Whig friends had gone home, and then call on me to have some matter explained that they would pretend that I had said at my meeting that night, and prove by some of their party that I had said things that I had never thought of, and when I would deny it they would frequently commence abusing me, and I would be under the necessity of drawing a weapon on them in self defence. When I spoke at large meetings in company with such men as James Cooper, Thaddius Stevens, Judge Sargent, Charles Penrose and others, the most distinguished speakers in the State at that time, the Democrats would in publishing an account of the meeting, merely name those destinguished speakers, and devote a whole column in misrepresenting and abusing me, misquoting almost every thing that I had said, and then call on their party to stay away from my meetings; this they did to poisen the minds of the working men of their party against me, and thereby prevent them from attending my meetings. But notwithstanding all their efforts to keep the honest portion of their party from hearing me they failed, for the people would come, and I have no doubt, but many of the moderate men of their party, who had read so many of their denunciations against me, after hearing me themselves, left their party and voted our ticket. It must be conceded, that many a good man has been misled by them into the Democratic ranks, who when he is convinced of his error, will forever leave them. Not all Democrats are bad men, but my experience is, that all bad men are Democrats; there seems to be a natural affinity between a loafer and a Democrat, a kind of drawing together; so much so, that my experience of fifty years in politics, has led me to believe that it is safe to bet five to one, that every drinking disorderly loafer you see is a Democrat.

I often hear it said, that the Democratic party, was once a pure party, I would ask in all seriousness, when that was, it has not been in the last fifty years, it was conceived in sin and brought forth in inequity; it was started by the rabel of that day, against one of the best men that ever lived; it never has appealed to the understanding of man, but to his baser passions. It was gathered up in the interest of the whisky insurrection in the early part of the present century, and as a party opposed to collecting the excise duty on whisky, that was levied to pay the national debt. So you will see that it was the same party then that it is now; I have often thought that as the party was organized in the interest of whisky, that it had something to do in giving the party of this day, such an appetite for the article, that it has, for every body knows that without whisky the Democratic party could not exist long, neither could they carry on a successful campaign.

I will now relate an incident that occurred at Millerstown on the Juniata river. While I was speaking on the subject of Van Buren's Sub-Treasury scheme, I exhibited a Sub-Treasury note for fifty dollars, with one cent interest, payable one year after date, it had nine months to run before it was due; I held it up and asked if any person in the audience could redeem it, that was not an office holder. I said the people must pay all their postage and other debts to the government in gold and silver, and these bits of paper are good enough for them; the office holder must have gold and silver for his work, and these are good enough for the people, when up raised a man and sang out, "I will give you fifty three dollars for that bill, it is worth a premium of six per cent." The Democratic portion of the audience raised a terrible yell, when I said you must be an office holder; "yes" said one of the crowd "he is the post master of this town," oh said I, no doubt but he can raise the gold and silver for it, but can any other but an office holder do it, I will wait a moment to see, no other person seemed to respond, I said, you can have it, sir, bring on your cash, when up he stepped and poured out on the stand the fifty three dollars in silver; after I had counted it, I said, "it is all right, sir, I am much obliged to you, I have made five dollars on it for I can buy as many as I want in Philadelphia for forty-eight dollars; they are four per cent under par. Said he, "is this a genuine note," I said, "I don't know, it come from the Democratic party at Washington and I have some doubts about it, for I never have seen anything that did come from your party that was genuine, but said I, "have you any more silver about you, or was this the size of your pile, (pointing to the silver lying on the stand,) I have another note here, pulling out another fifty dollar note with eleven months to run, drawing five mills interest, and shook that at him, said, "come on now don't back out," but he did back out and then my party raised a yell, and the post-master and his friends sneaked off very much chap-fallen, for they knew that the note was only worth fifty dollars and a half in gold when it was due, but he had paid this premium, in order to get this note out of my hands not knowing that I had another.

The next day I was to speak at Mifflintown, a few miles up the river, and had to pass a place known as the Narrows, a short distance from Millerstown, where the rocks for some distance, were fifty feet high, projecting over the road, where some of those malicious men, no doubt prompted by the postmaster, had by the aid of hand spikes worked a large rock loose that would weigh at least three tons, and had it all ready when I came along in a carriage, in company with Charles B. Penrose, a member of the State Senate, and a gentleman that owned the carriage; just as we got under the rock they tipped it over, and if it had not been for the horses being very active and had sprang forward at the noise made by the crushing of the rock above as it tipped over we would have all been crushed into the earth. We only escaped by a few inches as the rock struck the edge of the hind wheels of our carriage as they passed under it merely touching them, hard enough, however, to break one or two spokes.— After our narrow escape we went around the narrows and got on the rocks and there saw their tools that they had used in working the rock loose. Hundreds of people visited the spot to see for themselves, and that rock bears the name of the Buckeye rock until this day.

You may see my kind friends by this what I have had to endure and to suffer for my principles, and the cause of right, and I have no doubt but that there are but few men but what would have become discouraged and given up and gone home, and I have often since wondered how it was that I endured all that I did, the half will never be known that I did endure.

From Mifflintown I was to attend a meeting, a barbacue, a mile or so from Lewistown, a few miles up the river. Here the Democrats had been very active in preparing a plan to keep their party from hearing me speak; they had gotten up a meeting at the same hour of our meeting not twenty rods from ours, and as we were to raise a pole at twelve o'clock, they were to raise one also at that hour; well, we both had good sized meetings, and at twelve o'clock the fun commenced; our pole was a nice dressed pine pole, and was light and easy raised, we run it right up in a few minutes, they, however, were determined to outdo us, had got a large green hickory pole and could not raise it nor never did raise it half way up. As soon as our pole was up and we had cheered awhile, our meeting was organized and I began to speak; no sooner than I began to speak than the whole of the Democratic crowd left their pole and came over to hear me, speaker and all. I told them that I was glad to see them, that it did me good to see men, and particularly workingmen, have independance enough to hear for themselves what the opposite party had to say. In a few moments their speaker called on me for the proof of something that I had said, when some of our men were for putting him out of the crowd; I said, no, the gentleman has a right to call for proof, and I am bound to furnish it, which I will do if the gentleman will take a seat on the stand; he came forward and took a seat, I handed him the proof; when he had read it I said, are you satisfied. sir, that I made a fair statement? He said, yes, it is all true. I went on and as fast as I read a document, I handed it to him to see if I stated it right, and as he would read them he was honest enough to admit their genuineness. When I had concluded my speech, I invited him to reply, when he immediately came forward and said that the proofs that I had produced were so unanswerable, that he should not make any attempt to do so, and unless his party would produce testimony, by the next Tuesday, to show that they were false, he should take to the stump for Gen. Harrison. This, as a matter of course, raised a shout from the Whigs, but the Democrats began to abuse him and accuse him with being bought, and to say all manner of things against him, and even made loud threats of personal violence against him, but I was their match, when they made threats against him, he being quite a small man; I said, if I hear another threat out of one of you, I will come down from the stand and thrash you out of your boots.—This raised a great laugh, and Doctor Swartz, for that was their speakers name, had to seek safety from them on the road back to town in our procession, and that night made a Whig speech with me in the Court-house in Lewistown, where he handled the Democrats without gloves; he remained a true man during the campaign, and was the means of doing our cause much good. I received great credit from the Whigs for bringing over this man, and for the manner in which I succeeded in doing it.

From Lewistown I was to be at the great convention at Lancaster, and in going there had to travel by Canal in packet boats, as far as Harrisburg, where we could take the cars; they ran that far West at that time. The Canal being in the hands of the Democrats, they concluded to not let us go through, and in order to stop us, drew off the water from one Canal that was a mile or more long, but we beat them at that, by all walking along the tow-path with long ropes and hauled the empty boats through the mud until we reached the next Canal and arrived in Harrisburg in time to meet the evening train for Lancaster, and arrived there the night before the Convention met.

At this meeting a large number of the roughs from Philadelphia, of the Democratic faith had assembled, for the purpose of aiding the Lancaster roughs in breaking up our convention, but there were too many Whigs there for them to undertake it in the day time, so they waited until night, when they supposed that the most of them would leave, and they would be better able to manage the balance; so at night they made an attack upon a meeting in the Public Square but made a bad bargain of it. They then went to the public Hotels and attacked every Whig they met and beat many of them severely. As I was walking up from one of our stands, for we had meetings at several places that night, I met three or four of the Philadelphia bullies, who enquired of me if I knew at which meeting they could find the Buckeye Blacksmith, for, said they, we are after him. Well, said I, he was right down yonder, where you saw those lights a few minutes ago. Thank you sir, said one of them, we would give fifty dollars to get hold of that fellow. I thought to myself and you would give a hundred to get away from him again if you were by yourself.

They went on and I went down the street a considerable distance and called into a small tavern and ask d if I could get lodging, when I was told that I could. I made some inquiry about what was going on in the street and was told all about the meeting, and that the Democrats intended to get hold of the Buckeye Blacksmith that night if they could, and the landlord, although a Democrat, expressed some fears that the mob would attack the City Hotel, for he said this man was stopping there, as also the rest of the speakers, and he would not be surprised if some of them were killed before morning. I thought to myself that I should be surprised if they found the blacksmith at the City Hotel that night. What has this blacksmith done, said I, that they are after him to mob him? "oh, said he, "they say that he is very abusive in his speaking and pretends that he can thrash any man in the country." Did you ever see him, said I. "No I never did," he said, "but I always liked a spunky man."— The conversation ended here and I went to bed, for no person would ever think of looking for me in this little out-of-the-way place. So the next morning at breakfast I said to the landlord, I wonder if the Democrats found the blacksmith last night. "Yes," said a fellow at the table, "and gave him a good licking at that. — I'll bet he don't come to Lancaster to lie again very soon." "He lies, does he," said I. "They say so," said he, "I never heard him." "Where did they find him," I asked. "At the City Hotel," was the response. "Gentlemen," said I, "that blacksmith was not at the City Hotel last night; he is a plain man, as plain as I am, and prefers to stay at a good plain tavern like this." There were four or five men at the table and they seemed to be pleased to hear me speak as I did. "Then you know him, do you," said the landlord. — "Oh yes," said I, "he slept in this house last night. I can swear to that, for he slept in the same bed with me." "I don't understand you," said one of them, "if he slept in the same bed with you last night where is he now?" "Why, gentlemen," I remarked, "he is sitting at the table eating with you." "What! are you the blacksmith they talk so much about?" "I am the man," I said, "and am very much surprised to see that you hard-working men would lend your influence to a party that would stoop so low as to hunt down a man whose only crime is that he is poor and chooses to speak and act for himself; you gentlemen have the same right to speak and act in politics as though you were worth a million of money. They were very much pleased with my conversation, and the landlord and his wife were elated because of my stopping with them and speaking so well of their house as a good, plain tavern, which it was. The leading roughs however would not have been pleased to think that I was so completely in their power, if they had only known it.

From here I went to New York to speak one week until another meeting could be called for me, this was an arrangement between the two State committees.— This was my first visit to New York. The committee had called six meetings at different parts of the city, one for each day, the last one to be at the City Park. This was one of the largest meetings at which I had ever spoken and was held on Saturday afternoon. It was known that I was to speak on the Currency and Van Buren's Sub-Treasury scheme, which brought all the business men of the city to hear me. A. G. Clarke ex-mayor was chairman of the meeting; when I concluded he came forward and told the people that I was a poor man, and he proposed that the meeting should make me a present of a farm by a public collection that day, and said "I will give ten dollars and I know that a thousand of you will do the same," when thousands responded, and a committee sent around. I very foolishly stepped forward and said, gentlemen I am not out speaking for money as the Democrats say, I am out for the great cause of the Whig party. This put a stop to the collection, and the result was I paid my own bills at the hotel. This, I consider, was the most foolish act of my life, for I have no doubt but I would have received at least five or six thousand dollars that day if I had kept my mouth shut, for money was plenty and I had pleased the people to such an extent that they were ready to give their last dollar to me, but in the excitement of the moment I refused to let them raise me a dollar, which I ever afterwards regreted

I left New York and spoke next at Harrisburg, Pa., at which place I met several that had known me in my boyhood days when I had worked a few miles below there. Some of the Democrats had intended to kick up a fuss at my meeting, but when they heard that I was the same blacksmith that had been such a good fighter in that country, when but a boy, they concluded to let me alone. I took advantage of that and told them that I generally thrashed any man that interrupted me; I told them, that I had licked some of their best men when I was a boy and I had not forgotten how to do it yet, and the best way for them was to keep quiet, which they did.

I next went to York, where I had once lived, and many of the older citizens remembered me. Here I got the Democrats in a bad way; one of them came on the stand to make me take back something that I had said, but I soon made him leave the stand without accomplishing his object, amid the laughter of the whole crowd.

From York I began a tour along the Southern tier of counties westward, so as to reach Ohio in time for the election. I spoke at all the principal towns going West until I reached Erie, Penn., and then made my way directly to Cleveland, Ohio, where I spoke to a large meeting the night before the election. I was one hundred miles from home, but determined to reach there in time to vote the next day.

The Whigs of Cleveland had made arrangements with the Ohio Stage Co., to run me through by express in time to vote, which they did, and I arrived just one hour before the polls closed amid the shouts of the Whigs of our little town. I doubt if ever a man went to the polls with more friends around him than I did that day, it was a day long to be remembered by me. I had been gone nine months from home, went away a plain man and come back lionized by the whole country, so much so, that my friends and neighbors of all parties not only respected but felt proud of me; I was well received by all, and a meeting was called at once to hear a short history of my travels, which I gave them; while relating some of the amusing scenes that I had passed through, many of my friends were convulsed with laughter.

I went to Columbus, a few days after my arrival.— I gave a full history of all I had seen and heard while away, and thus ended my first political campaign.

CHAPTER IV.

AS SOON as it was ascertained that Gen. Harrison was elected, I concluded to pay him a visit. I was warmly received not only by him, but by all his friends around him at his headquarters in Cincinnati; he and his friends gave me great praise for what I had done, and were very much pleased with the history that I gave of my travels. They all agreed that I must be taken care of at the proper time, the old General saying that he had a nice little place in view for me.

When it became known that I was in the city, a meeting was called and thousands of people responded to the call, to hear me relate the various incidents that occurred during my travels, and when I finished I was very much lionised by my Whig friends. After remaining a few days in the city, and having been nearly shaken to pieces by my friends in their congratulations of my success in the campaign, I left for home.

On my arrival there I found a number of letters from members elect to the legislature, from various parts of the State, inviting me to become a candidate for Sergeant-at-Arms of the House, the coming session that was about to commence. I went to Columbus and consulted some of my best friends on the subject and concluded through their advice to let my name be used for that office.

A few days after I went to Columbus; the Legislature met, and I soon saw the game that was about to be played. The usual rule of the caucus was to nominate the Speaker first the Clerk next, and last the Sergeant-at-arms, but in order to secure a speaker from the Western part of the State, they balloted for Sergeant-at-arms first and nominated me, I living in the middle part of the State, they then nominated a man from the Eastern part of the State for Clerk, so as to secure the Speaker from the West; I concluded to block that little game, so I came forward and declined the nomination in favor of a western man, that would entitle my district to the Speaker. I no sooner declined than my friends saw the point and nominated the Western man in my place, and then gave my friend the Speakership.

I thus made a sacrifice of myself to promote the interest of one of the best men that ever lived in Ohio; he still lives there, and has faithfully served his country and his party in many high positions since that day. I need not name him, my readers, no doubt, will recognize him by what I have already said. Many of my best friends since that day have blamed me for sacrificing myself for others, for had I stood firm for myself that day, I might have gotten a start that would have enabled me in future years to have become one of the leading men of the State.

Nothing unusual occurred until the time for Harrison to take his seat. I was there, of course, and made several speeches congratulating my friend on his success. A few days after the inauguration I called on the President and was admitted without a card, which gave some offence to the great crowd who were trying to gain access to him; the President told me to rest easy a few days and he would have my place ready for me, which was an Indian Agency among the Wyandott Indians; so I went away contented and in a few days I received my commission, but before I had given bond (which I did) and had gotten my instructions, the President got sick and died.

Mr. Tyler succeeded him and it was some days before I got my final instructions and started to my field of labor, which was at upper Sandusky, Ohio, among the Wyandotts. I soon became very popular with the Indians by attending strictly to their interest; soon after my arrival among the Indians the Government commenced negotiations with them for their lands, and sent a Commissioner there to treat with them; he was an excellent man, and with my aid finally made a treaty by which they were to receive lands in Kansas for their lands in Ohio, and were to move to their new homes within one year at the expense of the Government, and I was to go with them and continue to be their Agent; but about this ttme Tyler had sold out to the Democracy, and I had but little hopes of staying in office under him, as I was an unyielding friend of Henry Clay, and Tyler knew it. About this time I had business at Columbus and went there; no sooner had the Tyler party of Columbus heard of my arrival than they called a meeting at the Market House without consulting me and announced me to speak. As soon as the Clay men saw their bills, they too, called a Clay meeting at the opposite end of the Market House, and announced me as their speaker. What was I to do? Principle, and fidelity to my party stareing me in the face on one side, and bread for my family on the other. I was poor. If I spoke my sentiments, which would be for Clay, I would be turned out of my office. If I lost my situation I would have nothing to start with; what should I do? If I spoke at the Tyler meeting I would sacrifise my whole life's cherished principles. I must confess it was the severest trial of my life, both parties around me urging me to speak at their meetings. I had but a few hours to decide the matter. I finally made up my mind what to do, which was to go to both meetings, and decline to speak at either on the ground that I lived in the Indian Territory and had no right to meddle with State politics; I did so, but at the Clay meeting the President desired me to say who I favored for the next President. Without any hesitation I answered: when the time arrives to elect a President and Henry Clay is still living, I shall support him if nominated. This caused the wildest excitement among both parties, the Tyler men denouncing me and the Clay men shouting praises for my firmness in the matter; the end of the matter was, that in nine days from that Tyler discharged me; we had no telegraph then, so it took four days to go to Washington, one day to act on it, and four days to come back.

Well here I was in a distant country away from friends, with none but Indians about me and they to poor to help me to start any business, so I concluded to open up a campaign on temperance. I had sometime before that, taken a decided stand in the great Washington temperance movement of that day, so I moved back to my former place of residence, and started out speaking on temperance, and here again I was brought into direct antagonism with my old opponents the Democrats, for I was not only in their way as a party man, but assisting to destroy their most powerful lever that moved their political machinery, (whisky.) They immediately commenced a new attack on me wherever I went, they secured the services of their most miserable tools to libel me, and say all manner of evil things against me to destroy my usefulness as a lecturer, they followed me wherever I went, reporting that where I had spoken the day before, that I had been drunk, and that the Temperance men had refused to let me speak and would not recognise me. So unrelenting did they prosecute me, that I was compelled to get a certificate from the leading men of the place where I spoke, certifying to my conduct while at their place, and take it with me to the next town; in this way I managed to head them off; I have a large bundle of these certificates unto this day. On one occasion there was to be a Fourth of July celebration in an adjoining county by the Temperance people, and they sent a committee to my county to obtain speakers. I was the man recommended by several of the clergymen of our county, as the most effective man for them and was accordingly invited in connection with one of our leading clergymen to attend. The committee returned home and reported these facts to an adjourned meeting; no sooner had they done so, than a leading Democratic doctor who was one of the leading Temperance men of the county offered a resolution to notify me not to attend. This resolution was at once voted down on the ground that I had been recommended by the best men of the country. This Democrat at once withdrew not only from the Temperance cause, but from the church that had sustained me; this occured some two weeks before the celebration was to take place.

No sooner was it determined upon, that I was to speak there, than this doctor and his friends secured the service of a poor miserable drunken Englishman, to go to my county and obtain some claims, if any could be found against me, so as to arrest me as a non-resident debtor of the county, and thereby disgrace me, and if possible, destroy my influence. He succeeded in obtaining two small claims, one for less than two dollars, and the other for less than ten dollars; this they kept a secret calculating to arrest me on the morning of the fifth as I was exempt from arrest on the fourth by law.

The fourth of July arrived and with it myself and friend that was to speak with me. I spoke twice that day, and gave so much satisfaction that one of the leading Ministers of the county offered a resolution inviting me to speak again next day at ten o'clock and at night; it was accordingly so arranged. The next morning this drunken loafer went before a magistrate and made oath that I was about to leave the county with intent to defraud him out of his just claims, (when I had not any knowledge that I owed him a cent.) He got a warrant, and just as I was about to commence speaking, had me arrested on one of these claims; my friends were too strong for him and I made my speech before I went with the constable, and when I appeared before the Squire I beat him in the suit.— I did not owe the claim. As soon as I beat him on this claim, he got another warrant for the other, and had me re-arrested; this claim he managed to beat me in although it was another man's debt, still I was bound to see it paid; I took an appeal on this, and finally in the end beat him on that also, the real debtor coming forward and paying the debt.

There was a monster meeting that night and several Ministers and leading men came forward and denounced these proceedings in the severest terms. I left there in the course of a few days with flying colors.

My dear reader you will never be able to fully understand the amount of sufferings, persecutions and trials, that I have had to pass through for the cause of right, and for principles that I honestly believed to be correct; the half will never be known this side of eternity what I have endured in the last fifty years in advocating those great and fundamental principles that I have always believed would advance the interests of the laboring men of this country. I have labored honestly, fully believing that in the fulness of time, in His own appointed way God would bring about the accomplishment of these very principles I have so long and zealously advocated. Though I may not live to see that day, I have an unshaken confidence in their final triumph. May God in his goodness hasten the day!

On many occasions these enemies of mine would obtain the services of some abandoned woman to meet me on the street, and pretend that I was one of her old acquaintance, and insist on a renewal of our former friendship, when in fact she had never seen me before, but these games had but little effect, the better class of people understood them too well.

At one place during my absence a poor ignorant creature stole into my room at a tavern where I was staying, and put a pint bottle of whisky in my carpet bag, and then came to my meeting and offered to bet twenty dollars that I carried whisky in my bundle, (but in this I beat him.) Just before I went to the meeting I went to my room to get a handkerchief and there found the bottle and at once destroyed it, knowing that devil had put it there; so when he offered to bet the twenty dollars I asked him who gave him the money to bet, (for he looked like a man that never had any money.) He said: "never mind wnere I got the money; you dare not bet." "Yes, I dare" said I, "put up your money in the landlord's hands and appoint your own committee to examine my carpet-bag, I will bet you twenty dollars that I have no whisky in it." We put up the money and he appointed the landlord to examine the carpet-bag. The whole crowd rushed to the tavern to see the examination.— After everything was taken out of the carpet-bag and no whisky found, the landlord gave me the money amid the wildest shouts of the temperance men present, and I never saw such a chop-fallen set as these few red face, blear eyed Democratic rummies, who had made up the money for him to bet; they scarcely knew what to say when I told the landlord to give me a room with a good lock on it, for I feared some of those fellows who had such dirty shirts on might take a notion to some of my clean ones, and I had no notion to trade with them. The next night I spoke again and told the whole story, how I had found the whisky and destroyed it, showing the whole plan to disgrace me and win my money; this, as well as the most of their dirty tricks only served to make me more popular, at least it did me no harm.

At one place there lived a man who had considerable property; he had three sons, two were grown young men, and the other nearly so. They had all began to love whisky too well, and their father knew it. I had gotten up a great excitement in the place on temperance, when a venerable old Methodist minister, who knew the habits of these young men, went to their father and said: "my friend, you know that your boys are in danger of being ruined by whisky, had you not better join in with us in this great temperance movement that is now going on, you may thereby save your sons from ruin. "Parson," said the old man, "I would rather follow my boys to the grave than see them join the Temperance Society, for every man that joins that Society is forever lost to the Democratic party, and I would rather bury every son I have than see them vote the Whig ticket."

You will see my dear reader, the difficulty that I labored under. When I met a Whig that was fond of whisky, he said: "well you are a good Whig and I don't care if you are a Temperance man, I like you anyhow," but when I run against a Democrat that loved whisky, and the majority of them do, I had no offset to make with him; he had a double hatred to me, and even the very few temperate Democrats that I met, threw every obstacle in my way that they could, even some of their best members of the church refused to meet me in a social manner, so much had the party press prejudiced their minds against me.

If a liberal Democrat was seen in a friendly conversation with me, he was at once set upon by the leaders and chastised for departing from the faith.— The poor fellows were afraid to be friendly with me, for fear they would be read out of the party, and you know it would be a dreadful thing to be read out of such an honorable and dignified party as the Democratic party has always been; this, and this alone kept hundreds, yes, thousands of their respectable men from leaving them, the fear of the abuse that would be heaped upon them by their leaders and the party press.

Without going into any further details on my temperance experience, I will only add that I continued to lecture on that subject until the fall of 1843, when I received a letter from a Committee of the leading Whigs of Columbus, Ohio, to come and speak for them a few times on politics. I went and soon found that their object in inviting me there was preparatory to sending me South in the interest of Henry Clay's nomination for the Presidency the following Spring. I stayed there several days, made several speeches, and got myself well posted on the various subjects that were then before the people.

My Whig friends had secured the services of a Southern man to pioneer me through that country (as I had never been farther South than Kentucky,) by the name of Mosely, who was styled the Kentucky Pumpmaker, and after fitting us out with every thing necessary for a six months trip, we started on the first of November for New Orleans, speaking at all the principle towns within fifty miles of the Ohio and Mississippi rivers, commencing at Cincinnati.

When we arrived in Cincinnati we found the papers full of notices of the meeting to come off that night, to be addressed by the Buckeye Blacksmith and Kentucky Pumpmaker. When the hour arrived for the meeting we found a monstrous crowd gathered in front of the Court House; my colleague was a well educated sensible man with good conversational abilities, but not a great speaker. It was not, however, intended for him to do much speaking, but merely to introduce me, which he could do in good style; he generally mixed with the best citizens through the day and prepared them to hear me at night. The subject that I generally spoke upon was the Tariff, which was a new thing to most of the people of the South.

Upon our arrival at Louisville we found the Whigs ready to receive us with open arms; they had not forgotten me since 1840, and we had a great meeting.— Here I began to impress upon the people of the South the great benefits t at would result from a protective Tariff, and the only hope that we had in bringing about these measures was the election of Mr. Clay, their own immortal statesman. This took like hot cakes with the people of that city, and I went away from there with more honors than I did in 1840. We next visited Frankford, the native place of my friend Mosely, where we met a very warm reception, arising no doubt to his being a native of that place.

From Frankford we returned and made our way down the river, spoke at several places until we reached the mouth of the Cumberland river, where we took a steamer for Nashville, the Capital of Tennessee. Notice of our coming had preceeded us; here I was met by the Hon. John Bell, former Secretary of War, under Gen. Harrison, whom I had served under while Indian Agent. No sooner had we arrived than we were taken in charge by Mr. Bell and Gov. Jones, and escorted to the State House; the Legislature being in session, we were introduced to the President of the Senate, who, although he was a Democrat, adjourned the Senate and introduced us to the members. He then escorted us to the House and introduced us to the Speaker, who left the chair and made a motion to tender us the use of the House to speak in, and although both the Houses were Democratic, the motion was carried by acclamation. Here I found the most honorable and manly set of Democrats I ever had seen, and began to conclude that there was some decency to be found among Democrats, and in my speech I tried to return their compliments to me by treating the party with courtesy.

My companion, however, made a great mistake by abusing Gen. Jackson at his own home, a thing uncalled for, as he was not before the people for their suffrages. I, however, smoothed it over the best I could; I pleased them so well, that the next day I was invited by the Democratic President of the Senate, to ride up with him in his carriage and pay my respects to Gen. Jackson, which I did, and received a warm greeting from him. He thanked me very cordially for the manner in which I had referred to him the night previous, in my speech.

The next day after my visit to the old General I spoke to a large meeting at Columbia, the home of James K. Polk, who was afterwards elected President. At this place as well as others, I advocated the principles of the Tariff in the strongest terms. This speech and the one at Nashville brought out a letter from Mr. Polk to the Legislature, condemning the Tariff of 1842 in the strongest terms, both in principle and detail; and on my return to Nashville, to address another meeting expressly for the benefit of the ladies who had a great desire to hear me, I found Polk's letter already in print. I secured a number of copies for Northern use; and after speaking to a monstrous meeting, at which the ladies turned out by thousands, I left Nashville, I believe, with the good wishes of all the people.

We continued our way down the river, speaking at most of the larger towns until we reached Memphis, where we had a great meeting, and I became very popular. A Committee went with us to Jackson, the Capital of the State of Mississippi, and here again we received a great compliment from the Democratic Legislature that was in session at the time; they, by a unanimous vote of the House, invited us to seats on the floor with the members, and tendered us the use of the House to speak in. Here again my companion pitched into Jackson in an uncalled for manner, and would have had considerable trouble, probably been shot, if I had not got the matter settled for him.

After we left Jackson we went to Vicksburg, and from there to Natchez, where we had a great meeting. I spoke twice there and left for Baton Rouge; here we had more trouble. My companion got into trouble about Jackson, and while I was speaking a drunken fellow came into the Court House and thought I was the speaker that had abused Jackson; he drew his pistol and fired at me, the ball just missed my head and struck the wall right by me; the mistake was soon discovered and he came to me after I was done speaking and offered an apology, and through me this trouble was settled.

I began to conclude by this time that I would be better without a pioneer than with one and told my companion so, and unless he would quit abusing Jackson in this Southern country we would both be killed. He agreed to quit it, but on our arrival in New Orleans we were met by a large committee, who escorted us to the St. Charles hotel, and as a matter of course we had to show ourselves on the balcony of the hotel and make a few remarks to hundreds that were waiting our arrival. Here again my companion pitched into Jackson in the very city he had saved from being burned by the British in 1814; I was frightened almost out of my wits, but managed to heal up the difficulty by telling a few laughable stories, in my funniest style.

The next day was to be our great meeting at Bank's Arcade, the largest hall in the city. The leading Whigs called on us, and in a very friendly manner told us that they would rather my companion would not speak for there was a bad feeling towards him and he had better wait a few days before he spoke; it was so arranged. Mr. Clay was in the city at that time and was desirous to hear me speak; accordingly the Whigs secreted him behind the stand, so that I might not see him, for fear that if I saw him I would become embarrased. I spoke over two hours explaining the great benefits to be derived to the country by the election of Henry Clay to the Presidency. During my whole speech I was listened to with the most profound attention; at the close of my meeting I was taken in charge by the committee and escorted to my hotel, where they made arrangements for me to speak in all sections of the city for ten days ahead.

The next morning I took a stroll to the Post Office, and who should I meet there but Mr. Clay. "Good morning Bear," said he, "how are you this morning after your great speech last night." "I am very well Mr. Clay, and hope to find you well; how did you know that I made a speech last night," said I. "Why I heard you," said he, "I was hid right behind you and heard everything you said, I was afraid to let you see me for fear it might embarras you," said he. He then went on to tell me that the course that I was pursuing was according to his judgment, calculated to do a vast amount of good, that he and some of his friends had concluded to keep me in the field until the election took place; he said the committee would take charge of me and provide for me, and write letters ahead, and fully endorse me to the people of the South and when the election was over and all went right, to come to him, and he would take good care of me. We had a hearty laugh over the little incident of my bringing him fire to light his segar, when I was a boy; he was much pleased when I told him that all I was and ever expected to be I gave him credit for; had he not advised me to go to a free country and get education, I never could have been what I now am. He said he felt proud to have such a friend as I, coming as I did, from the working class.

My friend spoke once or twice with me after that, and then the committee sent him to Mobile, to prepare the way for me. When I was ready to leave, the committee furnished me with plenty of money and the best of endorsements to the people throughout the South. The ladies made me many very valuable presents of clothing for myself, also many rich presents for my daughter. I left New Orleans with the best wishes, not only of the Whigs, but many of the Democrats also.

When I arrived in Mobile my comrade had got the people on tip-toe to see me, so much so, that when the boat arrived there were hundreds waiting to get a glimpse of me. Mr. Wm. E. Preston of South Carolina, had me in charge, and introduced me to the chairman of the committee who took charge of us, the crowd following us to a hotel. As soon as we arived I was taken to the balcony of the hotel and introduced to the people; order being restored I said, Mr. President I feel very proud of this reception, at the hands of a people that I have never until this day met. Indeed sir, I have met with nothing but the kindest and most courteous treatment since I left my Northern home and come to the sunny South, for which I feel very proud. I know not sir, why it is that the people of all classes seem so anxious to see and hear me; it certainly is not because of my eloquence as a speaker, or the fine language I use? I am a plain mechanic, without the advantage of a classical education, and am therefore unable to use the fine words that a more gifted speaker can. I can give no other reason for my popularity than this, that I am a very liberal man, believing that there are honest men in all parties, and churches, and though I may differ with you sir, on politics and religion, I still believe you are as honest as I am, and that your opinions ought to be respected. I hope sir, that during my stay among you, that we may all become better acquainted, and warmer friends. After inviting them to come and hear my speech the next afternoon, I retired to my room to prepare to receive those that wished to call on me. During the afternoon all the leading men of both parties in the city called on me, and we had a very pleasant time.

I had by this time discovered that the poor or laboring men of the South took but little interest in politics; they generally voted as their employers or owners of the land they lived on, did; they paid no attention to me or but little to my speeches, so I had become satisfied that in order to reach them I must mix with them. I told the Whig committee that it was important for me to visit the various work-shops and houses of the poor classes of the people, in order to have them hear me speak; they saw the point and accordingly next morning I was taken around to all the work-shops and places of business in the city, and was introduced to working men generally. I cracked a joke or two with each, and gave them a special invitation to hear me speak; this seemed to have a very good effect, as many of them were much pleased with me, inviting me to their houses, and one poor Blacksmith insisted on my taking dinner with him, which I did, and it was a good one; his wife and friends were delighted with me they said that I was not a big bug like other speakers in that country, but a plain man.

I would here remark that many of our best speakers make a great mistake in failing to notice the poor men who largely compose their audiences; they generally speak highly of the poor man in their speeches, but never notice him before or after the meeting. This is a great mistake, for the poor men notice this and talk about it. I have often been told by poor men, the reason they liked me was that I would talk to them as well as to rich men after I was done speaking, by these means I have brought many hundred of men to hear me and vote my way, that never could have been reached in any other manner.

The result of the course that I had pursued since my arrival in the city, brought together that afternoon one of the largest meetings ever held in that country. The meeting was held in a beautiful grove in a public square and we had rich and poor, ladies and gentlemen, Democrats and Whigs, in fact every body was there. I was introduced as a plain mechanic from the North, who had come South well recommended, and the attention of the audience was requested to hear me on the great tariff question.

I commenced by saying that from my extensive acquaintance throughout this broad land of ours, I had become satisfied that the American people were politically honest, one party as well as the other; so well satisfied was I of this fact, that I would have no hesitation in trusting my life on the prosperity of the country in their hands if they could only be well informed on the great issues before them. I then went on to answer the Democratic objections to the protective system, and the great advantages arising from protecting American industry; showing that no country could become great which depended on other countries for supplies; that in order to become a great and prosperous Nation we must sell more than we buy to bring the balance of trade in our favor; we must divide our labor; let some produce from the soil and others manufacture, and thereby create a home market; showing that the nearer we could get the producer to the consumer the better for both; while thousands of boys and girls were idle in this country they were shipping their cotton to Europe and paying boys and girls there for manufacturing it into cloth, and then paying for shipping it back again.

In this way I talked for over two hours, and when I closed I was warmly applauded by the great crowd that was present, and I was pressed by the Whigs to speak again for them that night, which I did to another monstrous meeting.

I left next morning for Montgomery, but shall never forget the people of Mobile, nor the warm reception I met at their hands; I was followed to the boat by hundreds of them and was cheered loudly until the boat was out of sight.

My companion had preceded me to Montgomery and had gotten up a little excitement about me, but I soon found that the people of that place had no great opinion of greasy mechanics; they treated me very well however, and we had a large and very interesting meeting. There were few working white men there, and I therefore mixed but little among the people.— I made my speech and left the next day for a great barbecue that was to be held at Watumkee, a new county town some twenty miles from Columbus, Georgia.— Here I had a fine time of it; the main speaker that was to speak there failed to come and I had to do all the speaking; here I became very popular, so much so that I had some trouble in leaving them. A committee from Georgia had met me to take me to Columbus, but the Alabamians would not let me go but took me away to a small town that night to speak again and then sent me in a fine carriage the next day to meet my engagement at Columbus, Ga.

My experience in Alabama satisfied me that my popularity among them was not their love of a working man, but simply for the effect I could produce among working men. This, my dear reader, is generally the case everywhere; leading men care but little about us working men only for what they can make out of us. Therefore we should work and vote for our own interest which is the protection of our own labor by standing by the Tariff.

CHAPTER V.

CAMPAIGN IN GEORGIA, SOUTH CAROLINA AND VIRGINIA.

UPON my arrival at Columbus, I found the people on tip-toe to see me. Here I found the finest water power I had ever seen, but none of it in use; the water seemed to tumble from one rock to another, as far as I could see up the river, and I made good use of that circumstance to aid me in my speech on the tariff that night. I told them that I had seen five hundred young negro boys and girls, since I had come to their city, running about doing nothing, that could manufacture all the cotton goods needed in the place, if they only had one live Yankee to put up a factory for them. Here said I, you have the water that God has given, you have the idle laborers, and you have the raw cotton and plenty of money to build factories with, and yet you ship your cotton all the way to old England and pay her laborers for spinning and weaving it for you, and then pay for shipping it back again for you to use, and let all the young negroes run idle. You must think a great deal of the English to spend so much money to give them employment, when you could manufacture all the cloth that would be needed in your State, within two miles of where I now stand. There is wealth enough in this town to build factories sufficient to supply all the wants of this country, and in place of letting these young negroes run idle, they could earn their masters two or three hundred dollars a year working the mills for you. The result of my speech, was, that before I left Columbus, they had appointed a committee to go to Lowell, Massachusetts and investigate the plans of manufacturing, and very soon after commenced the manufacturing of their own cotton goods.

I became very popular at Columbus, so much so, that they would have given me any amount of money to settle there and make it my future home. I have often been sorry that I did not do so; for they were a warm hearted, liberal class of people. And whatever may have been their faults since, in the rebellion, I must say, that in all my travels in life, I never found a more high minded, liberal, social, kind hearted set of people, both Whigs and Democrats, than I found in Georgia.

I have often wondered how it was possible that there could exist so much difference, between a Southern Democrat, and a Northern Copperhead, but such is the case. When I meet a Southern Democrat I meet a gentleman who will converse freely and in a friendly manner with me, invite me to his house, and if I go, treat me most kindly, and we part in friendship, but when I meet a Northern Copperhead, he is very likely to insult me the first word he speaks, either directly or by insinuations, attacking my character or that of some friend of mine; no wonder that I had such a poor opinion of the Democratic party before I went South. I have not changed my opinion of the Northern wing yet.

I next visited Macon, one of the most beautiful little towns I ever saw, situated on a small river in the interior of the State, about two hundred miles from Savannah, a very aristocratic place, but very few poor whites living there. I had been so highly spoken of by the Whig papers of the country, for my liberality toward the opposite party, the Democrats as well as the Whigs gave me a cordial welcome among them. I spoke there twice, the second time by the invitation of the ladies; they were not present at my first meeting, and hearing of my good natured way of speaking, insisted on hearing me, and by the way they smiled and waved their kandkerchiefs, I must have pleased them.

I spent one of the happiest Sundays there that I ever spent in my life, and on Monday left for the city of Savannah, in charge of a committee of both places. On reaching Savannah I met the grandest reception I ever met except in my own native town (Frederick City, Maryland.) Here I found more mechanics than I usually found in small Southern cities; there were over three hundred men who met the cars some three miles out of the city, where myself and the committee were received with great pomp, and escorted into the city to the head quarters of the Young Men's Clay Club, where there were hundreds of men, women and children, white and black, all anxiously waiting to get a glimpse of a live Northern working man who could make a speech.

I was taken into head quarters by a back way, and hastened to put on a good suit of clothes and was at once brought forward to a front platform and introduced to the people to make a short introductory speech. No sooner had I commenced than a young sprig of a lawyer after eyeing me very closely, turned on his heel and started away swearing, (a blacksmith the devil,) that is a gentleman, he is no blacksmith, why look at his clothes that will satisfy you. I only spoke a few minutes when I was taken to my hotel for dinner. Shortly after dinner in came a committee who said they were a mixed committee of the two parties, and had called on me to ascertain whether I was a blacksmith or not. One young man (a Whig) said that he had bet twenty dollars that I could beat any man in Savannah making a horse shoe, and from what he had read he believed I could. I laughed and told him that I thought he would win; this created great merriment among the crowd present.

The bet was made with a boss horse-shoer; he had a black man that made his shoes, and on the strength of this man's work he had made the bet. I told them I would bet fifty dollars more that I could beat any man in the State making a horse-shoe, and let my Democratic friend, who had made the bet of twenty dollars, be the judge. This was a clincher for the Democrats; they backed down at once, being satisfied with the twenty dollar bet. We soon made arrangements to go to this man's shop who had made the bet, to prove who could make the best shoe, (as horse-shoeing was my trade I had no fears of the result.) There went a great crowd with us, so much so, that they had to take several boards off the shop for the people to see me make the shoe. I went to work and fixed the punches to my mind and made the shoe. Before I had it done the boss spoke up and said, gentlemen, it is no use to talk, I have lost the bet, that is the finest formed shoe I ever saw. So I left the shop amidst the shouts of my friends. The young man who made the bet on me was rich and did not want the money, so he handed me not only the twenty dollars he won but the other twenty also. That was the biggest price I ever heard of for making a horse-shoe.

In Savannah there was a small dirty little Democratic sheet that had attacked me several times before I arrived, as also on the morning after I had made the shoe, (but to the honor of the South he was a Northern man,) so when I made my main speech that day I pitched into him, (the Whigs having posted me.) — Soon after I had finished my speech and was entertaining some friends in my room at the hotel, I was waited on by two young gentlemen, bearers of a challenge from this editor, to fight a duel. I read it, smiled, and handed it to one of my friends to read aloud. What answer will you make to it, said my friend. Accept it, said I. This of course pleased my friends. I told the young men to be seated a few minutes and I would give them my answer in writing. Gentlemen, said I, the challenged party has the choice of weapons and the mode of fighting I believe, in this country. Certainly they have, said my friends. Very well, I will fix that chap pretty soon, I said, and commenced and wrote the following answer :

SIR! Your note of this date inviting me to give you satisfaction in mortal combat for words spoken in my speech of this date, has been duly received, and in answer I beg leave to say that your invitation is accepted.

I propose to meet you in front of Whig Headquarters at 6 o'clock this afternoon precisely. The weapons used are to be our heads— we will butt out the difficulty.

Very respectfully,

J. W. BEAR.

To J. H. S.

When I had finished it I handed it to my friend who looked over it, and after letting my other friend see it I thought they would go into fits laughing. The young men refused to carry it so I sent it by one of my friends. At the appointed hour I was on hand, but the editor failed to come to time. I made a short speech to the crowd that gathered around explaining the whole affair of the challenge and answer amid the wildest laughter of all present.

The result of this affair caused so much amusement that my Whig friends put out posters that night for another meeting the next day and it was a monstrous affair. My antagonist failed to put in an appearance. I paid him up fully in that speech with compound interest, to the entire satisfaction of all present Democrats as well as Whigs. Many of the leading Democrats of the City called on me that afternoon and expressed great pleasure at the manner in which I treated him, declaring that his attacks on me were uncalled for and unmanly. Some of them concluded that he would not challenge another Blacksmith very soon.— I told these gentlemen that I had not received one insult through my journey in the Southern States from any man born in the South. Whatever insults I had received in the South came either from foreigners or Northern men, and to the latest hour of my life I should never forget the kindness I had received from the Southern people. This kind of talk was the crowning point of my visit to Georgia. I was to leave that night at 10 o'clock in the boat for Charleston, South Carolina. When the hour arrived for me to leave the hotel, more than five hundred men of both parties escorted me to the boat, for fear this editor would make an assault on me. When on the boat in charge of a committee I made those on shore a short farewell speech until the boat left. As she pushed off from the shore the crowd made the welkin ring with hurrahs for the Blacksmith.

There had been great preparation made in Charleston for us, my colleague going there with me. We arrived in the morning and were met at the boat by a considerable number in carriages and taken to the South Carolina hotel, one of the finest hotels in the city; we were visited during the day by many of the leading men of both parties; the Columbus, Georgia, committee on their way East had given them a history of my tariff speeches, as also the history of my colleague's speeches; he had been in the habit of abusing Gen. Jackson to such a degree that he had become very unpopular with the people wherever he spoke; I had great trouble to keep him down, indeed in many places they refused to let him speak, putting him off with the pretense that one speech was all the people cared about listening to. The people of the South are a very sensitive kind of people, they will listen all night to argument but not to abuse; in Charleston, Calhoun's home, it was necessary to treat him as well as Jackson with the greatest respect, they were not before the people for office and it was impolitic to say anything about them unkindly, this I urged on my colleague; I hated them as bad as he did but still I let them alone and if I spoke of them at all I made some favorable allusion to them; this course rendered me very popular with all parties; the committee arranged for me to speak in the theatre that night, my colleague to only make a short speech introducing me. He could make an excellent introductory speech and he did so that night. It was arranged that I should speak on general politics that night and on the tariff at the mass meeting the next day. We had a large meeting that night, and in urging the claims of Mr. Clay for the Presidency I spoke of him as one of the great luminaries of the age, not to be equaled by any man living except one, need I say who that one is, I am too near his home to be misunderstood, I mean gentlemen, your own idol John C. Calhoun ; it appeared that they would shake the house to pieces with their stamping and cheers.— This course, my dear reader, is the best policy in all cases in politics or any other subject, if you can't say any good of a man don't say anything. You cannot trap flies with vinegar, molasses is better ; if you want to win men to your cause don't abuse their friends, differ with all men honestly, and don't think because they differ with you that they are bad or dishonest men. In this way I made many thousands of friends to my cause.

That night when I arrived at my hotel I was for two hours in the parlor receiving the crowd that wished an introduction to me, among them, all the leading Democrats of the city, they telling me they felt proud to take a mechanic by the hand from a Northern State, who could speak such favorable things as I had about one of their citizens whom they all so much delighted to honor.

The next day we had a monster mass meeting in a grove. I made my tariff speech; when I made the allusion to the thousands of idle young negroes I had seen in their city who could earn their masters ten per cent. on their value, it pleased them very much, they saw the point very clearly through my explanations, so that when I was done I met a very warm reception, everybody seemed to want to shake hands with me from the richest to the poorest.

I was met here by a delegation of men representing the ladies, inviting me to speak for them on female influence at the theatre that night. I accepted it.—We had the place packed an hour befor the time for speaking, by the elite of the city, all anxious to see and hear a blacksmith speak; at the close of my speech the chairman said that many of the ladies wished to shake hands with me, which I considered the greatest compliment I ever received, and told them so, they were as fine a specimen of Southern ladies as I ever saw. I stood for a long time and was introduced to many hundreds of them, many thanking me for the favorable allusion I made to them as well as their gentlemen friends, particularly Mr. Calhoun. I left the next day for Columbia, a beautiful little inland town some forty miles from there; I spoke to a large meeting there, and then returned to Charleston on my way to North Carolina.

On my arrival at Wilmington, N. C., I found a very different class of people, they were not as intelligent as I had generally found them through the South, there were more poor white men and less negroes, and more of the middle class than I had found through the Southern States. We had a large mass meeting the night that I arrived there, and the first time for months I spoke to a large proportion of working men. This brought me into my right element for my hobby had been the workingman's interest. I spoke at length on that subject in connection with a protective tariff. My speech that night would have been a grand success had it not been that just before I got through a fire broke out in a large hotel in the vicinity of the meeting which broke it up, and it was an awful fire, it burnt up nearly the whole city; myself and colleague could get no quarters that night, but worked all night helping in extinguishing the flames; the next day we left for Raleigh, the capital of the State, had a fine time there, and then left for Petersburg, Va., where we arrived two days in advance of our meeting; my colleague had relations in Richmond so he went ahead to prepare the way for me. I had a fine time in Petersburg making them a short speech the night after my arrival to prepare the way for our great mass meeting that was to come off. In my speech that night I spoke very flatteringly of their pretty town and also their ladies. The result of my speech that night had the effect of bringing out the largest meeting ever held in that place; the ladies turned out by hundreds not only from the city but from the surrounding country; here I had a fair chance to speak on my great hobby the advantage of protection to American industry; a large number of laboring men were present, and they were much pleased at my allusion to them in my remarks on the subject of the tariff. I made some very happy allusions to the ladies in saying that with their smiles and influence we expected to win.

> We gained the day four years ago
> For all the girls helped you know,
> And now they all enlist again
> And go for Clay with might and main.

CHORUS—
> Then get out the way with your foul party,
> We are the girls of 1840.

I sung them this song that I had composed for the campaign.

This brought the meeting down with the wildest applause, everybody wanted a copy ; a printer present agreed to furnish them with plenty of copies, which he did in a few minutes.

I left there the most popular man that ever lived, not only the ladies but the working men flocked around me to bid me farewell as I was to leave for Richmond that night in charge of their committee.

The next morning soon after breakfast the Whigs began to call on me, and to show me the *Richmond Enquirer* which had mistook my colleague's speech the night before for mine. I have not yet made a speech there having only arrived at a late hour at night, but my colleague had spoken to a large meeting and had pitched into Jackson and the editor of the *Enquirer* in his usual way, so the editor pitched into me by mistake. My friends told me that I must go to him and make him agree to make an apology in his paper, and if he refused, I must shoot him down in his office. They supplied me with a pistol and I went for him, two of my friends going with me. I called on the gentleman, and asked him if he was the author of the article in his paper alluding to me. He said it was handed in by one of his local editors, he had not written it himself. I told him the whole thing was a falsehood as I could prove that I was not at the meeting neither had I ever made a speech in Richmond, and I therefore demanded a retraction of the whole matter in his next issue. He very politely told me that it was not his desire to do me or any other man injustice and would very cheerfully exonerate me the next morning, which he did. I invited him to come and hear me speak, he did so and I treated him very politely. So the next morning he spoke in very honorable terms of me, only saying that I had better be at home in my shop, than learning Virginians politics. My meeting was a grand affair, the Whigs had built a large wigwam, the largest I ever saw, it would seat ten thousand people and was packed to overflowing. My colleague having prepared the people the night before, there were thousands of ladies there and I sung my song with good effect and think that I made the best speech that night, that I ever made. Several gentlemen present who heard me before, said that I outdone myself.

That night at the hotel the State Committee paid me a visit to engage my services for their Spring election that was to come of in about six weeks. They told me that I should have all the money I wanted to spend and for my services also, but that I must get rid of my colleague, he would undo all that I could do. So the next morning I frankly told him what they had said, and that we now must part, and each one take his own course. He felt very much hurt at the arrangement, got angry and left for Ohio, his home. I stayed with them until their election came off, speaking in all the principle places in Eastern Virginia. In many places in the lower part of the State I found a very ignorant class of people, the most ignorant I had ever met with. At one small place, some of the men refused to hear me speak on the tariff for fear they might catch it, thinking it was a disease that was catching; some of them refused to shake hands with me. On one occasion I was travelling along a country road and was quite sick. I came across a small country tavern. I called and although I was not in the habit of drinking liquors, I asked the landlord, a big dirty looking fellow, if he had any good brandy, he said it ought to be good, for he paid eighty cents a gallon for it by the wholesale in Norfolk, for he had bought two quarts at a time, and it was old, for he bought it last Fall. I said I am sick let me have it without so much talk. He set out the bottle, I poured out some and asked him for some sugar; he reached his hand into a gourd hanging against the wall and took a little brown sugar in his fingers and put it into my brandy, took his pocket knife, with which he cut his tobacco, and stirred it up. I said give me a little mint, I saw some growing near the house, he stepped out and got some and stirred it in the brandy. I said now a little ice if you please, he looked at me and said, look here man, I thought you was a fool when you first came in, now I know it, who the devil ever heard tell of ice this time of the year. Now this man was fifty years old and a good Democrat, and had never heard of ice being kept for use in Summer. This fellow was and is now a fair specimen of many of the poor whites of the South, and one of course opposed to negro equality as they call it.

I found soon after my arrival in Virginia that the Democrats were more of the stamp of the Northern than the Southern. They were envious and ready to do any dirty job that their leaders want done. They were destitute of that high sense of honor that I found in the Democrats further South. On my arrival in Norfolk I found that they had got a poor drunken creature of foreign birth to go before a Magistrate and swear that a few weeks previous he traveled with me in the cars from Baltimore to Washington and I had publicly declared, that I would never vote for any man but an Abolitionist. This they had printed in circular form and scattered all over the town. My friends came to me and told me that I must satisfy the people that it was not true, or my influence would be destroyed; well gentlemen, said I, that is easily done. I did not say such things, neither was I within a thousand miles of there at the time he swears I was, neither have I been in Washington for three years. I will show you where I was at the time sworn to. I went to my trunk and got the New Orleans paper, which contained a long account of my ten days speaking there, as also my departure for Mobile, and speaking in the highest terms of me. There gentlemen, you see that I was speaking in New Orleans on the very day that he says I was in Washington. You see that I have no wings and the impossibility of my being there. I also have papers here for almost every week fer three months before that time, giving an account of my speaking in the South and Southwest at the same time handing them a bundle of papers, to prove my statements. They said that I had so fully vindicated myself, that they would stand by me at all hazards.

The next question was, what shall I do with this fellow. Shoot him, said one. He is not worth it, said another. Said I, gentlemen I think the best way for me is to denounce him at my meeting as a liar, a scoundrel and a coward, and that no man of respectability dare take it up, and if they do, shoot him. That's the plan, they all cried and raised to their feet gave me three times three cheers.

Well, at 3 o'clock that afternoon our mass meeting came off. As soon as I was introduced I took the circular and read it and said: Now Mr. President and gentlemen, I will show you that this whole thing is as false and as base as hell, and that the author of it is a liar, a scoundrel and a coward, and I here say, that no man of respectability dare take it up for him. This created some exitement for the moment, I then took out my papers and read the articles above referred to, handing them to the President to look over; he immediately arose and said gentlemen of this large meeting, this gentleman has so fully shown his innocence in this matter, that I propose three cheers for him and three groans for his adversary and they were given with a will. I then went on and made my speech to the entire satisfaction of all my friends, and at the conclusion of my speech I said, that if any gentleman wished any satisfaction from me for anything that I had said, they would find me at any hour at my hotel during to-day and to-morrow until 3 o'clock. This raised a monster shout on my side. But none of them called, they were ashamed of their conduct. 1 left Norfolk with flying colors, and spoke the next day at Portsmouth to a delighted audience; hundreds of the Whigs came to me and congratulated me on my success in backing down the Democrats of Norfolk.

After speaking at several other small places, I returned to Richmond to speak at Hanover Court House, the birth place of Mr. Clay. It had been arranged for me to debate the tariff question. We spoke two hours each, although he was a fine speaker he did not understand the practical workings of a protective tariff. At the close (for I had the closing hour,) many of his Democratic friends acknowledged that I had the best of him. Mr. Hunter paid me a compliment, he told the audience that he had spoke with me on the Whig stump and that he knew me to be a very clever fellow, and he was sorry that I was not a Democrat.

From there I commenced a tour up the James river, speaking at various places, without anything occuring to mar my happiness, until I reached Lynchburg; here I met a very dirty editor of a very dirty sheet; he had pitched into me before I come, and at my meeting I let him have a few shots with the tongue; he was there and began to growl a little, he wondered how I knew so much about him; he forgot that my friends would post me,—I knew all about him before I began to speak, he knew nothing about me; when I was told that it was the editor that was grumbling so much, I said: "what noise is that, I hear something like the bleating of a calf, I wonder if the old cow its mother knows it is out." This raised a loud laugh, the poor editor began to back out; I sung out, "don't leave I will let up on you," this only increased

*6

the merriment, when I spoke up and said: "gentlemen, men's heads are like tubs, they don't all hold the same quantity, you can only fill a tub full, whatever you put in after it is full will run over, so it is with men's heads, you can only fill them so full, and if you undertake to put any more in it will run out; now I have filled that fellows head full, and the noise you hear is the overplus running out." This set the crowd wild with laughter amid which the poor editor made tracks for his office, and I finished my speech.

What fools men are to insult a stranger that they know nothing about, they may be certain that some friend will post him, and that he will have the best of it, this has happened with me hundreds of times. The next place I spoke at after I left Lynchburg, a drunken fellow contradicted me when the chairman whispered to me, and said: "don't mind him, he is of no account he has been in jail for stealing geese and corn." I went on and very soon he began again, I said: "I hear a goose making a noise out there, will some gentleman be so good as to give it a handful of corn to keep it still until I am done speaking." Well, that was enough, the crowd roared and clapped for a long time, and finally this fellow dared me down to fight; I jumped down and made for him, but he took to his heels across the field and I after him, but he out-ran and got away from me; when I got back to the stand there was the wildest excitement I ever saw, everybody, Democrats and Whigs congratulating me on my success in ridding the meeting of such a noisy customer. I finished my speech and left the same evening for Staunton, a beautiful town in the Valley of Virginia; here I had a fine time; this was the home of A. A. H. Stuart, the then great and active Whig of that part of the State. We had a large meeting and I fully met their expectations. Mr. Stuart had made an appointment for himself and me at Harrisonburg for the next day.

Harrisonburg was the great centre of the tenth legion as it was called, the whole county was one way, it was the Gibralter of Democracy; they had bid defiance to any Whig speaker and dared them to come there; we went and found the town alive with Democrats swearing that if we attempted to speak there, that they would duck us in the river; we had but three or four friends there to sustain us against more than a hundred drunken men, so we quietly got into our carriage and left. This was the first and only time that ever I was backed out from making a speech in my life.

I then had but a few days to speak before the election, so my next appointment was Winchester; here I met some of the best Whigs I ever met, we had a fine time; I had a debate with one of their candidates on the tariff, we debated part of two days; I beat him and he was defeated at the election a few days after and all hands gave me the credit of defeating him. I spoke at Charleston, Martinsburg and finally wound up the campaign at Shepardstown, and returned to Winchester to stay until the day after election, which resulted in favor of the Whig ticket in that county, and I got the credit for it.

I then left for my home in Ohio to rest until the campaign opened in Pennsylvania which was in a few days.

CHAPTER VI.

TOUR THROUGH PENNSYLVANIA.—VIEWS UPON THE TARRIFF.

I ARRIVED safe home in Ohio about the 10th of May, after an absence of over seven months, and after having travelled many thousand miles and averaged about one speech per day, I was worn down and needed rest very much. I had kept the Ohio committee posted with my operations. I had sent the papers regularly, so that when I returned they understood all about my trip. I was sent for however and had to make a speech and give a general detail of everything that occurred of any interest.

I intended to remain at home and rest myself until the first of July and then open a campaign in Pennsylvania. But in a few days after my return home I received and accepted an invitation to attend the Young Mens ratification meeting to be held inSyracuse, New York, which was to come off on the 12th of June, so on the first of June I packed up and started for another tour. I went to this meeting, spoke there twice amid the greatest enthusiasm. The New Yorkers tryed their best to keep me in their State, but I had made an engagement with the Pennsylvania committee to speak for them. I have often been sorry that I did not stay in New York. I might have been the means of carrying the State for Clay and thereby have elected him. But he never was intended for President of the United States, he was too great a man for that.

By the time that I got into Pennsylvania both parties had fairly opened the campaign. Mr. Polk had been nominated, and the Democrats knowing that Pennsylvania would not vote for an anti-tarriff man, got up a letter, known as the Kane letter, pretending that it came from Mr. Polk; Mr. Polk however never saw it until it was published in the news papers. I had taken the precaution when in Tennessee (having brought Polk out with a letter by my tariff speeches in that State to the legislature in opposition to the whole system of protection, they had it printed and circulated in pamphlet form) to supply myself with half a dozen copies, not thnking however that he would be the candidate, he aspired to the Vice Presidency.

When this letter made its appearance, I at once offset that letter with his letter to the Tennessee Legislature, I had plenty of the original pamphlets from Tennessee. The Democrats, James Buchanan at their head, pronounced my pamphlets a forgery. I went to their committee and offered to enter into bonds of ten thousand dollars for the faithful performance of our contract, which was this: The Whigs should appoint a man of character and the Democrats should also appoint one. These two should take the Kane letter and Polks' Tennessee letter and go to Mr. Polk in person and present them to him. If he denied the Tennessee letter to have been written by him or if he said he wrote the Kane letter, the Whigs were to publish the facts on his return. But if Mr. Polk owned that he wrote the Tennessee letter and not the Kane letter, the Democrats were to publish the facts on their return, and the Whigs to pay all expenses. Their committee only laughed at me; they said, we understand our own mode of electioneering, and although we published the whole proceedings and challenged them to deny it, they only answered us by making personal attacks on my character.

On one occasion Mr. Buchanan spoke at Northumberland, and in my presence declared that he knew Mr. Polk to be a better tariff man than Mr. Clay, and when I replied to his speech that night, the Democrats stoned me from the stand, and it was some time before we could rally a force to sustain me until I got through. In this way they have always met our arguments. As soon as it was known that I was using this Tennessee letter with some effect, they commenced to slander me in all their dirty papers throughout the State, and many of them went so far as to advise my assasination. At that time I carried a revolver and a bowie knife, and on several occasions had to walk from the stage to the hotel door with pistol and knife in my hands; they very often made attacks on me in the cars and stages, and sometimes in private carriages and at hotels.

On one occasion on the Sabbath day I came to Philadelphia in the cars, and while the cars were being switched on the right track to be taken into the depot, several rail road men, who had been insulting all the way from Harrisburg, jumped out of the cars and ran to the depot and collected a large crowd around the cars wherein I was and surounded me as I got out. I suspected them and told them to let me pass. Before I left the cars I had my hand at my revolver, and when they refused to stand away, I drew it and said if you don't stand back, I will kill six of you with this, and hauling out my big bowie knife that weighed two pounds, and with this I can cut my way in any crowd. Several of the passengers from the other cars saw the trouble, and after finding that I was to be mobed, interfered, and I was thereby enabled to make my escape.

The Whig papers denounced this outrage on Monday morning, and in reply on Tuesday, the Democratic papers said, if I did not like Pennsylvania treatment, I had better go back to Ohio, thereby virtually giving encouragment to the mob to take my life. Almost every place I went I had to let them know, that I was well armed to save myself from an attack, and on several occasions I got down from the stand where I was speaking, and thrashed one of them.

I have spoken in and travelled through some twenty six states and am bound to say that the Democrats of Pennsylvania are the most ignorant and meanest Democrats that I ever saw. In the seven months, that I spoke in the South, I did not receive one insult from any Democrat that was born in that country. They always disagreed with me in an honorable way, but the Pennsylvania Democrats were always for insulting me without hearing me. At one place an old chap got up while I was speaking and said the Democrats ought not to let me speak. Why not, said I, aint this a free country? Yes, but I heard that you said, you could whip any Democrat in the county, did you say that? I looked at him and laughed. I answered yes, I did say it and I never tell lies. This raised a great laugh. I told the old man, that I would make a fair bargain with the county committee. I would give a bond for ten thousand dollars and they should do the same, conditioned that I was to fight every Democrat in the county. Every one I whipped should vote for Clay, and for every one that whipped me I would furnish a Whig to vote for Polk. I told him that I could make votes faster that way than by talking. This created quite a laugh in the crowd, even among some of the Democrats, who admired my pluck, as they called it.

I have no doubt, but that the great opposition that

was brought to bear against me, was on account of the manner in which I presented the tariff question to the people. I have often been amused at the way that some of our great speakers talked about that subject. They would talk very loudly about a protective tariff and tell the people that it was their interest to stand by protection, but never once tell the practical workings of this system. My plan was to go into the practical workings of a protective tariff, first show them that if they depended on Europeans for their supplies, that they would first have to find a market for their products, convert it into money and then send that money to Europe, pay for these goods and never see that money again, that in the course of time they would exhaust the country of money and then we would be a nation of paupers.

I told them that the same rule that operated on a farmer would operate on a nation. If a farmer produced from his farm five hundred dollars worth of produce to sell, and it cost him six hundred to produce it, he would loose a hundred dollars and have to pay the difference from his own pocket, and be the looser of a hundred dollars every year. So it was with a nation; if we bought a million every year from other nations more than we sold, we would have to pay the balance of trade out of our treasury, and in this way become a bankrupt nation. But, says the freetrader, a tariff for protection is a tax on the consumer. I admit that it is. But I will show you the consumer can pay the tax, and have more money left, than he would have if we had no tariff. First you will admit that without any protection our laborers would have to work at the same prices that European laborers do, which is about forty cents a day, with this small pittance they could not support their families. The result would be that they would have to turn their attention to agricultural pursuits, this of course would lessen the demand for produce and increase the supply. This course would increase the products of the soil, and destroy a home market for it, which would be the means of lessening its value. Foreign countries only buy from us the amount they need for their consumption, and no more. They would buy just as much from us, as they now do, if we manufactured all our own fabric and did not buy a dollars worth of theirs.

Our true policy therefore is to divide our labor, let one portion of our labor be turned to manufacturing iron, others cloth, others cotton goods, others boots and shoes, others the thousands of other small articles needed by every body. All these men and women and their families have to eat, and will consume all the surplus produce that the farmers have, thereby giving a home market to them, and save them the trouble of finding a foreign market.

Take for example, a farmer wants a new coat, there is now English cloth in the market, he can get it for four dollars a yard for cash; he has plenty of produce, there is no demand for it at home, every body else has plenty as well as himself, he is compelled to seek a foreign market for it, the result is by the time he converts it into cash, he gets but a small price for it. But suppose that there is a factory in his neighborhood where cloth is made, employing three or four hundred people, who all want to eat; the farmer loads his cart with the necessaries of life, goes down to the factory, tells the foreman that he wishes two yards of cloth, but has no money, but that he has a cart-load of provisions at the door. All right, says the man, we have five hundred hungry men, women and children here, that must have their breakfast; unload, that's what we want this morning, sir. The result is, he sells his produce at a fair price, gets his cloth and is back home again by breakfast time. So it is with iron, boots and shoes and every article commonly used.

Now I ask you Mr. Freetrader, is this not better for all hands? which is best, give a man fifty cents a day and let him buy flour at three dollars a barrel, or give him one dollar and fifty cents a day and compel him to pay nine dollars a barrel for his flour. At fifty cents a day it would take him six days to earn a barrel of flour and he would have ten dollars left for his other twenty days work for a month; give him one dollar and fifty cents a day, and let him pay nine dollars for a barrel of flour and he will have thirty one dollars left for twenty other days of that month and thus it is with every other article he uses. The more wages you pay a man for labor, the better not only for him but for the whole country. An Irishman on one occasion grumbled at the price of a peck of potatoes that the market man wanted two shillings for. Faith, said Pat, but I could buy them in Ireland for six pence. You ought to have stayed there, said the market man. But, said Pat, the divil of it was to get the six pence to buy them with. Thus you see, a man can better afford to pay nine dollars for an article at one dollar and fifty cents a day, than he could afford to pay three dollars for an article at fifty cents a day.

I have in my young days bought in Ohio as good beef and pork as ever went on a table, for one dollar and fifty cents per hundred, and as good flour as bread was made from at one dollar per hundred pounds, and the finest chickens at fifty cents a dozen, ready for the oven, and every other article in proportion. Why was it so? I will tell you, there was no manufacturing going on, every body was producing and very few buying; no home market.

Well, says my free trade friend, why can't we compete with foreign markets? I will tell you. As soon as we establish our factories and get them under way without a tariff, these old foreign establishments having millions in their hands, put the prices down below the actual cost of making them at home, and flood our country at a loss of a large sum. People will buy, where they can get the cheapest: the result is, our factories are compelled to stop, they have not the capital to stand the pressure. As soon as our works stop, goods take a sudden rise in the foreign market, and they make up all they lost last year and a good profit on the whole, then if our works start again, down goes foreign goods, it is their large capital, that thus enables them to crush us.

I once knew a Company to put an opposition boat on the James river from Richmond to Norfolk, the old line charged five dollars fare, without meals, the new line charged three dollars without meols. The old line was very rich, had plenty of capital, they immediately put the fare down to nothing, and in a few weeks, because the new line hung on, the old line gave their passengers their dinners in the bargain. Every body knows that they could not afford this. They did operate it at a dead loss for six months, and as soon as the new line was taken off, for the want of passangers, up went the old line again to five dollars and meals extra.

Now if the travelling public had patronised the new line in place of travelling on the old line for nothing, they would always have had the fare at a fair price, but as it was they had cheap fare for a short time and then as before had to pay double fare. So it is with American manufacturers in competing with those wealthy foreigners; they have not the capital to do it with. It is our best policy to sustain our own workshops in their infancy; but they say our manufacturers are getting rich too fast. Which is best I pray you, to help to build up rich establishments at home where the money that they make, will be spent among us, where we can have a chance to get some of it, (for these men do not make their money, it is made by others, and while they are making their boss rich they are making some foi themselves; stop the boss from making anything and you cut off the supply of his workmen,) or help to make the foreign manufacturer rich in a foreign nation where we will never see a dollar of it while we live.

The best plan is to keep money at home, these rich men can't eat money, neither can they get fine horses carriges and fine clothes without money; it takes money for everything they get, and it is impossible for money to circulate without all hands getting a share of it, in some way or other, this is my plan.

In this style I talked to the people at that time, my friends saw as well as the Democrats that this plan of presenting the subject, was calculated to do our cause good, they at once made arrangements to send me into the manufacturing portions of the State, and for this purpose hired a horse and wagon and started me in company with another man on a tour through the Northern portion of the State.

As soon as we commenced our tour, I found the country flooded with hand bills, calling Democratic meetings at the same time and place that my meeting was called, heading their bills with Polk Dallas and the Tariff of '42; this they done to off-set my Tariff speeches and to draw their friends from hearing me speak, and when I would urge the tariff question these fellows would say "that is just what we are for," when they knew it was a falsehood.

On one occasion after I was done speaking I went over to their stand to hear what they had to say, their speaker was reading the *Congressional Globe*, giving a speech as he said of Mr. Clay in the Senate against protection, which was very bitter against the tariff. This said he is the opinion of Mr. Clay their great champion. There were plenty of Whigs there to sustain me, so I sung out, that what you have read is false, that is not Mr. Clay's speech, but C. C. Clay's speech of Alabama, a full grown Democrat. This created a terrible commotion among the Democrats, he claimed that his friends had not interrupted me while I was speaking, and that I must not interrupt him while he spoke; tell the truth said I and we will not interrupt you; I dared him to show the speech to his audience that he had just read, and if they did not say that it was C. C. Clay's speech in place of Henry Clay's speech I would apologise. He insisted on his rights to speak and read as he pleased at his own meeting, and I insisted that he had no right to falsify the records of the Senate of the United States; I said that I had one of the same records at the hotel, and could prove in five minutes that what he had read was a falsehood. He still refused to let me have his book; all right said I and I went to the hotel got my book and returned to their stand, with my *Congressional Globe* of the same date of his, and sung out, now gentlemen all of you who wish to hear me prove that fellow a liar, step over to our stand and I will show you that what he has read as being Clay's speech is false, All of the Whigs and half the Democrats followed me, and in five minutes I had them convinced of the truth of what I had said; I came off that day with flying colors.

Their plan was not to organize their meeting until we got about half through, then organize and endeavor to draw the people away from our meeting; at this they generally failed, as the people would stay to hear me through. At one place their committee called on us and said as the people all wanted to hear me, they would not begin their meeting until I got through with my speech; all right that is fair, said I, in that way the people can hear both sides. As soon as they had left I told my committee my plan, which was to speak all the afternoon or until I had drove the people all away.

The meeting was organized at two o'clock, and I was introduced and commenced speaking. I went on slowly, read long paragraphs from papers and continued to speak until eight o'clock that night; by this time I had driven every Democrat, but their speaker from the ground, and then said, with these few remarks I will leave the subject with you until I hear the other side, I hope gentlemen, that you will remain and hear what the honorable gentleman before us has to say. There were but about thirty present who at once retired. My friends surrounded me that night at the hotel congratulating me on my success in so completely putting down the Democracy that day.

I continued on from day to day to speak snd debate with the leading men of their party, for a week or two after the meeting just referred to, when the State election took place in that State. Gen. Markle was the Whig candidate for Governor and was defeated by Mr. Shunk the Democratic candidate, by near five thousand majority. Markle was a weak man and never ought to have been nominated; he had no strength with the people, and was put on the ticket by a set of tricky politicians, who expected to use him for their purposes, if elected.

I never doubted his defeat from the time I began to canvass the State, and quietly told some of the leaders so. I saw very plainly in mixing with the people, that Shunk had a stronger hold upon them, than Gen. Markle had. He was very popular being widely known and known, only to be loved; while I was satisfied that Shunk would carry the State in October, I was equally satisfied that Clay would carry it in November.

The election came off and I had a day or two to rest; we had no telegraph then, and very few railroads, the result was we were some days without knowing who was elected. As soon as it was known that Shunk had carried the State by five thousand majority, the Democrats became very jubilant, and the Whigs were a little down in the mouth, but went to work with renewed energy, to regain for Clay, what we had lost on Gen. Markle, and accordingly made arrangements for me to speak through all the Western counties, closing the campaign in the city of Erie, the Saturday before the election on Tuesday the 4th of November.

I found it up-hill work after being defeated, to rally the people around me. The Democrats took another plan of electioneering, in place of holding meetings; they went around among the people and said the State election had settled the question, and that the Whigs only held those meetings to keep up appearances; that it was all a lie that the Buckeye Blacksmith was to speak there; that he had given it up and gone home. In this way they managed to keep thousands of their own party and many of the Whigs from our meetings. The only course we had to pursue, was to get to the town early and go around among the people through the day and show ourselves and tell them that we were going to have a meeting that night. Even this plan they tried to baffle, by following us around and swearing that I was an imposter; that I was not the original blacksmith, and some went so far as to come and tell me so to my face. I had on several occasions to find some person who had heard me speak in 1840, to come forward and vouch that I was the man. In this way I fought my way through from town to town, until I reached Erie, where I made the last speech in that ever memorable campaign of 1844.

The defeat of Mr. Clay was the hardest blow that I had ever recieved; he had been the idol of my life, I had learned to love him when a boy, and as I grew older my friendship ripened almost into idolatry, so much so, that I really believe that I would have given everything that I possessed on earth to have elected him to the Presidency, but an all wise Providence willed it otherwise.

I now made up my mind that I would forever after abandon politics, which resolution however to my sorrow I failed to keep, being satisfied that the slave power of the South had such a strong hold upon the Democracy of the North, that no man could be elected to the Presidency who was not in full sympathy with the slave interest, which Mr. Clay was not, (although he owned a number of slaves at the time ;) and this was one of the causes of his defeat, (and the principal one) They were afraid to trust him on that subject, and in order to defeat him sent millions of dollars to the North to be put into the hands of their allies to defeat him in New York, and Pennsylvania, and through trickery and falsehood and ballot box stuffing, were able to accomplish their object. There never was a more villainous or deeper laid plan to defeat the wishes of the people of any nation, than that laid to defeat Mr. Clay. I will here give you some of their plans, and you can judge for yourselves of the fairness of them, (no wonder God frowned on them.)

During the campaign in which Clay was defeated, the Democrats throughout Pennsylvania and other Northern States, who were interested in a tariff, headed all their calls for meetings with, Polk, Dallas and the Tariff of '42, thereby misleading many thousand of the honest, hard working men of the country, when at the same time they knew that Mr. Polk was opposed to protection and would sign a bill for the repeal of the tariff of '42, if elected, which he did among his first publc acts after he came into office. And as soon as he signed the bill that was passed by the casting vote of their Vice President, who was a strong tariff man, a few months before, the party with one voice declared that the whole system of protection was a wrong, and that every body knew that the Democracy were opposed to the tariff of '42. Why was this done, the slave power gave the command and the doe-faces had to obey.

It was necessary in order to elect Mr. Polk that he should appear as a free trader in the South, and a tariff man at the North. And when the Whigs confronted them in the South, with a Northern handbill for a meeting, they would get around it, by calling it a Whig lie; so also in the North. In this way they cheated the people into voting for Mr. Polk in both sections of the country. Mr. Polk was said to be an honest man, at least he was called so by his friends, now I submit it to any candid man to say, was it honest in him to allow his friends to declare him a tariff man in the North to deceive them, when he knew he was not, answer me if you can.

CHAPTER VII.

DAGUERROTYPING—SCOTT AND PIERCE CAMPAIGN—KNOWNOTHINGISM—SICK AND PENNILESS.

ON the day of the election I returned home in time to vote, almost penniless and broken down in health after a years hard labor speaking in the South in favor of Henry Clay's nomination, and in the North in favor of his election after he was nominated in Baltimore in May of that year.

As soon as the election was over and I had got a little rested, I concluded to leave the West and go East where I thought there was a better chance to get a start in life than in the West; I therefore went to Philadelphia where some of my old Whig friends assisted me with funds to learn and start the daguerrotype business. I started my business in Philadelphia, but owing to its being a new thing I did not succeed as well as I expected, so I packed up in the Spring of 1845 and went to Boston, believing that if ever I got a start in life again it must be among the Yankees; accordingly I opened up in Boston where I had but one or two oppositions to contend with; I hung out my sign and at the end of the first month I found I had made a failure; I could not get the people to come into my place; I saw plainly that I must burst up or use some other plan to attract the attention of the people; we were charging three dollars for a small picture in a morocco case which was considered very high. So I concluded to reduce the price, and in order to attract attention to the price, I concluded to play a Yankee trick on the Yankees. I got up a large placard on each side of a frame that I fixed on the top of a pole ten feet high and hired a boy to stand at the corner of Court and Hanover Sts., the most popular corner in the city, and hold this pole so that all the passers-by could see it, (from five to seven in the evening when thousands passed on their way home from work.) The people of the country had just began to talk about a war with Mexico; this subject was in everybody's mouth, I took advantage of this and had my placard headed in large letters: "War with Mexico, (then under that) or not (in small letters) J. W. Bear will furnish beautiful daguerrotypes at No. 17 Hanover street, colored, true to life, in fine morocco cases for one dollar and a half, with a premium to the first setter every morning." This was all that I had on my large placard.

I stood a short distance off to see the effect it would have; it had the desired effect, for the people came running from every direction to see what that war news meant; after reading the whole bill they would go away laughing, saying, "that it was the best dodge of the season."

The bait took like hot pancakes, for next morning early when I got to my rooms I found a score or more waiting ready to enlist as they said for one of my cheap pictures. I gave a premium of fifty cents to the first one that came every morning, (this hurried them up.)

The result of my experiment was: that rich and poor, high and low, all flocked around me, and many of them said that I must be a Yankee for none but a

Yankee could ever have got up such a good dodge as I had to get custom, and many of them offered to assist me with means to increase my business, and I have no doubt had I have stayed there that I should have been a rich man to-day, for the Yankees are the best people I have ever seen to help a stranger along in business who is willing to help himself, and I would here advise every young man who wishes to make a good start in the world to make that start among the Yankees.

I stayed in Boston until the winter set in, and then concluded that the climate was too cold for me and that I had better go South. This was the greatest misfortune of my life. I had made money enough to furnish myself with the finest set of instruments that the world could produce with a fine stock of materials for a tour to the South and a nice little pile o cash in my pocket.

The first place I stopped at was Wilmington, Del., where I stayed a few weeks, but done but little business, owing, I suppose, to its being a new thing it did not take with the people there. I very soon saw that it was no go at that place, so I pulled up stakes and went to Annapolis, Md., where I opened up in the Court House with an excellent light for the business. I had no sooner hung out my sign than the people began to crowd around me, and for five or six weeks I done a most excellent business; I took in over five hundred dollars in less than two months, then when all that wished pictures had been supplied I packed up and went to Alexandria, Va.

I opened up in a fine room and went to the printer to get some bills printed, when he frankly told me, that he would charge me five dollars for them and that I would never get it back for pictures in that city, for said he, "daguerrotypes are played out here, there are three men at it here already that can't make their rent, and they are citizens, so it is no use for a stranger to try it." All right, said I, "print my bills, I will try it a few days and see what I can do."

I changed my bills from what I had intended to put up; in place of putting the price at two dollars I concluded to play a Yankee trick on them, so I got up the following bill:

Only $1.50 for the best daguerrotype ever seen in Alexandria, put up in fine morocco cases; colored true to life and warranted not to fade at —— Washington street, (adding below,) how many have lost a father, a mother, a sister, a brother, or an innocent little prattling child, and have not even a shadow to look upon after the separation; some little toy or trifling article are often kept for years and cherished as a token of remembrance. How more valuable would be one of the Buckeye Blacksmith's beautiful pictures of the loved and lost.

Reader you could not do a better thing now, while your mind is on the subject, than to take a stroll to the Buckeye's Place, you may have reason in future years to feel thankful for these gentle hints from a stranger:

> For think not these Portraits by the sunlight made,
> Though shades they are, will like a shadow fade;
> No, when this lip of flesh in dust shall lie,
> And death's gray film o'erspreads the beaming eyes,
> These life like pictures mocking at decay,
> Will still be fresh and vivid as to day.

A call is respectfully solicited. I hung out my sign at 12 o'clock, went to my dinner and returned at 1, and found a dozen or more looking at my pictures. "Are you the gentleman that makes these pictures," said a pretty young lady to me. I told her I was. "Will you make me as pretty a picture as this (pointing to one in my frame) for a dollar and a half?" "oh, yes, and prettier too, for you are a better looking young lady than the one that set for that picture," said I. This raised a great laugh among the crowd; we went in, and I not only took her picture but nine others, thus before night I had taken in fifteen dollars. I went to the printer that night and told him what I had done, "that I had taken fifteen dollars the first day and intended to take in fifteen hundred before I left," he said, he hoped that I would but doubted it. The next day I was full from morning till night with the fashion and beauty of the city, and so I continued from day to day, until finally the families of all three of the other operators came to me to get pictures, for none of these operators knew how to take good pictures and had quit the business as soon as I got under way.

The result of my operations in Alexandria was, that in seventeen weeks I took in over fourteen hundred dollars in cash. But notwithstanding all my prosperity in my business going to Alexandria was the most unfortunate step of my life for the following reasons:

At the time I commenced business there, they had the Virginia lotteries drawn in Alexandria. I was induced to try my luck in them, hoping from day to day to make a fortune in that way, the more I lost the deeper I went into it, for I was made to believe that if I would hang on I would certainly get a prize sometime. Well I had got such a mania for the lottery that I could scarcely eat or sleep without a ticket in my pocket. I kept this all a secret from my true friends and seemed to allow those lottery swindlers to have full control of me, the result of the matter was that when I left Alexandria and went to Frederick, Md., I had but about ten dollars to begin with, all the money that I had made in Alexandria and over five hundred dollars I took there with me, was gone for lottery tickets and I had no prize yet. So you will see that this move in going there was a very unfortunate one, for I commenced there to lead a life that has ruined thousands of good men, and next to rum has ruined more men and women than anything that has ever cursed our country, and I would here say, my dear young reader if you value prosperity, if you value happiness and character, I warn you to let liquor and lotteries alone; for the two together or one alone must in the end prove your ruin; I know what I say, for I have travelled that road.

I went to Frederick, opened up my business, but soon found that the old proverb is a true one, when it says, that a prophet is not without honor save in his own country; I was borne there and the people thought it was impossible for me to take as good pictures as a stranger that was there at that time. He professed to be from New York, and the people of course thought that he knew more about the fine arts than a man that was born a poor child in their own county, when at the same time his pictures could not compare with mine, the result was, I stayed there several weeks and then had to go away without being able to pay all my board and rent.

I packed up and went to Hagerstown and left my instruments in pawn for my board, until I could get something to do. I got to Hagerstown without a cent in my pocket and over twenty dollars in debt at Frederick. I felt like the old irish woman, who said while drunk and being hauled to the watch house in an ashcart—"I have been in many a scrape before and got out of all of them, but this one," so I thought that I had been in many a tight place in my life and had got out of all but this; and although I felt a little down hearted, felt certain that I could work my way through this difficulty also.

While in Boston I had got hold of a receipt to make cement for mending glassware, crockery and all earthen wares. I concluded that I would try that business in Hagerstown, so I went to a druggist and got credit for eight cents worth of the materials for making the cement; went to the hotel where I had put up at, got to work and prepared it for sale. I had enough cement to bring me ten dollars, (it was nearly all profit.) I went to work to sell it and succeeded first-rate that afternoon, and by night everybody found out that I was in town. During the evening many of the leading Whigs of the place called on me at the hotel (which was kept by Mr. Robert Fowler, who has since that become a very active politician in the Conservative party of the State, and is still living.) After conversing some time with them, I told them that I was considered the best daguerrotypist in the country, and that I had failed to do anything in Frederick and had to leave all my aperatus there in security for my board and rent, and that I had taken this method of raising money to pay this debt and get a small stock of materials to begin with, when I intended to start business in their town. They asked me how much it would take to start me. I told them fifty dollars would get me a good stock of materials and twenty dollars would redeem my tools; with seventy dollars I could make a good start.

Mr. Fowler, the landlord, proposed that seven of the party then present should advance me ten dollars each to start on, and take it out in pictures after I got under way, (for he said that I had done enough for the party to entitle me to a living as long as I lived;) he had no sooner made the proposition than every man present (one or two Democrats among them) responded that he would be one of the seven; and in a few minutes the money was raised, and before I went to bed I had started fifty dollars to Philadelphia for goods and twenty dollars for my tools, (well, you can bet your bottom dollar that I slept good that night.)

The next day I got a first-class room in the Court House, rent free, and went to work to fit it up by the time my tools and goods would arrive, which they did in due time; in the mean time I kept on selling cement so by the time that I got ready to work I had several dollars picked up in that way. I put out the same handbill that I had at Alexandria and it took well, all declared that my specimen pictures were the best they had ever seen; I got several prominent men to let me take their pictures to hang at the door in my show case before I opened up for the public, so that when I did open up everybody admired my work and commenced to crowd around me by dozens at a time, all anxious to have their pictures taken.

I never shall forget to my latest hour the people of Hagerstown, for no sooner than they found out that I was poor and needed a friend than they came as one man to my relief; from the morning that I hung out my sign to the day that I left their town they never ceased to patronize me, but here also as well as in Alexandria I found a lottery office, I had not gotten over my mania for tickets notwithstanding my sad experience but a short time before, and here, too, I had the misfortune and weakness to spend nearly all that I had made; I made up my mind to leave the South where lotteries were tolerated and go to Pennsylvania where there were none, so I packed up my kit and went to Chambersburg, Pa., almost penniless but enough left to stand a decent business.

I opened up there, and for several weeks done a small business, so very small that I began to fear that I should make a failure of it at this place as I did in Frederick, Md. About this time the Methodists had a great meeting to dedicate their large new church, and Bishop Janes, one of their big guns, was to preach the dedication sermon for them; I was not long in making up my mind what was best for me to do.—I went to hear him preach on Sunday, and when he was through a celebrated preacher by the name of Collins, from Baltimore, was to do the begging of money to pay for finishing the church. I immediately bit at that bait; at the proper time Mr. Collins called on all that felt like giving anything towards

*7

paying the debt, that were not members of the church, should raise up and say what amount they were willing to give; I took advantage of this and sung out, "I will give you ten dollars." "Your name, sir," said Mr. Collins, I told him, when he sung out in a loud voice: "the Buckeye Blacksmith gives ten dollars." All eyes were on me for a moment, and I felt that I had gained a point.

The next morning early I went to see the Bishop, invited him to my rooms, took a splendid large picture of him, made him a present of it, and also made one for myself for my show table; this had the desired effect, for in less than twenty-four hours everybody knew what I had done and commenced to call and see the Bishops picture and to get a copy of it, and in less than ten days I sold over a hundred dollars worth of copies. I had raised myself in the estimation of the Methodists so high that they came in droves to my place and got their pictures taken, and I done excellent business for a number of weeks after that and had succeeded in saving several hundred dollars.

I then concluded to go to Carlisle, Pa., where the people had the name of being very high minded and aristocratic, here, I thought, would be a fine field for me. When I got there I found two men engaged in the business but neither of them understood how to make a good picture. I went to see them and one of them told me that he was not a country artist as I was but a New York city artist that took pictures by an entire new and improved plan; that his pictures could not fade and therefore were more valuable than any others, and even dared me to open up against him.— I told him the people would speak of him as they would of Noah of old, as one that once lived, but was no more, as soon as I opened for he would not get another picture to take after I got under way.

The other fellow came frankly to me and said that he knew that he did not understand the business, and asked me to learn him so that he could make a living for his family. I told him I would do so, which I did, without charging a cent. As soon as I got open for business I hung out my sign and filled the town with flaming hand-bills, and in three days had the pleasure of seeing my New York artist take the cars body and baggage for parts unknown, and have never heard of him since nor never expect to.

I stayed at Carlisle some four months and done a most unparalled business; I had sent to Vienna, in Austria, and got a set of the best instruments made that was ever imported, and was in a fair way to make a fortune again, but the devil or something else put it in my head to go to the South again; I started for Winchester, Va., with the finest outfit that ever crossed the Potomac in my business; my outfit was so extensive that I had to pay some eight dollars extra fare on the cars. I had also a nice roll of cash in my pocket.

When I arrived in Winchester I found a young man engaged at the business, but as he was rich he only followed it for pleasure and was glad that I came to relieve him of the bother of taking pictures for the public; he rendered me all the assistance he could in getting a suitable room to operate in and issued a card recommending me to all his friends as a first-class artist; this was very valuable to me as it brought me at once into notice, he being one of the first families of the place, his father was a Senator and stood high among the people of Winchester, which gave a decided advantage over any place that I had been; here I had no opposition, and with a fine stock of the best materials and the finest instruments extant I was prepared to do a fine business.

I opened my business here with the fairest prospects that I had ever had. The people had never had a picture taken for less than three dollars, so when I hung out my sign at one dollar and a half everybody came to see me; in this place I reserved every Friday afternoon for colored people, this seemed to please both white and colored; I also published that slaves would be taken for fifty cents less than others, this made me very popular with them, they came in droves to see me on their day, the white people all agreed that my plan was a good one, so much so that the owners of them willingly gave them time to get their pictures taken, and many of them came with them to see that they got good ones taken. I had lots of fun with them, no odds how black they were I made their pictures light, this would please them, they would say "bless de Lord it looks just like dis chile," and when a black man and a yellow girl would set together I would throw the largest amount of light on the man so as to make them both as light as possible, this took with them like hot pancakes, and pleased their owners also.

I very soon became very popular, not only with the white ladies and gentlemen, but with the colored ones too; the result of my popularity with the people here, was, that I had a successful run of business from early in the Fall of '47 to the Spring of '48. I took over fifteen hundred pictures there, the lowest at a dollar, the highest at five dollars. But lo! and behold, right opposite my place of business was a lottery office and, here, as before, the mania took hold of me, and every dollar that I made as well as what I had taken there with me was spent in that way, and before I left there I was compelled to sell one of my instruments to get away.

I now made up my mind fully that I would forever leave the South to return no more, but I stopped at Charleston (a place that has since been made memorable in this country as the place where the first martyr to liberty was hung.) for a few days, just long enough to make a raise to take me to Pennsylvania. I done an excellent business for a week or two, and then packed up and went to that State, fully intending never to return. I arrived there safe and sound just about the time the Presidential question began to be talked of, but had not made up my mind what I should do on that question. I had not taken any interest in politics since the defeat of Mr. Clay, and thought that I never would, but as soon as the Whigs at their National Convention of that year had nominated Gen. Taylor as their candidate for President, I saw very plainly that the South had gained their point in placing a strong pro slavery man on the Whig ticket against Gen. Cass one of the best men that the Democratic party ever had placed before the people. I had known Gen. Cass well and had known him to be an honest man, which was more than I could say for the most of them. I knew very well that the South would not trust Cass, although he was a much superior man to Taylor. Yet he was a man that they could not use, and they knew it, hence their lukewarm support of him. Although I knew him to be the best man for the place, party lines were so tightly drawn that I could not vote for him.

I took but little interest in the election, further than to speak three or four weeks around through three or four counties of that State. I saw from the first that Cass was beat, Taylor's war record was carrying him flying over the Presidential race course, like a tornado, and that nothing but a miracle could stop him. I told the Democrats so, but they were foolhardy enough to think up to the day of election that they would carry their point, and I could not pursuade them that the South would not allow him to be President. Well the election came off, and the result was just as I had told them, Taylor and Filmore were triumphantly elected. I had told some of my friends that men were like water, it would seek its level, so would men. Cass had not equals enough he was too distinguished a man, the same as Mr. Clay was. Polk and Taylor were ordinary men, and a very large majority of the voters of this country being but ordinary men, sought their level by voting for them in place of Mr. Clay and Gen. Cass, hence their defeat.

Gen. Taylor took his seat with as little pomp and show, as any other President had done; and I have no doubt, but had he lived, that he would have made a pretty fair President; but before he had been eighteen months in office, he died, and Mr. Filmore took his place, then came the tug of war. Mr. Filmore very soon became the pliant tool of the slave power, and through him, as the best compromise that Mr. Clay (who was in the Senate at that time) could get, we got the fugitive slave law. That law made every white man in the North a negro-catcher for the South, for if one of their slaves ran away and got into one of the Northern States, and his master followed him and called on you to assist him to catch his slave, that law compelled you to help catch him; if you refused to assist him and was worth the price of the negro, you would be compelled to pay for him. To this state of things I most positively demurred, and this law I refused to obey. Look at the unfairness of the thing.—Negroes in the South were by law goods and chattels, the same as horses and oxen are in the North—well let us see how this law worked; if my horse or yours ran away from us in the South, there was no law to compel them to help us catch him, neither could we make them pay for him if he got away from us; but if one of their black cattle got away from them, we must assist in catching or pay for him. Look at it, Northern Democrat, and tell me, did you ever support such a measure as that? I tell you you did when you supported Mr. Pierce in 1852.

After the campaign of '48 was over I concluded to go to work again at my business, but by this time every little town in the country had a daguerrotype saloon in it and the large places had two or more men running opposition in them. Every fellow who could raise a few dollars would get up a small outfit, mostly almost worthless, and put out into some country town and stick up his cards and pretend he knew more about the business than any man living, when at the same time all that he knew and his tools in the bargain were not worth ten dollars. Almost every town I went to I found one or two and sometimes more of these fellows blowing their own trumpets, and as soon as I would open up and commence business they would generally put the price of their pictures down to about half what I charged in order to burst me up, but I generally made them leave, and that very soon after I got under way.

The greatest difficulty I had to encounter with these men, was the want of a suitable room with the right kind of light to make good pictures with, they being there before me, would generally get the best places to be had, and I would have to take an inferior place to compete with them, but having more knowledge of the business than they had, and the best instruments in the country, I could always put them to flight.

I saw very plainly, that there was something wanting. I knew what kind of light I required to do good work with, and this light I could not get in country towns. There being a little Yankee in me, I set to work to build me a house adapted exactly to the business, with a large, splendid sky-light, made in such a manner, that I could, by taking off a few screws, take it all apart in small compartments and load it on a car or big wagon and move it to any place I might wish to, where, with the aid of two men, in three hours I could put it up, ready for work. It was three times as large as those saloons which were built on wheels years after that, and far superior; those saloons were too small and were never adapted to the business, consequently I never had one.

As soon as I got my house done I had no more trouble with opposition. My sky-light made such fine even shades over the face, everybody said they were just the thing they wanted, and everybody admired my enterprise in getting up such a novel plan of doing good work, and they fully rewarded me for my outlay and skill. I would go into a town, get a vacant lot whereever I could, get two or three men to help me, and have my house all ready for business before any person knew what whs going on. The first thing they would know about my being there would be when they read my bill, which I would have thrown into every house as well as all over the country around. I put up my bills thus:

> The great crowd you see moving from morning till twilight
> Are enquiring the way to the Buckeye's great sky-light,
> To have a daguerrotype view of their faces
> Put up for a dollar, in the very best cases.

A call is respectfully solicited—saloon on——lot —— &c.

This saloon as I called it was a decided success, for in it I did the best work I had ever done, and whereever I went, I did a very nice business. I continued to travel about through Pennsylvania, from town to town, from the time of Taylors election until the Spring of 1852, when another political campaign was about to open, but as yet nobody knew who were to be the candidates.

The result of the two National Conventions was that the Whigs nominated General Scott and the other side nominated General Pierce of New Hampshire. By this time the people had become very tired of the agitation of the question of slavery, and ready to vote for any party that would pledge itself to keep down the agitation of this vexed question. The Democrats took advantage of this, and placed in their platform at Baltimore, the day that they nominated Mr. Pierce, a plank, declaring that they would forever after discountenance the opening up of that question; and their speakers and their press during the campaign that followed pledged themselves, that if the people would elect Mr. Pierce, that question would be forever settled. Through these pledges and the weakness and vanity of General Scott, he having no strength with the people, they were enabled to elect Mr. Pierce by a tremendous majority.

On the 4th of March 1853, Mr. Pierce in his inaugural address, in the presence of the congregated thousands of upturned faces, declared that during his term of office the opening of the slave question would not be tolerated. This his friends received with loud applause and the country seemed to be satisfied with it; but lo and behold, Mr. Pierce had scarcely got warm in his seat before he and his party leaders began a system of agitation tenfold worse then ever by their plan to force Kansas into the Union as a slave State, against the will of a large majority of the bona-fide citizens of that territory. This they attempted to do by filling the territory with armed border ruffians, to stuff the ballot boxes to suit themselves and in order to assist them in this plan, Mr. Pierce appointed a Mr. Reeder of Pennsylvania, Governor of Kansas, hoping as he was a dyed-in-the-wool Democrat, that he would declare the fraudulent election that had just taken place, to be a legal one, but notwithstanding Reeder's powerful democratic proclivities, the dose was too bitter for him to swallow, and after investigating the whole matter, he wrote back and declared the thing an outrageous fraud. The result was, that he was immediately recalled, for he had refused to do the dirty work for which they had sent him there.

The next man they tried was John W. Geary, also of Pennsylvania, supposing that they would find a pliant tool in him. Well, Geary went out there and in six weeks he returned, also declaring the whole thing a fraud, so he could not swallow the Southern pill. They then boxed the compass about for awhile to find a man to suit them, and at last picked up ex-

Gov. Shannon of Ohio; he had heretofore always been willing to do any dirty work that the Democracy wished him to do, so they sent Shannon out there; but willing tool as he had always been for them, he also came back disgusted with Kansas and the whole proceedings of the election.

They now saw very plainly that there was no use in trying to get a Northern man for that job, so they concluded to try a Southern man. Although they preferred a Northern man for the job, they could then go before the people of the country and declare that the election was a fair one and had been so decided by a Northern man. This they preferred but they found it impossible to get one to suit them; they therefore sent all the way down to Mississippi and got one of the large slave holders of that State, Mr. Robert J. Walker, who was a strong Democrat, supposing as a matter of course, that he would bite at the bait. But slave holder and Democrat as he was, he too utterly refused to enter into such a damnable plot as that was, and he as well as his secretary, also a Southern slave holder, came back perfectly disgusted, not only with the Kansas question but the Democratic party also.

My dear reader you will thus see how the Democratic party have kept their pledges in former years, when the party was comparatively pure, and if they failed to keep them then, in the name of common sense, what can you expect of them now, when their leaders are composed of the worst men of the nation. I would here state with all due respect to many honest Democrats, for they have honest men among them, that I have never known them as a party, to keep a pledge they ever made, except to protect the whisky rings of the country; this they have always done to the letter, for the simple reason, that much of their success in politics depended upon the influence that whisky brought to bear in their favor, for without whisky you could not carry on a Democratic campaign.

I was told once, by one of their prominent men that he could make more votes in his county with a barrel of whisky than I could make with the ten commandments, when I told him the Democrats were like the man who sent his child to the grocery to get sixpence worth of bread and six pence worth of whisky, the child returned and said they had no six pence loaves of bread, nothing less than eight cent loaves, when the father replied, damn the bread we can do without it, go back and get the whole shilling in whisky; therefore I conclude you can do better with whisky in your party than you could with the bible or bread either.

But my dear reader the question very nuturally arises, why did the South have such a strong desire to extend slavery into the free territory, I will try and explain it to you: there were four millions of slaves in the South that had no voice, part or lot in the administration of the affairs of the Government, they were only goods and chattles, but at the same time they were counted in the ratio of representation, at the ratio of five slaves to three free citizens; this gave them about two million four hundred souls to be counted in the representation. At that time every ninety six thousand souls entitled a State to a member in Congress, counting the two million four hundred thousand slaves, at ninety six thousand to the member, they had twenty seven members, thus representing their property, in the place of free white citizens, and also twenty seven electors for President and Vice President; what right I ask you had they to count a negro if he was common property, in their ratio of representation, unless they allowed us to count our property also. To show you how this system worked, and the advantage it gave the South over the North let me call your attention to a few facts. Vermont with a free population of more than nine thousand more than South Carolina, had but three members of Congress, while South Carolina by counting three out of every five of her slaves had six members, thus making one free citizen of that State equal on the floor of Congress to two free citizens of Vermont; then take New Hampshire, if you please, she had a free white population of over thirty one thousand more than South Carolina, yet she had but three members in Congress, thus making one South Carolinian more than equal to two white citizens of New Hampshire. Then take Rhode Island with an equal population of South Carolina, she has but two members, thus making one South Carolinian equal to three Rhode Islanders, and so it worked throughout the entire South, but in less proportion in some of the States than it did in South Carolina, Georgia and Mississippi.

It will thus be seen the great advantage slavery gave them over the free States. You will very readily perceive that with the twenty seven members representing their slaves added to those they were entitled to, they only needed a few votes from the North as well as a few electoral votes to elect a President of their choice or carry any point they wished. In this way they held the balance of power on almost every important question that came before the people. It was this balance of power which elected Mr. Van Buren; it was this balance of power which repealed the tariff of 1842; it was this power which elected Mr. Polk; it was this power which gave us the fugitive slave law; it was this power which repealed the Missouri Compromise; it was this power which elected Mr. Pierce and also Buchanan; it was this power which prevented a system of free education in the Southern States, which left a large majority of the poor whites in ignorance and the servile tools of the slave drivers; it was this power which filled the poor houses of the South with hoards of poor, ignorant white females, who had fallen a prey to the slave driver and his sons, and were left to endure their own shame in the county poor house, until some poor, ignorant white tool of their destroyer could be hoodwinked into marrying them.

Is it any wonder my dear reader that the great ruler of the Universe in the fullness of time took this matter in hand to destroy the fountainhead of all these monstrous evils as well as the Democratic party, which had been the instrument in the hands of the devil to produce them, it is God that ought to have the glory and not man for their destruction.

I had taken but little interest in the election of 52, other than to make a few speeches through the county where I was working, for I saw very plainly that Scott was defeated three months before the election, and that all efforts to create any feeling in his behalf was labor in vain, hence I spent but little money or time in that direction. I always thought it was folly to spend money or labor in a hopeless cause. So I continued on at my business going from town to town until the beginning of the year 1854, when the great Knownothing party began to attract considerable attention throughout the country. I began to look at the question in all its bearings, and finally made up my mind that through that party we might possibly be able to break down the corrupt Democracy, for about this time they had become about as corrupt as they well could be. I therefore concluded that it was every mans duty who loved his country to assist in putting down this monstrous evil, I therefore made up my mind to unite my destinies with them.

Here was the Democratic party in power, had gotten that power through three of the most powerful influences in the country, viz: slavery, whisky and the foreign vote, which they had enlisted in their favor through the heads of one of the powerful churches of this country. Here I found a large mass of foreign voters from one end of the country to the other, all as one man throwing their entire vote to one party; this I considered a very dangerous thing, I feared that at no distant day this influence might and would endanger the liberty of the people of this country. I found the churches composed of the native born citizens of the country divided in politics the same as those who where not members of the church, but when I found a church of foreigners, I found them solid for the Democracy. This I thought, and think so yet, meant something, and would some day be used to our sorrow, therefore I felt that there ought to be a stop put to it, hence I united with the Knownothings with all my heart.

As soon as the campaign opened I was appointed one of the officers for the eastern part of the State with full power to establish lodges through any district; I had saved some money at my business and concluded that as it was the Whigs that had gave it to me for my work that I would spend every dollar that I had, for the Knownothings who where mostly Whigs to help them to break up the Democratic foreign whiskey and slavery party. I therefore sent to Pittsburg where the head officer of the State lived and bought with my own money two hundred dollars worth of blank charters, and quit all business. I commenced to travel, establishing lodges from night to night, and day to day, paying my own expenses, never asking a cent for the charter of a lodge, for fear that the people might think it was only a moneymaking scheme of mine, although I had paid two dollars for every charter that I had. My plan was to go to a place, feel around and find a friend or two, send them among their friends, appoint a place to meet that afternoon or night, under some big tree in the woods or some cornfield or old out house, or any other place where we could meet secretly and th re I would initiate them into the order; they very soon began to write or come for me to visit all parts of the country, which kept me going constantly for near three months.

I had many pleasing incidents in that campaign; on one occasion a Democratic Congressman sent four of his Democratic friends to different schoolhouses to watch if any Democrats met with us. At the same time all four of these men belonged to our lodge, and in place of going to the country and schoolhouses to watch Democrats, came into the lodge and told all about it, and had a hearty laugh over it; on another occasion they sent a fellow to watch us when he got into a pig pen among some pigs. The owner heard a noise among his pigs and supposing some persons were stealing some of them he took down his shot gun and fired at the fellow, peppering his whole hips with fine shot, which gave the doctor a pretty good job picking them out.

Finally the election came off, I was the last one to vote, when the polls had closed, the Democratic Congressman alluded to above, took up a collection among the Democrats to pay the Telegraph Co. for the use of the wires that evening for political news, when I stepped up and offered to pay a part of it but he declined to take it from a Knownothing, at the same time saying that although I was the great Mogul of the party, that I had got but two of their men from them, and that the Democrats would still have forty seven majority in the Borough. I told him that I had no doubt that he spoke what he thought, but I would speak what I knew, we would beat them twenty for the whole ticket except Congressman, and would beat them eighteen for that. This raised a great laugh among the unterrified, they said I had gone crazy and ought to be locked up for safe keeping. Very well gentlemen, said I, wait a few minutes till the tickets are counted and you will see that I know what I am talking about. We continued to crack a few jokes for awhile until at last the vote for Governor and Congress was handed out of the window to us, when lo and behold we had beaten them just as I told them we would, and in five minutes there was not a Democrat to be found on the ground. I hunted up the

Congressman and found him in his office without a light, asked him how the election was going, for you have the telegraph said I, when he replied, "its all gone to h—l and you can go there too if you choose." I went away laughing at the top of my voice. Thus ended the success of the great Knownothing party.

The Knownothing party was a short lived party, owing to the fact that it proscribed the children of foreigners and also the children of American Catholics; had they have left that out of their creed they might have built up a party that would have ruled this country for many years to come; another cause of its downfall was that the great men of the country who were capable of being leaders never took hold of it, they stood aloof and looked on to see what effect it would have but took no part in it, and thus it died out for the want of great men to lead it; the principle was a good one, that Americans should rule America, this was the doctrine of the Father of Our Country (George Washington) when he said, "put none but Americans on guard," which doctrine I endorsed then and do to this day, but as it is dead and buried I will let it rest in peace.

After the election was over I went to work again, but was very much broken down in health by my constant exposure to the night air, for I had been for near three months exposed all hours of the night in the open air until I was nearly prostrated; the result was, that I was taken down with the typhoid fever, forty miles from home, and lay there for five months before I could be taken home, and this sickness added to what I had just spent in politics took every dollar that I had on earth; it left me penniless without any means to begin my business or without bread to eat, or a home to put my head into. I had to sell nearly all my tools to sustain myself until I got able to work which was two months after I was able to be taken home. My services were not needed then in politics and I found but few friends that were willing to assist me. Thus I have found it with politicians, you are everything when they want to use you, but after they have used you and got out of you all they want, you can go to the devil for all they care. There are some exceptions to this rule, however, they are not all of that stripe but unfortunately a large majority of politicians soon forget and desert their best friends.

Henry Clay, Daniel Webster, General Harrison and Mr. Lincoln were among those that are dead that never forgot or deserted a friend, and one of the main reasons why General Jackson was so popular was, he was never known to desert a man who was his friend. These men are all dead but their deeds of kindness still live, and will continue to live long after you and I, dear reader, are forgotten. The best living man I ever knew in my fifty years experience in politics to remember a friend or services rendered, is Simon Cameron of Pennsylvania. I have watched him closely for more than forty years, and can truly say, that I never knew him in one single instance to go back on any man that ever rendered him any service. And this accounts for his great popularity with the people of that State. I hope all young politicians will profit by his example.

CHAPTER VIII.

CAMPAIGN OF 1856—STARTED OUT FOR FILMORE, BUT AFTER FIRST SPEECH WENT FOR FREMONT—A FRIEND IN NEED—PLOTTING OF THE SOUTH.

DURING the Summer of 1855, after I had partly recovered from my long attack of sickness, I went to Philadelphia where I found a friend to loan me money enough to start my business in a small way, but by this time the city was full of operators, and my means being so limited that I could not do much. I was not able to make much of a show, and that was every thing in a city, it made no difference how I made my pictures, I had no show to draw the people into my place; therefore I made but poor headway during that Summer and the following Winter, only doing enough to keep soul and body together. But I had confidence that I should get out of my difficulty after a while, my organ of hope was very large, and always has been, or I should have been dead long ago.

Early in the Spring of 1856 there began to be considerable talk about the Presidential question, and there was much speculation about who the candidates would be. The Whig party had been swallowed up in the Knownothing party, and Mr. Filmore seemed to be the choice of the American party and was finally chosen their standard bearer, and Mr. Buchanan was chosen by the Democrats; thus matters stood for a while, but there existed a powerful feeling throughout the country in opposition to the extension of slavery into the free territory of the country. The good men of all parties were uniting in opposition to it, and it was plain to be seen, that the men who composed this opposition meant business, and would make themselves felt, and that very soon, in a way that would not be very palitable to the Democratic party. These men were opposed to Mr. Filmore, owing to his affiliating too much with the South, and were determined to ruu a ticket of their own. They claimed that Filmore was the nominee of the South, and if elected would be as he had been before, their pliant tool. They called a National Convention to meet in Philadelphia in July. Accordingly when the Convention met it was one of the largest and most respectable one that ever convened in this nation, and almost by a unanimous vote nominated John C. Fremont for President and presented him to the people as an opponent to the extension of slavery.

Mr. Fremont in his letter of acceptance of the nomination, came out boldly in favor of free soil for free men, and in opposition to the extension of slavery, thus we had three candidates before the people. Living as I was in Philadelphia, where Filmore had all the strength that he had in the State, and where Fremont had his least strength, I made up my mind notwithstanding Filmore was not my choice and Fremont was, that it was my duty to go for Filmore, as the available man to beat Buchanan, not knowing that Filmore had no strength out of Philadelphia. I had been made to believe by the Filmore organ, and the Democratic papers of Philadelphia, that he was carrying everything before him outside of the city. They were giving the most glowing accounts of the outpourings of the people in his favor; to read these papers you would have thought that Fremont was not running at all. I therefore made up my mind to go for Filmore with my whole heart, as the only hope of beating Buchanan, and commenced to speak at meetings about the city in his favor.

About two months before the election the chairman of the Filmore State Central Committee sent for me to call at his office to see him on business connected with politics. When I called on him he told me that he was authorized to send me through the Western counties as a speaker; and that he would pay me a hundred dollars a month and all expenses for my labor; he said that the West was in one blaze of enthusiasm for Filmore, and that the people wanted me out there; and if I would consent to go on a certain day, he would send large bills through that country announcing my meetings for me. As I was doing but little business I consented to go, and the next morning it was announced in the city papers that the Buckeye Blacksmith was to stump the State for Filmore. Almost every person I met congratulated me, and wished me success..

The day arrived for me to start, and I called on the chairman for the money and letters of introduction to the different committees. He gave me a check on the Northern Liberty Bank for a months salary, and a ticket to Pittsburg, my first stopping place, also a letter to the chairman of the committee there, saying that he should take charge of me while in that city, and forward me to my next appointment. I went to the bank with my check and presented it to the paying teller, who told me there was no funds there to cash it with. This rather surprised me; I walked to the door and just as I got there I met the chairman of the Democratic State Central Commiteee going in. I stopped at the door for a moment considering whether to take the check back or go home first. The chairman stood at the bank counter and then passed out; as soon as he had gone this same teller came around the counter and tapped me on the shoulder and said he could cash my check now, when I turned and went back to the counter and received my money.

I now began to fear that all was not right, and that Filmore was running in the interest of the Democratic party, but I said nothing about my fears to any one, for fear that I was mistaken. I was determined if it was Democratic money that I had got, it never should be used to their advantage; so at twelve o'clock that night I packed my kit and started for Pittsburg, with my mind fully made up concerning the course that I intended to pursue, viz: that if the great ado about Filmore was only a hoax I would use their money against them for the Fremont party.

Well, the next morning a number of the gentlemen passengers recognized me and began to plague me about Filmore, offering to bet me a hundred dollars that I could not find fifty Filmore men West of the Alleghany Mountains, this, I confess, rather staggered me for they seemed to be candid men and meant what they said, and the nearer we got to Pittsburg the more I became the butt of ridicule. I finally arrived there, and very soon found my committee man who received me very cordially and sent me to one of the best hotels in the city, which I soon found to be the Democratic head-quarters; the Democracy flocked around me and treated me with great respect, which was not very pleasing to me but I said nothing and thought a great deal.

In the evening the committee man called for me according to promise and gallanted me to the meeting which was held in Liberty Hall, a small hall by that name, which, if well filled, would not hold more than five hundred persons; I found about two hundred noisy men and boys there all clamoring for the Buckeye. I was introduced to the meeting by my committee man and made but a short speech, being fully satisfied the Filmore movement was a failure at that place.

After I had returned to the hotel I was called on by several gentlemen who had once known me, when one of them said: "Bear what are you doing; have you forsaken all your old friends and your life long principles and turned over to the Democratic party that you have always opposed, or what do you mean by coming out here making Filmore speeches, when there are not ten Filmore men in the county that are residents, what few there are here, belong down South, and are only here doing business; further, the very man or men that have had you in charge since you came here, and nearly all that heard you speak to night are Democrats and you are here in one of the worst Democratic holes in the city. We do most positively assure you that there is no Filmore party in this part of the State."

I told them all about the manner in which I had been started out, and how I had got the money and pass to come on; and also what I intended to do with the money that I had. I told them that I had been deceived into the belief that there was no Fremont party in the State, and that I had thought that Filmore was our only hope to beat Buchanan with, but I was now satisfied that it was all a Democratic dodge to weaken Fremont, and that I should change my whole course hereafter, that I should fill the appointments that were made for me, but the Democrats would make little by the operation. This pleased them very much and they left with a better opinion of me than they had when they first called on me.

The next morning when I called for my bill, preparatory to leaving the city, I was told that it was paid and a ticket had been left for me to take me to Kittaning, where I was to speak that night. I asked who the kind friend was that paid my bill and left the ticket, when the clerk said it was a friend of the cause ; here you perceive there was some more Democratic money used. I took the cars and in due time arrived at Kittaning and as soon as I got out of the cars I began to look around for the notices of my meeting, but saw no bills ; I asked several persons present if there was to be a Filmore meeting there to night, a Filmore meeting said one of them, what kind of a meeting would that be, there aint a Filmore man in the county. Yes there is said another, there is a fellow down the country about ten miles from here that swears he will vote for him ; oh well said the other he will be allright before the election. Then there is no Filmore hotel where I can stop at, said I ; no said the man, but that omnibus, pointing to one, will take you to a good hotel, but I hardly think you will find many Filmore men there.

I went to the hotel, registerd my name and asked the landlord if he had heard of any meeting that was to come off there that night, he said not, when a servant man spoke up and said that some bills had come there a few days before to the landlords brother, for a Filmore meeting, and they where laying in the closet then, and went and got them, when all present had a hearty laugh over them. The landlord said, his brother was a halfway Filmore man, but had gone to New York, so there was no Filmore party in town at this time. About this time the high sheriff of the county came in and the landlord introduced me as a Filmore speaker, who had come there to make a speech and that the bills had not been posted. That dont make any difference, said the sheriff, everybody is here today attending the county fair, and we can get up a meeting without any trouble. I am a Democrat, but you shall have a meeting to-night, and a big one at that, we all want to hear the Buckeye Blacksmith, the man that we have read so much about.

After dinner the sheriff took me all around town and introduced me to all the big bugs of the county, telling them that I would speak at the court house that night, but I soon found that he was introducing me generally to Democrats. The Chairman of the Republican County Committee had a store opposite the hotel, where all the principal men of the party were collected looking daggers at me. I finally asked the sheriff to go over with me and introduce me to them, which he did; they treated me very kindly and asked me how many Filmore votes I expected to make in their county. I told them that I expected to convert all of them to my doctrine before I left town. This caused considerable merriment among them. The sheriff then took me out to the Fair ground where I had a nice time with the ladies, and returned to town with the sheriff in time for tea, well pleased with that days adventure.

At the hour of meeting, my friend, the sheriff, escorted me to the Court House which I found packed to overflowing with men; every available spot had a man in it so that I could hardly get a place to stand and speak; there was no chairman appointed, the sheriff telling me to go ahead and make my speech which I did; I commenced by a violent attack on Buchanan, I raked up everything he had ever done, and gave him the best drubbing I could; this the Democrats only smiled at, supposing, of course, that I would give it to Fremont worse after I had gotten through with Buchanan. I spoke a few things in favor of Filmore, spoke of him as having been a good and true Whig that we old Whigs had delighted to honor, &c., when all at once I stopped short in my speech and said, but, gentlemen, there is another fellow running, what is this they call him I have forgotten his name, when a dozen voices sung out Fremont, ah, yes, said I, Fremont is his name, well I don't know much about that fellow, all that I do know is what the Democratic papers says about him, (I must confess that it is not very good authority.) They say that in 1846 while he was in charge of the Commissary department in Mexico or some other place, that he stole eighty thousand dollars worth of Government cattle, well, this I believe for the strongest reasons that a man could have that was not an eye witness to the fact, he was a Democrat then, and was elected to the United States Senate by them about that time as such, and as stealing had ever been the order of that party, I had no doubt but that he thought it was his duty to follow in the footsteps of his party.

But, gentlemen, I am free to say that I have never heard of anything wrong against that man since he left the Democrats and got into decent company ; this fixed matters, all the leading Democrats raised up and said they had heard enough of the Buckeye, and made for the door amid the shouts of the Republicans who gathered around congratulating me on my success in putting down the Democracy that night; when order was restored I finished my speech to the entire satisfaction of all the friends of Fremont and some of the Democrats.

After I was done speaking and returned to the hotel, the Chairman of the Fremont Committee with many of the leaders of the party of that county called on me and complimented me very highly for the manner in which I had turned the tables on the Democrats who had been the means of sending me out to speak for Filmore, for I had told in my speech all about the way that I started out, and where the money had come from to send me. The next morning the Fremont men would not allow me to go in the stage but sent me to Brady's Bend in a carriage in charge of a committee, and when we got to Brady's Bend the Democrats, what few there were in the place, had posted the bills and had made arrangements for me to speak at a tavern of theirs, but my committee took me

*8

to a Fremont house and went and saw all the leading men about the mills and works of the place, and told them all about my plan of speaking, and by night they had got up a large meeting at the hotel where I was staying, so when night came everybody was there except a few leading Democrats who were at the other tavern; I therefore told them that I would speak where the crowd was and therefore did speak at the hotel where I had put up.

The next day I went over to another town where I was to speak and here also I found my bills up for a meeting, but at this town the Democrats had been posted by some of their friends, who had been to the fair at Kittaning; so they stood aloof and paid but little attention to me, but the Fremont men made up in attention, what the other side neglected to do. Here we had a day-meeting and a pretty stormy one it was, for the Democrats undertook to use their old and only arguments, that is, when they can't answer your questions, to kick up a fuss. This they undertook at this place, but got the worst of it by getting two or three of their men whipped.

From this place I took a stage for Clarion the county seat of Clarion county, where I was told in Philadelphia they had fourteen hundred enrolled names for Filmore; I had also been told that they had eight hundred enrolled names in Armstrong county, where I had just left, but I had failed to find one man, so I supposed it would be in Clarion, but I was mistaken, for on my arrival there I was met by a delegation of real bonafide Filmore men; it is true, it was not a very large delegation, but what it lacked in numbers it made up in zeal, it was composed of three Journeymen painters from Philadelphia who were up there painting a large church. They received me very cordially and introduced me to most of the leading men of both parties of the place.

The Fremont men were pretty shy and said but

little to me, but the Democrats seemed to delight in talking to me; I said but little on politics, talking mostly about county affairs, crops &c. I had invited all that I talked with to come to my meeting that night and hear what I had to say, so that when the hour arrived for our meeting, I found the courthouse full. It was a Democratic county and as a matter of course there was a majority of my meeting of that stripe; they organized with one of my Philadelphia painters as chairman and another as secretary. When I was introduced, I said, gentlemen I am a very fearless speaker, I generally speak my own sentiments without fear, I generally take the responsibilty on myself for what I say, and I never allow any man to interrupt me while I am speaking; I hope you will all listen to me until I am done then I will answer any question that you may ask me.

I took about the same course that I had taken in Kittaning, pitched into Buchanan, spoke well of Filmore and then took up Fremont as I had done before. I told all about my start from Philadelphia and said, that every dollar that I had to electioneer for Mr. Filmore with, had been furnished by the Democratic party, and that the whole Filmore movement was a Democratic dodge to weaken Mr. Fremont; I told of the fourteen hundred enrolled Filmore men that were claimed for that county and showed the Philadelphia papers as proof, which caused great merriment among the crowd; I spoke for two hours, and when I closed I was taken in charge by the Fremont men and seen but little of the Filmore party in that place.

I was to speak in six places in that county that week. So the Fremont men sent a man to all these places to post their friends about me, so as to get up good meetings and they sent a good speaker along to help me. I had a very lively time that week among the unterrified, got into several fusses with them, but always came off victorious. After speaking a week in the principal places in the county finding but three Filmore men, I left for Jefferson county, where I was to speak for another week.

Here I found five live Filmore men, although that county was said to have eight hundred men enrolled for him. Here I had a monster meeting, it was court week and almost everybody was in town that week; they knew nothing of my manner of speaking, and when the time came for the meeting, the Judge of the court was nominated for chairman; he declined, saying that he could not be chairman of a meeting in the interest of Democracy. We got a man to act in his place, who introduced me as a Filmore speaker who would address them. I began by saying, that I had no doubt but that there would be more disappointed people there to night, than was ever in that court house before at one time.

I began my speech in my usual way, and when I got to that part that alluded to Fremont stealing cattle and being a Roman Catholic the manner in which I got around it, and brought it to bear upon the Democrats, brought down the Fremont men with loud and continued applause. When order was restored up jumped a fellow from Philadelphia, that had been sent there under pay of the Democratic party to intercept me (for they had heard the turn that I had taken on them) and he began to denounce me, and had the impudence to ask me, if that was the kind of a speech that I was sent there to make. You were sent here to make Filmore speeches, said he, and here you are making Fremont speeches, Hold on, says I, you shall have a chance when I am done. I then commenced and gave the whole history of the case, how I had been deceived into the belief that Fremont had no party, and that Filmore was going to carry everything before him in the western part of the State; I told how and where the money came from and who paid my bills at Pittsburg, and how opposed I was to the Democratic party and then asked the people present, wether I was not justifiable in the course I was pursuing, when the old judge raised up and offered three cheers for the Buckeye Blacksmith and the whole house came down with loud applause. I then told this fellow he could take the stand, which he did, and commenced to abuse me, but was soon told by the crowd, that if he did not want to be ducked in the mill pond, he had better stop that kind of talk, when many sung out in the crowd, duck him, duck him, duck him, let us duck him anyhow, he has no business here, and if the Judge and myself had not interfered, he would have got into trouble there that night, but we got the people quiet, and he left at a late hour that night for a town some ten miles away.

In all the travels of my life, I never made a speech that gave more satisfaction than that speech did that night; I had shown so conclusively that the whole Filmore movement was conducted in the interest of the Democratic party and with their money, that every Fremont man in that great meeting was ready to fight if necessary for me. They said, that I have done them more good than any other man could have done in the country; I have no doubt, but that fellows interrupting me in the way he did, done us great good. The effect of that meeting was, that the whole five Filmore men who were there when I began to speak, all came out boldly for Fremont as soon as the meeting was over. I filled all the appointments that had been made for me in that county and two or three in Snyder county and then turned my face toward home again, arriving there a few days before the election, where I spoke three or four times every night until the election.

After I returned to Philadelphia and began to speak at the various Ward meetings, speaking at two and three meetings every night telling them about my travels through the western part of the State, declar-

ing to them that there was no Filmore party outside
of Philadelphia. The Democrats and the leading Filmore men and their papers began a tirade of abuse
against me, and even had the assurance to declare in
face of all the facts of the case, that Filmore was the
only opposition that Buchanan had, and many of them
came to my meeting and denounced me as a liar when
I was telling the truth. But notwithstanding all their
abuse I went ahead, well satisfied that the Filmore
men were coming over daily not only by hundreds, but
by thousands. And I have no doubt, that if we could
have had ten days more to have worked in, that we
would have been able to have given Fremont the
State. I certainly never did see such a revolution in
politics in one week as there was in Philadelphia the
week before that election, for as soon as the people became satisfied that their was no Filmore party outside of the city, they came around by thousands; a few
days longer to have worked in would have accomplished all we wanted. The people were honest and
wanted to vote right, so as to beat the Democratic party.

Soon after the nomination of Fremont, his State
Central committee proposed to the Filmore committee,
to run a joint set of electors, pledged to cast the vote
of the State to the man that had the largest number
of electoral votes in the nation. If the vote of the
State would elect Fremont, they were to be pledged to
cast it for him, or if their votes would elect Filmore,
then they should cast it for him. This the Filmore
committee utterly refused to do, saying that they would
not affilliate with Abolitionists. They saw very plainly
that with a union ticket the State would go against
Buchanan, and Fremont would be elected; the Democrats saw it too, hence they paid any amount of
money to this committee to keep up a separate organisation. Had they accepted the offer of the Fremont
committee six weeks before the election, we never
would have been cursed with Jimmy Buchanan's ad-

ministration, we would have elected Fremont, and then we would never have been cursed with that terrible rebellion; for weak a man as Pierce was, he never would have suffered the seceeding States to have withdrawn from the union.

And I would here state, that the leaders of the Filmore party of Pennsylvania, stand to day responsible before God, for every drop of blood that was shed in that rebellion, and poor as I am, I would not take the Presidencey and be compelled to meet those four hundered thousand martyred soldiers and their starving wives and childern at the bar of God on the day of judgement, as they will have to do; for be you well assured that every dying groan of the soldier, and every sigh and tear of their bereaved families at home, God will bring up in that Day against them, and I am proud to day that my soul (whatever my other faults may be) has never been stained with the blood of my countrymen.

The reader will thus see the various tricks and plans that the Democratic party resorted to, in order to cheat the people into electing an objectionable man. For unknown as Fremont was to the people and as little time as we had to bring him before them, he would most assuredly have been elected if he had not have been cheated out of it. Thus Mr. Buchanan carried the electoral vote of Pennsylvania by a minority vote of the people, and was therefore elected by that vote. Hence our country was cursed with the greatest calamity that ever befell any nation from Adam until the present time.

After the election was over, I began to turn my attention to my business again, but here I was broken down in health without much money, for I had spent all I had in the campaign that had just closed, and had been defeated in my undertaking. How to start again, I could not see, but my doctrine had ever been to hope on hope ever. So I looked a round a few days, and at last found an excellent opening, provided I could raise two hundred and fifty dollars, but where that was to come from I knew not, I had but a few days to raise it in; so I went to my friends, that were able to help me, but the election was over and they had no use for my services, and therefore were not willing to assist me with a dollar. The last day that I had to raise the money in, had arrived, and I was no nearer it, than when I began; (so I thought at the time.) I had become very low spirited and out of heart, so I sat down on the curbstones to rest myself, meditating upon my hard fate, thinking over the old proverb, that Republics had always been ungrateful, when who should walk up, but a prominent Democrat, and said, well Buckeye, what are you studying about, grieving I suppose over your late defeat, aint you well; no, said I, but I am grieving over my misfortune in not being able to find a friend to help me out of a tight place, and then told him all about the place that I could buy out, if I could raise the two hundred and fifty dollars; well said he, if you can get it for that sum, you can get it for two hundred cash and your note for the balance, this I am certain of; but where is the two hundred dollars to come from, said I; he then said, I have it my pocket and will lend it to you, provided you can get the place in that way, and took out the money and gave it to me, with the understanding, that I was to give it back to him if I failed to get the place, and if I got it, I was to pay him as fast as I could.

This raised my spirits up to fever-heat; this caused tears of gratitude to rise in my eyes to think, that after I had failed with all my political friends to raise a dollar, that God had sent a political opponent to raise me as it were from the grave. I at once went to the party that had the place and told them that all I could do with them, was to give them two hundred dollars in gold for the place, if that would suit them there was the cash, they owed some rent that I told them must be left in my hands. They consulted awhile and said, that they could not accept it, so I started to leave the place, but before I had got down to the street they called me back and accepted my offer, and gave me a bill of sale on the place and keys and walked out; well I went home that night a very happy man I assure you, but before I left for home I went to the *Ledger* office and put a card in that paper for a partner with a cash capital of two hundred and fifty dollars to join the Buckeye Blacksmith in a money making business well understood by the Buckeye.

The next morning when I went down to my place I found a number of men waiting for me to understand what business I wanted to carry on, and before night I had near fifty applications for the places; I made a contract with one of them who paid me two hundred and fifty dollars cash for one half of the place that I had only paid two hundred dollars for the whole; I had here made a pretty good thing of it so I went to my friend, paid him his two hundred dollars and had fifty dollars and half the place left, thus you will see that I had a pretty good start again.

I went to work and learned my partner as soon as I could and we were doing a very nice little business, but unfortunately for me, we did not agree very well, he was not the clear thing, for he took every advantage of me that he could, which was very unpleasant to me, so much so that by the next summer I sold out to him for two hundred and fifty dollars for the other half of the place; this was just about the time that Mr. Wilmot, the great Wilmot Provisoman, was nominated for Governor of Pennsylvania, and as I was out of business I thought I would make a little tour through the State until the weather got a little cooler and then open up business again for myself.

I therefore went to the committee, and they, through

their chairman, agreed with me to stump the State for
them, and as it was early in the campaign they had
no funds collected, they arranged with me to pay my
own expenses and keep an account of it until the end
of the campaign when they would pay me my expenses and something for my services. So I started
and stumped the country until a few days before election and returned home. When I got back I found
that everything was excitement in Philadelphia owing
to the great panic in money matters, for it was during
the great crisis of 1857; the result was that the people
had failed to pay the committee what they had subscribed and they had adjourned and gone home and
let the election go by default and I never got a dollar
of the money that I had advanced to pay expenses nor
a cent for my labor, which left me with but about
ninety dollars to begin business with.

I took what money I had and started in a small
way and thus continued doing a small business during
the years of '58 and '59 when the Presidential question begun to be agitated throughout the country,
but I made up my mind that I would take no more
part in politics for the simple reason that there are
but few politicians that have any other principal than
self-aggrandizement, they too soon forget the men that
do the work for them, and for this reason I would advise all young men to beware of politicians and in
place of being a politician engage in some honorable
business.

Although I had taken but little part in politics
since Buchanan's election, I had kept pace with all
that was transpiring in the political doings of the
country. I saw the inroads the South was making
upon the North; the plans that they were laying to
get the whole Government into their own hands, that
whenever they might pretend to have cause for a
separation from the North, they would be prepared
for it, they had been steadily preparing for secession

for a number of years, by getting a large preponderance of the officers of the Goverment both civil and military of Southern birth.

During the administration of Mr. Jefferson he inaugurated a system of equalizing the Federal officeholders at Washington, so as to give each State its proportion of officers according to their representation in Congress; this system seemed to give entire satisfaction to the whole country, and indeed this seemed to be the only fair way of disposing of the matter for each State to have its share of the public patronage of the Government.

This system was continued without much deviation through the various administrations that followed Mr. Jefferson's until Mr. Pierce took his seat as President, he commenced to deviate from that rule, by appointing a large excess of these officers from the Southern States; this, of course, was done as a reward for his nomination for the Presidency by the votes of the South in the National Convention.

Will any man pretend to say that Franklin Pierce himself, or any other Northern man for one moment ever thought of Mr. Pierce as a candidate for President of the United States, and it was said at the time that when the news reached Mrs. Pierce that she took it as an insult to her husband, and could scarcely be made to believe it, but the South had sprung him on the ticket as an available man to suit their purposes, for with him at the head of the Government as their tool, they could have things pretty much their own way, which they had, and thus were able to force upon the country a large overplus of their friends in the Federal offices at Washington.

In the campaign of 1856 when we charged it upon the Democracy the unfairness of the distribution of the public offices at Washington they readily acknowledged the fact, but pledged themselves to the people that the election of Mr. Buchanan would remedy that evil as he was pledged to walk in the footsteps of his illustrous predecessors Jefferson, Madison and Jackson. But alas how very soon are the promises of politicians forgotten. As soon as Mr. Buchanan was installed in his office instead of going back to the old Jeffersonian doctrine in the distribution of those offices equally among the States he not only followed in the footsteps of Mr. Pierce, but went far ahead of him in his appointments of Southern men to office, so that by the close of his administration eleven out of every fourteen of the officers at Washington both civil and military according to the blue-book or department register, were of Southern birth, why was this done, there must be a motive for it, well I will tell you why it was done.

The South had been preparing for a separation from the North for a number of years, they desired a Government with slavery for its basis and were sooner or later fully expecting to get it, and in order to be fully prepared, whenever they were ready to strike the blow, it was necessary for them to have not only the army and navy in the hands of their friends, but the Treasury also, as well as all the archives of the country; this they had been gradually securing by getting a large majority of both civil and military offices in their hands during the administration of Pierce and Buchanan.

Thus they were in the closing year of Mr. Buchanan's administration about as near ready to make their contemplated blow at the Government as they ever could possibly get. But before it would be safe to make that blow it was necessary to divide the Democratic party, for they saw very plainly that the Republican party of the North would run a candidate on free soil for free men principles, and there was a large vote in the North opposed to Democratic principles, that would not unite with these free soilers, and that if they run a strait Democratic candidate he must be elected, as the opposition would certainly be divided, and thus they would be left without a pretext for a separation, hence it was necessary to divide the Democratic party also.

Well about this time the opposition or a part of the opposition to Democracy met in convention and nominated John Bell, of Tennessee, for President, and very soon after the Democrats met at Charleston, S. C., to nominate a candidate of their choice, no I can't say of their choice for they had no choice, they did not intend to make any choice, the Southern portion of that convention only met there to mature their plans for dividing the Democratic party and not to nominate a candidate; if they had met for that purpose why did they not make a nomination. Stephen A Douglas went into that convention with a clear majority of over forty votes on the first ballot, why was he not nominated, I will tell you.

Mr. Bell had been nominated by a large body of men, and the Republicans had already called a convention to nominate their candidate, this would so divide the Northern opposition that if Mr. Douglas was put on their ticket he would most likely carry the North through this division in the opposition party, hence they were compelled to break up the Charleston convention in a row, and adjourn to meet in Baltimore some weeks later, and when they did meet what was the result, Mr. Douglas had a large majority on the first ballot, after which the Southern wing of that convention kicked up another row and withdrew and organized another convention, and nominated John C. Breckenridge, a fire eater of Kentucky as their candidate, while the regular convention nominated Mr. Douglas, as their standard bearer, and thus we had two distinct and separate Democratic candidates in the field.

Douglas got but few votes in the South, as it might well be supposed. It was not their intention that he should, neither did they intend that he should have too many in the North. Their plan was to so divide the Democratic party in the North as to make the election of the Republican candidate, whoever he might be (although he was not yet nominated) certain. Then they could go before the rank and file of the Southern people and inflame their hearts against the North, by telling them that the North had decided against the South and her institutions, and in favor of the freedom of the negroes. This of course would be a sufficient cause for breaking up this government.

The great Republican party met and nominated Abraham Lincoln of Illinois, and thus we had four candidates in the field. Each party seemed to hold up their man as the only fit person for the office he aspired too. And from the way matters stood at the beginning of the campaign, it bid fair to be a very lively as well as very exciting one. The Federal officers were nearly to a man enlisted on the side of Mr Breckenridge, while the farmers and working men of Democracy generally preferred Mr. Douglas. While in the opposition ranks Mr. Lincoln appeared to take the lead, he was a working man himself, and appeared to take well with that class of voters. I as yet had taken no part in the matter, but was determined to go for Lincoln, for the reason that I knew him personally and knew him to be an honest man, (and Henry Clay once said that an honest man was the noblest work of God.) I was therefore determined to do all that I could for him.

CHAPTER IX.

CAMPAIGN OF 1860—SECESSION—19TH APRIL IN
PHILADELPHIA—AN OFFICE HOLDER IN
THE CUSTOM HOUSE.

MR. LINCOLN was a strong man, I knew that he was hard to beat, that he had scarcely ever undertaken anything that he did not succeed in, I therefore felt every confidence in his success, and tendered my services to the State committee, as a speaker, so that they could use me whenever they wanted me. During the several years that I had travelled through various counties of the State as a daguerrotypist, I had always told the people that my pictures would not fade, while most of the others would, in this I knew I was right, as a few years had proven; this circumstance I took advantage of. I had told them the truth then, so they would be more likely to believe me now than they would other speakers. I therefore sent out small bills to a few places that were strongly Democratic, to try what effect I could produce among them. The first place that I went to I found a very large meeting collected together, both ladies and gentlemen. They had brought a grand supper with them, each farmer had brought a basket full of nice things to eat, and had arranged a long temporary table in an orchard near by, and had it filled to overflowing with the best the country could produce. I did not arrive until the time for speaking, and was taken on the stand at once.

When I was introduced to the audience, I told them that I was glad to meet them after so many years of separation; that I had formed a friendship for them when among them some years ago taking their pictures, that I had never forgotten, and I was very certain that I never forgot their kindness to me at that time. I had come among them a stranger, and had told them that I would do them good work, and that my work would not fade as most others had, and would; you believed me then and got me to take your likeness, and I feel very certain that none of you have had reason to regret having your work done by me. No, no, said a hundred voices, at the same time holding up their pictures, saying here they are as good as ever. Well gentlemen, I told you the truth then, and I have come here to tell you the truth now; when many of them cried out that is what we want to hear. Then gentlemen if you will give me your attention, I will try and tell you all I know about the questions that are now before the people.

I told them that the election of a President was similar to a farmer employing a man to superintend his farm for him, we had a large farm to take care off, the whole United States, and we wanted to employ a man to superintend it for us. We had four gentlemen applying for the situation, and it was for the people to decide which of these men are best qualified for the place. If you farmers wanted a superintendent on your farm, who would you employ, you would employ a farmer, one that fully understood farming would you not, you certainly would not employ a lawyer or a merchant, for the simple reason that he did not understand the business. So it is with all other trades, if you want a coat made, you go to a tailor, not to a shoemaker, because he would not understand the business. So it is in choosing a man for President, we should throw aside politics, and try our utmost to get a man who understands the wants of the working men, as a large majority of us are working men; we should get a man who knows how to feel for us and one that understands our wants. My friends I am well acquainted with Mr. Lincoln, and know him to be the man who does understand our wants. He has been a working man himself, and knows what a hard days work is worth, he has worked many a long day, hard for fifty cents, and knows exactly what it is worth, and what kind of laws the working man needs to protect his industry. They say that he was once a rail splitter, well, so have you and I split rails, but is that any disgrace to him or us; no my friends it is an honor to any man to have earned his own living by the sweat of his brow. Does it prove that because you and I or Mr. Lincoln or any other man has had to work for our living, that he is not capable of doing any thing else? No my friends, the best and greatest men that this nation has ever had, were self made men.

Another reason why we should elect Mr. Lincoln is, that he is an honest man, and every man of all political views, that ever knew him, will say so. There is not a farm in Illinois where he is known, that he cannot buy on his word, there is no need of a written contract with him, his word is law, and every body knows it that knows him; therefore I think he is decidedly the best man to go for. Mr. Bell is a good and an honest man, but he has no show to be elected, and therefore the fight is entirely between Mr. Lincoln and Douglas, against whom I have not a word to say. Mr. Douglas is a great Statesman, probably as great a man as we have now living in this country, but gentlemen Mr. Douglas is and has been raised a lawyer and cannot understand the wants of the people as well as Mr. Lincoln does. It is not possible that he could, he never having done a days work in his life cannot know what it is worth, or what laws would be needed to protect him as Mr. Lincoln does. I therefore conclude that the best thing we can do is to lay aside all politics, and give an undivided support to the working man's friend, honest Uncle Abe, as he is called by the people who know him best. What do you think of it my friend, don't you think so too, if so in conclusion let us give him three cheers, when all hands joined in one shout for old Uncle Abe, ladies and all, after which an old Democrat raised up and said, "gentlemen Democrats, I move that we Democrats give three cheers to the Buckeye for the manly way in which 'he has spoken of his opponents, and the plain and acceptable manner in which he has presented Mr. Lincoln. This they responded to with thunders of applause.

As soon as the speaking was over, I was invited to the orchard where we all partook heartily of a fine colation that had been prepared for the occasion. After we had done justice to our appetites, and I had made a general round of hand shaking, we separated at a late hour of the night, or I might say an early hour in the morning, never so far as I am concerned to forget that nights proceedings. The most pleasing scenes that I passed through that night, was the taking by the hand of ladies who were now married, that I had nursed on my lap years before. when they were little girls. A number of old gentlemen would lead their daughters up to me and say, do you remember the little black eyed girl that you wanted to adopt as your daughter, when you took her picture ten years ago, well here she is, and here is her husband, pointing him out to me, when I would generally remark, that she was a pretty little girl ten years ago, and had not yet lost her good looks. This would please not only her but all her friends, and I am very certain that no man ever left that place more popular than I did when I left there the next morning, for the landlady told me at breakfast, that old as I was I could get any of the girls for a wife, that were there that night, for, said she, a number of them inquired of her, if I was married. This I told her was caused by my funny way of speaking, when the landlord spoke up and said, that he would give half of all that he was worth, if he could win the people over as I could. He said that a number of lifelong Democrats had come to him after our meeting was over, and said that I had told them the truth ten years ago about my work, and they believed that I had told them the truth to night, and that they intended to vote for Mr. Lincoln if they lived to the day of election, and the vote of that district on the day of election showed they did vote for him.

I went to my next appointment, and was met by a similar crowd, mostly farmers and working men, where I took about the same course that I had taken the night before, and was received in the same cordial manner, except the supper in the orchard, but had a fine one at the hotel after the meeting was over, where we ate and drank until many of us became merry. In this style I continued until I had finished the appointments that I had made, when I returned home and reported to the committee all that had occurred. They told me that they would have plenty of work for me in a short time. I went to work for a few days until they were ready,—but before I had been home a week they sent for me, and told me that I had to go back again to all the places that I had just visited, for hundreds of people who had not heard me, insisted on having me back again so that they could also hear me. So the county committee thought it very important to have me go over the same ground again, that I had just left. I therefore sent another set of appointments to the same places as before, and at the appointed time filled them to the entire satisfaction of most of the people who heard me. And I would here state that the main cause of popularity was the fact, the people had confidence in me, that I would tell them the truth, for I always made it a rule and it is the only true rule, never to make a charge on any man or party that was not strictly true and that I was not able to prove by authentic documents if contradicted. This has ever been my motto, and should be the motto of every speaker who undertakes to make a political speech before the public, if he wishes to become a popular man with the people.

When I had finished my last set of appointments in that county I returned home. The committee had made arrangements for me to travel through several of the northern counties of the State, to speak at mass-meetings, which was very much against my will, as I never had a very great opinion of them. I always thought that the five or six speakers who would attend a mass-meeting would do more good by scattering around the country and hold six different meetings, than to all speak at one meeting. There would be more Democrats come to the six meetings than to the one, and would have a better chance to be convinced by hearing one speaker fully explain his ideas than to hear six short little speeches all of different ideas. — But I consented to go, for I knew that if there were a dozen speakers at a meeting the people would not rest until they heard me through, and if I am proud of any one thing attending my public life, it is this, that but few people have ever left the ground while I was speaking, and that I never have found a man who could hold an audience longer than I could; this of course I am proud of; neither did I ever find many speakers that were willing to speak after me, but always prefering to speak before me, for the reason they said that I made the people laugh so much while I spoke, that they could not get a smile from them.

About this time there was a very lively contest going on in my district, for the nomination of a candidate for Congress, between Judge Kelly and Wm. B. Thomas. I felt a deep interest in that nomination I therefore went home for a few days to assist in the contest. Judge Kelly had done me a great favor in 1857, when I was sick and needed a friend, and as I had always considered that ingratitude was the foulest blot on any man's character, that could ever be found to stain it, I concluded that it was my duty to use every power at my command to aid in his nomination, which I did, and the country knows the result. We not only nominated, but elected him by a large majority to a seat in Congress, which he has satisfactorily filled ever since. I have always felt proud that I was one of the men that sent Judge Kelly to Congress, for I look upon him as one of the best men of the present age.

Mr. Thomas was also a good man, he was rich and very good to the poor, which made him very popular with the people, and had it not been for a little mismanagement he would have beaten Kelly for the first nomination. Mr. Thomas never forgave me for the part I took in favor of Kelly against him at that time and although I wrote Mr. Lincoln a long letter as soon as he was elected, giving many good reasons why Mr. Thomas should be the collector of customs for the port of Philadelphia in 1861; yet he refused to give me anything better than a night-watchman along the river which only paid one dollar and a half per night.

After the nomination for Congress was over and I had got a little rested I continued to speak all through the eastern part of the State until the election which terminated so successful to the Republcan party. Mr. Lincoln was triumphantly elected over all opposition, and the little giant, as Douglas was called, was quietly laid aside and Breckenridge and John Bell were left badly out in the cold; thus ended that great and never to be forgotten campaign. It had resulted just as the South wanted it to. They broke up the Democratic party for that purpose; it was for this reason that Mr. Douglass was not nominated at Charleston, it was for this that they withdrew from the convention at Baltimore, for no man who has a sane mind will pretend to say, that Mr. Lincoln with a divided party at the North and no party at all in the South, could have beaten Mr. Douglas if there had been no other Democratic candidate running. Mr. Douglas was popular with the people and would have been hard to beat in a single fight, and would have beaten Mr. Lincoln easy in a triangle fight, with Bell and Lincoln both running in the same party, but the South did not intend to have any other than a Republican elected from the start, so they sent millions of money to the North to keep up the split in the Democratic ranks.

As soon as the election was over I went to work again at my business in a small way, for I had but little cash to start on, so I done little work for the want of means to increase it; I struggled along until Spring, when I intended to apply for a situation under the collector of customs, but before Mr. Lincoln had taken his seat the entire South had organized a most powerful resistance and seven States had already withdrawn from the union and had established a seperate confederate government at Montgomery, Alabama, and to show you their sincerity in their opposition to Mr. Lincoln, I will only refer you to one fact. The Democrats had a majority of some six or eight in the United States Senate, that could have held a check on the President, so much so, that he could not have appointed his own cabinet or any other officer of the nation, and yet these southern Democratic Senators in the face of all these facts before them, resigned their seats in the United States Senate and went through the entire South inflaming the peoples minds against

Mr. Lincoln, in order to get them to assist in separating of the States, when they knew that Lincoln's hands would have been tied so far as doing them any harm was concerned. Yet they were only carrying out their intended plans of a separate government with, as I have said before, the intention of making slavery the basis of it.

And when the time arrived for Mr. Lincoln to take his seat, what do we find to be the facts of the case. The Government in the hands of the South, the army and navy in their hands, the navy had been sent into far distant seas, where it was impossible for them to be reached in time to render any assistance in maintaining the government, the army also was in their hands, had been scattered all over the South, ready to be used by them against the government they had sworn to defend. They had taken the precaution to remove all our guns and ammunition out of reach, and every dollar as well as every dollars worth of available funds had been scattered through the South, so that when Mr. Lincoln should reach Washington, if he ever did alive, he would find the capital almost entirely in the hands of his enemies, and a formidable army across the river and he alone without a dollar or a man to defend him, where he would fall an easy prey to their hellish malice.

But in this they were mistaken, as they were in many other things, they had no idea that the North was so easily aroused. They had already fired on Fort Sumpter, and the blood of the North had begun to warm up almost to fever heat and wanted but little more to set it a boiling. They were determined that as their President had been elected fairly, that he should take his seat at all hazards.

The threats had been so loud that the friends of Mr. Lincoln thought it the most prudent for him to change his intended route to Washington, and in place of going from Harrisburg to Baltimore, where it was they were prepared to assasinate him, that he should go by the way of Philadelphia and Baltimore disguised as a common old farmer, and thus escape his intended murderers. Thus he reached Washington where he was safe among his many friends who had preceeded him there. And on the 4th of March in the presence of the thousands of his friends, who had congregated took the oath of office which he never violated.

But he soon found that it was necessary to call out the military to defend the Capital against an army of rebels that were already organized to march against it. The people from one end of the North to the other responded to the call at a moments warning, and when they reached Baltimore they met the first armed resistance, and then and there was the first blood shed in that damnable rebellion; and had it not have been for Mayor Henry of Philadelphia, on that memorable 19th of April, the city of Baltimore would have been laid in ashes in twenty four hours after they fired on the Northern troops. But Mayor Henry prevailed on the people to have patience, saying at the same time that Baltimore would right herself in twenty four hours, and if she did not, he would not interfere with them, that they could do as they pleased. This had the desired effect of quieting down the excitement for that day. And if Baltimore had not righted herself and had fired on any more Northern troops, there were fifty thousand men in Philadelphia, ready to take an oath never to eat, drink or sleep, until Baltimore was in ashes. And that it certainly would have been, had they continued to publicly obstruct the passage of troops through it. But the worst thing they done after the 19th of April, was to send a committee to the President to say to him that he must not desecrate the soil of Maryland by sending Northern troops through it, but they came away with a flea in their ear, for Mr. Lincoln plainly told them that it was too far for him to march the troops around Maryland and he had not time to dig a tunnel under it and the men had no wings to fly over it, and therefore he should have to march them through it. This struck them like a bombshell. They found out for the first time that there was pluck enough in old Abe. as he was called, to take care of the Government, notwithstanding one third of the people in it were arrayed in arms against it. The only blunder that Lincoln made in the start, he placed too much confidence in some of his officers. Had he have had the right kind of a man at the head of the army at the first Bull Run fight, he might have ended the rebellion then, but he had traitors in his camp at that time, and a long time after. Had Grant have been at the head of the army at Richmond when little Mac was there, the war would have been ended then. But it was not little Mac's programme to whip his Democratic brethren too soon; he and his friends wished to prolong the war without the shedding of much blood, so as to create a large war debt to bring up against the Republicans as an electioneering scheme, and through that to break down the Republican party and elect him to the Presidency, when he could make peace on terms to suit them.

I shall now return to the 19th of April at night in Philadelphia, which was the greatest night that I ever saw; the whole people were in the wildest state of excitement that was ever known in that or any other city. There was one outpouring of the people, and meetings were held at various points. I went to the National Hall to hear the speaking, but found more than ten thousand out side unable to gain admission. I was soon called for, and I mounted a segar show case and commenced to speak, and the crowd becoming larger and larger every minute, until Market street wide as it is, was packed with people as far as I could see. I continued to so speak for more than three hours to the largest mass of human beings that I had ever seen at one time. At one time in my speech some copper-head interrupted me, when he was seized by the excited people and hoisted above their heads and knocked and thrown from one to another as far as I could see; what became of the poor devil I never knew, but one thing I do know he got a pretty good thrashing before he got out of their hands. When I concluded my speech, the whole crowd seemed to rush upon me to take me by the hands to congratulate me on my great speech as they called it, and many of the leading men of the city declared that my speech that night was the greatest effort of my life; and I suppose myself, that I made the best speech that night that I ever did make, for the simple reason that I had more material to speak about than I ever had before. I was done speaking but how was I to get out of this mass of humanity, crowding as they were upon me, while six or eight would have hold of each hand and arm, shaking me nearly to pieces. At last ten or fifteen police managed to form a hollow square around me, and gallanted me home, amidst the shouts of ten thousand people, all crying let me shake that man's hand. And after I did get home, they continued to shout for the Buckeye, until I got out on a balcony and made them another speech of over an hour; when I closed they gave me three cheers and left. It was now near two o'clock in the morning.

The next day very early the mob began to assemble about the Court House yard to hear the news and prepare for the defense of the capital at Washington, and when the call was made for all those who felt like fighting for the flag to step across a certain line which was made, I was the third man who stepped over and offered my services to my country, and in less than ten minutes, more than five thousand had crossed the line to fight for the old flag. (God bless and protect that dear old flag, and forbid that its folds shall ever be trailed in the dust.)

The mob then organized a large force and made a raid on every house which was suspected of sympathizing with the South and gave the occupants but five minutes to hang out the stars and stripes, and God help the man who would have refused to hang them out—they would have hung him as high as Haman, and nothing could have saved him. Some hung them out and others ran away before the mob got to their places and thus saved their lives. Robert Tyler, son of ex-President Tyler, was one who escaped by jumping over the iron railing of the State House yard and running for life with five hundred men and boys after him with ropes to hang him, but Bob's legs were too long and nimble for them, and therefore he made a masterly retreat, as they say McClellan did from before Richmond, at the time that it took him weeks to advance ten miles forward, but was able to get back in a few hours. This they called a grand retreat, and thus it was with many of the Southerners who were in Philadelphia on that day, they saved their necks by making a grand retreat.

The Monday following the 19th, those who had volunteered went forward to prepare to be examined and mustered into the service. I was there with thousands of others, ready to shoulder my gun, but the examining Surgeon refused to pass me on account of my age, and a small defect in one of my hands. This came upon me very unexpectedly, so much so, that I sat down and shed tears of sorrow, to think that I was not permitted to assist in the defense of my country. The captain of the company in which I had volunteered said that he would rather have had any other man in his company rejected than me, for which I thanked him publicly for his good opinion of me, and told him that I would try it again in another company, which I did, but was again rejected.

About this time William B. Thomas was appointed Collector of Customs for the port and as I had been one of the men who had assisted in procuring him the appointment, I had supposed that there would be no difficulty in my getting an appointment under him, but to make the thing more sure, I went to work and got up three different petitions, one of them I sent to John Sherman of Ohio, a Senator in Congress, who got twenty-three United States Senators names to it,— to another I got seventy-two of the leading Bank-Presidents and Importers signatures, the other one I got over eight hundred leading active politicians to sign, and thus fortified I went to the Collector and handed him my papers, and desired him to read them, which he did; after reading them he said, you are the best recommended man that I ever saw—out of eight thousand applications which I have on file, you are stronger recommended than the whole of them together,— but I have no place for you except a night-watchman's place along the river.

Now dear reader, you can see the principles of a politician; he had used me to get the office he had, but as he had no more use for me, he turned his back on me. Well, what was I to do, out of business with no money to start on and nothing to eat? I was therefore compelled to accept this small place until I could do better, but why did Mr. Thomas refuse me a genteel place when I was so well recommended? It was because I had used my influence for Judge Kelly's nomination for Congress the previous Fall, and I was not the only man he punished, for no man in Kelly's district who had supported him, got anything under Mr. Thomas better than a night-watchman's place.

I had applied for captain of night-watchmen but in place of giving it to me, he gave it to a man who never applied for it and was not able to read and write; why was this done? Why, because the man was a Thomas delegate in the Congressional Convention when Kelly was nominated and had knocked down a Kelly delegate for something which he said against

Mr. Thomas. So you see that this was qualification enough for him. As soon as I was appointed to be under his direction, he commenced to impose on me in every way that he could by detailing me to every mean and dirty job there was to do; I was kept constantly on duty whether it was my turn or not, and if I grumbled or refused to obey orders he would report me and recommend my suspension, (at which game I always beat him, as it was the Surveyor and not the Collector who had the trying of the case.) The Surveyor of the port was a good man and understood my captain very well, and on one occasion told the captain that he would believe me as soon as any man on earth, for I had never told him a lie.

My captains continued failures to have me suspended or disgraced only increased his hostility towards me and mine towards him. I felt determined to have my revenge on him (you know that revenge is sweet) so I concluded to put up a case on him. I knew that I was not able to whip him myself, for he was young and a good fighter, so I concluded to hire a big fighting Irishman who lounged about the docks along the river, to give him a thrashing, as some satisfaction for his treatment to me. I saw the Irishman and agreed to give him two dollars and a half in gold if he would pick a quarrel and whip him. Well, the next night they met, when the Irishman picked the quarrel with him, and at it they went, but instead of the Irishman whipping him, he gave the Irishman a terrible beating, so the Irishman got the two and a half dollars and a sound drubbing in the bargain.

Well, here I had made another failure, but I concluded that my time would come some day, and sure enough it did come very soon. The captain heard of a large lot of sheep which were for sale very cheap some eighty miles up the country, so he and another man started off to buy them, the captain leaving his duties to be performed by his lieutenant. I found out that he had left without leave ; I went at once and reported him absent from his duty, and summoned all the watchmen along the river, as also the lieutenant to prove his absence. The result was that when he returned he was summoned before the Surveyor when I proved my charges and had him suspended for ten days, (and ah how sweet was my revenge.)

When he returned to duty I told him that if he would treat me fairly hereafter, I would treat him with respect and obey all lawful orders which he would give me. He however never abated his hostility towards me and continued to use undue authority over me, so much so, that I appealed to the Collector for protection, but he gave me no satisfaction further than to say that he supposed that I was as much in fault as the captain, and that it was my duty to obey him. I thus found that I had no remedy for my troubles in that quarter, so I concluded that I would write to some of my friends in Congress, they having just convened for the session of 1862. I wrote to Judge Kelly and laid all my troubles before him and asked him to lay them bofore the President and Secretary of the Treasury, and see if something could not be done for me.— He did as I requested and the result was, that John Covode, a member of Congress came over to see Mr. Thomas, the Collector, and sent for me, and in my presence told Mr. Thomas that it was the desire of not only the President and Secretary, but of a large majority of both Houses of Congress, that I should have a respectable place in the Custom House, to which Mr. Thomas replied that he intended to give me the first vacancy that occurred. Well, said I, there is a vacancy now, just the thing that I want, why not give that to me? He said he had promised that to another, but I should have the next chance.

As soon as Mr. Covode had left town Thomas sent for me and asked me if it was me who was kicking up all this fuss at Washington with the members, and whether it was through me that it was done? I frankly told him that I had written to a friend in Congress about the manner that I had been treated, and had asked him to get me a better place. He then told me that if I kicked up any more fuss about my place that he would discharge me altogether.

I now saw very plainly that there was but one thing left for me to do, either to put up with my ill-treatment without making any more fuss about it, or, give up my place and seek some other employment. This I thought hard, after all I had done for my party; I therefore made up my mind that I would go to Washington and see the President if I had to walk there, so I gathered up what little money I had and went to the Surveyor, who was my friend, and got leave of absence for a week. I left to try my luck with the President, the Surveyor having often told me that I ought to go to him, that he was certain that the President would see me righted, and that I was very foolish to put up with the treatment that I had received when I could so easily remedy it.

I went to Washington, saw several of my friends, and told them my troubles. They all advised me to go to the President which I did. He received me very kindly and told me that I ought to have come to him long ago, when he had plenty of places to give, that he hardly knew what to do with me now, but would look around and see what he could do; that I must stay a day or two until he could find a place for me. He said that I must come to see him every morning until he got me a place. When I started to go away he followed me to the door and asked me if I had any money to pay my way for a few days; I told him that I had but very little as I was very poor just now; he took from his pocket a "greenback" saying as he did it, this will keep you until I can get you a place. I left and was surprized to find that he had given me twenty dollars.

I went to the Capitol and told some of my friends what the President had said and done, which seemed to please them very much; they said that he would not forsake me as some others had done, that I might rest contented, that I was certain of a place. I felt so too, for I had every confidence in Mr. Lincoln's honesty and integrity. I had known him for a long time, having spoken with him on the same stand for Henry Clay many years before, therefore I felt satisfied that I should not make a failure this time.

The next morning I called at the White House when the messenger told me that the President wished to see me and to walk in; as soon as I went in the President said, how would you like to go to Baltimore to live; I have telegraphed to the Collector for a place for you and he says that you can have an easy place there at three dollars per day, how will that suit you, it is the best that I can do for you at this time; it will suit me first rate said I, it is just the thing that I want, and I am under a thousand obligations to you for your kindness to me. Never mind that, said he, you are entitled to something better than that, for your valuable services to our cause, but I have nothing better to give you at this time; go down to Mr. Risley, the supervising special agent, and he will give you your commission, which you will present to Mr. McJilton, the surveyor of the port of Baltimore and he will set you to work. After thanking him again for his kindness, I left him and made my way to Mr. Risleys office where I in due time got my commisson and left for Baltimore, in better spirits than I had been lately.

On my arrival in Baltimore, I went to the Custom house, found Mr. McJilton and presented my papers to him, when he very kindly introduced me to all the employees of his department; I told him, that I wished to return to Philadelphia and settle up my affairs there, before I reported for duty, which would take me until the next Monday; he said it was all right, so I left that evening for home.

The next day I went to see the Surveyor and showed him my commission. He congratulated me on my success, saying that he was certain that Mr. Lincoln would take care of me. I got him to write me a very saucy letter of resignation to Mr. Thomas, which I copied and went in to see him, in order that I might ask him again for a promotion. There was to be a vacancy in the Inspectors department, a place that I wanted, and if he would give me that, I would send my commission back to Mr. Risley, but he told me that he could not promise me anything better than I had before, until next Fall. When I handed him my resignation he read it and said that I was pretty independent about my place. Why should I not be, said I, when I have been to see the President who has given me a better place if I choose to accept it, at the same time handing him my commission to look at, which seemed to take him by surprise. But, said I, if you will promote me I will send this back as I would rather stay here than go to Baltimore. He said that he could not give me a better place just then, but if I would hold on to my old place for a short time he would do something better for me. I could not see the point however, so I picked up my hat, bid him good bye and left, never to meet him again as a friend.

That night I went down to the night-watchmen's office to bid them farewell, showed my commission to the captain and told him that I now held an office above him, and that if I ever caught him in Baltimore he should be the worst whipped man that ever left home. He only laughed at me and said that I was not the worst fellow in the world and thus we parted never to meet again on this side of Jordan, (as he is dead, he having died suddenly while attending a State Convention at Harrisburg some two years after I left. So let his ashes rest in peace.)

I returned to Baltimore on the following Monday morning and reported to Mr. McJilton for duty, when

I was assigned to the Permit Department as one of its officers, whose duty it was to examine and pass goods to be taken out of the city by and to loyal people.

CHAPTER X.

APPOINTMENT TO OFFICE IN BALTIMORE CUSTOM HOUSE
—GUBERNATORIAL CAMPAIGN IN PENNSYLVANIA,—
VOLUNTEERED TO DEFEND BALTIMORE—
CAMPAIGN OF 1864—A DREAM.

IT WAS on the 18th day of May, 1863, that I reported in Baltimore, and I had not been there but a few days before I discovered that "all is not gold that glitters," neither did all that held office under the Government at Baltimore, love the flag of their country as they should have done; disguise it as they would I could see the rebel in them, and the hatred they had towards me as a Northern man. Baltimore was under bayonet rule, and no man was allowed to say aught against the Government for fear of being sent to the Fort for safe keeping, so hundreds of wool dyed rebels pretended to be loyal in order to get some of the loaves and fishes. That portion of them who held hatred in their hearts against the flag, also hated me and I could see it. They took various plans to drive me from Baltimore; when I would leave my seat for a few minutes, they would have pins doubled up and placed in my seat in such a manner as to stick in me when I sat down, and when I complained about it, they would tell me if I could not take a joke, I had better go back to the North where I came from. At other times they would slip my coat that I wore in the street, into some other room, and sew the sleeves together from one end to the other; and smear mucilage in my hat so that it would stick to my head, when I put it on, and when I said anything about it, they would tell me if you don't like it go back to Pennsylvania where you come from, old Lincoln had no business to send you here anyhow.

I put up with this for a few days until I became convinced that I could not stay among them unless this thing was stopped. So one morning when I went down I called on Mr. McJilton and asked him to step into the Permit Room, which he did, at the same time asking me what he could do for me. I said Mr. McJilton am I a regular appointed officer here, and am I entitled to the same respect and pay that others are? He said certainly you are, why do you ask me that. I then told him how I had been treated since I came there. He looked at me in surprise and said, it has been done without his knowledge, and must not be repeated, if it was, he would discharge every man who had a hand in it; this had the effect that I desired.

They then changed their mode of devilment, they all refused to speak to me, although it was their duty to tell me by whose authority the goods were permitted, so that I could enter it on the permit. I could hear them say he came from the North, let him find out from whom the order came. I went to Mr. McJilton and told him again about their capers, when he walked out and told them very plainly that unless they treated me in all respects as they did other officers he would at once dismiss every man who violated this order.

This last reprimand had the desired effect, they came to me and apologised for their rudeness as they called it, and promised to treat me better in the future, which they did, and we got along very well together after that, until about the first of August, when the State Committee of Pennsylvania sent for me to stump the State for Gov. Curtins second election. I got leave of absence for that purpose and left for that field of labor.

When I got to Pennsylvania this time, I found a great change in the sentiments of the people. The Democrats had carried the State in '62, under what was known as the peace policy, and were very sanguine of success in '63. They had been doing all that they dared do, to discourage enlistment and had since the war commenced condemned every act of the administration in putting down the rebellion, but never had a word to say against Jeff. Davis or Lee, for carrying it on. They had always heard of a rebel victory before any one else, and never believed the news of a union victory when they heard it. When you told them of a union victory they were in too much of a hurry to stop and listen to it, their whole cry was, let us make peace with them, for we never can whip them, there has been too much blood shed already, so for God's sake let us call in our troops and let them go out of the union in peace.

Andrew G. Curtin had been called the soldiers friend. Mr. Lincoln had said that he had done, and was doing, more to assist the Government in putting down the rebellion, than any four Governors in the country. This we had as a rallying word all through the State, and I made good use of it. But with all of Curtin's popularity at home, as the soldiers friend, he never could have carried the State that year, if it had not have been that Congress had taken the precaution to pass a bill allowing the soldiers in the field to vote. Pennsylvania had too many Republicans in the army, and the Democrats too few for the Republicans to have carried the State without the vote of the soldiers. This was one of the reasons, and the main one, why the State went democratic in '62.

After the war was over the Democrats claimed that there were more Democrats in the war than Republicans; if so why did every Democratic Legislature and member of Congress from one end of the country to the other vote against allowing the soldiers to vote in the field, answer me Democrats if you can. The facts are these, every leading Democrat in this nation, not only opposed every measure for putting down the rebellion, but every man who assisted in putting it down, both North as well as South. And I am very certain that the Southern rebels as they were called, are a better class of men than the Northern Copperheads who were too cowardly to fight for what they desired to see effected, viz: a separation of the States, and I am certain that they are more to be trusted than a cowardly Northern Copperhead. I have never found one of them yet who was afraid or ashamed to maintain his principles, and that is more than you can say of one of those slimy reptiles of the North.

But all their peace policy and loud talk about the enormous debt that Lincoln was building up for the people to pay, with all their hue and cry about high taxes that were crushing the people to the earth, they were not able to meet us on the stump; why because we would ask them what made the taxes so high, they would have to answer, the debt; we would then ask them what made the debt, they would answer, the war. Your answers are very correct gentlemen, but please tell us who made the war, and who are opposed to putting it down. Was it not Democrats who fired first on the flag? Was not every State that withdrew from the Union democratic? Was there one Republican Governor in one of these States, if this is true, please tell me who made the war. These and similar questions they dared not meet before the honest people, and consequently refused to meet us on the stump, but contented themselves with going around among the people crying taxes, high taxes, millions, yea hundred of millions of dollars of debt to pay, and increasing every day, and will continue to increase as long as these Republicans hold the reigns of the State or National Government in their hands ; elect a Democratic Govenor if you wish to put a stop to these things. This was what I and other speakers had to contend with in that campaign ; they were afraid to meet us with such arguments, for fear that we would ask too many questions that they would not like to answer before the honest people. I for one, sent out a challenge to meet the best speaker and discuss these questions with him, but it was no go, they got out of it by calling me one of Lincoln's hirelings.

Well the election came off and we beat them out of their boots, as the saying is. Curtin was triumphantly elected, as well as a majority in the Legislature, and other State officers. I returned to Baltimore full of glory, and was complimented by all those who knew me and loved the flag. I reported for duty a few days after I returned, and had no difficulty after that with any of the men connected with my office, but had many flare-ups with the rebels of the city,—some of whom boarded in the hotel where I did, and many of the customers who visited the house were such, although the landlord and his sons were good Union men.

I was boarding at the Franklin House at the corner of Howard and Franklin streets at the time that Harry Gilmor made his great raid through Maryland, and there were some thirty others boarding there, who were mostly pretended Union men, but I could see that they hated a Northern man. There were but two of us from the North, and their constant talk was, that no man ought to come to Baltimore to make a living, who was not willing to defend it. This was on Thursday and Friday and on Saturday it was supposed that Gilmor would be in or near Baltimore before morning, so those fellows talked very loud about defending Baltimore. I knew who they were striking at, and said, why in the devil don't you go and defend it you want it defended so badly, and not talk so much about it. Why don't you go and defend it, said some of them? Because I don't think that it needs defending yet, said I, when it does I will go and defend it without saying half as much about it, as you have. Well the next morning about daybreak the bells began to ring the people to arms, Gilmor was coming, myself and room-mate put on our clothes and hastened down stairs to find all these fellows nearly panic stricken. I sung out come on you brave Baltimorians who have such a great desire to see Baltimore defended, now is the time to show your pluck, I am going to help defend Baltimore. Wait till after breakfast said some of them, and we will go too. No man ought to live in a town who is not willing to defend it without his breakfast, said I. And I and my friend went down to the city hall and offered ourselves as volunteers. There was a company forming and a Colonel commanding the people to fall into ranks.— We stepped in and before 8 o'clock had our guns and forty rounds of cartridges in our cartridge boxes, and had marched up to the Lexington market and stacked arms for thirty minutes to provide some provisions to take with us out to camp Bradford. And before nine o'clock we were marching past the Franklin House where we saw most of those brave fellows who felt so much like fighting a day or two before.

Come on, said I, boys we are going out to meet your old friend Gilmor ; but nary a one came, they thought best to keep away from the smell of gunpowder. We marched out to Camp Bradford, where we were soon joined by several other companies, when we were placed on picket duty during the whole night without anything to eat except what we had in our pockets. The next morning Gilmor burned Gov. Bradford's house, which was within two miles of where we were ; we were joined that day by a part of the 6th army corps, and they were worn out by their long march; we had to do picket-duty again all that night without anything but raw bacon and bread to eat. In ten days we were marched to "Druid Hill Park" in company with the 6th corps and there I got a furlough to go to town and get something to eat. I went around-about way, so as not to run afoul of the 6th corps pickets and when I got to the Franklin House, I found several of these plucky fellows sitting outside smoking; well Buckeye, said one of them, how many rebels did you kill; I said I killed as many of them as they did of me, when another one spoke up and said, he kill a rebel, he would run if he saw one; would I, said I, setting down my gun against the house, you are a rebel and you can't make me run, and at him I went, but he backed out so completely, that I let him off with a good cursing. I picked up my gun and told him, if he was worth shooting, I would put a bullet through him, but as he was a villianous, cowardly rebel I would let him off.

I got a basket full of bread and meat and a bottle of good whisky, and left for my camp, but just before I reached there I was picked up by a picket from the 6th corps who had been posted there after I had passed out; he took me into camp a prisoner, where I was kept under guard till morning, when I was taken under guard to my own company, amid the laughter of all hands. I enjoyed it finely and had many a hearty laugh about it afterwards. The second night that we were at Druid Hill, I was placed on the extreme outer picket with two others of my company; we were standing under a large tree near the top of a small hill; it was about two o'clock at night when I saw seven men coming over the brow of the hill; I told the boys to prepare to fire and stepped out and said, who comes there, halt and give the countersign, when to my surprise they all fired on us, and started to run into the bushes; we returned the fire and then retreated into camp, where we found the whole camp under arms, but we saw or heard no more of the enemy that night.

On Friday night ten of us were posted in a small grove of timber, that stood in an oatfield on the Liberty road, a short distance from our camp, when about midnight some persons unknown to us, fired a volley of bullets into the trees above our heads and made their escape before we could find them, although it was light enough to see a man for a long distance; we searched the field over but saw no man in it. On Saturday afternoon we were marched into town and by seven o'clock that evening we were all mustered out of service and honorably discharged, without the loss of a man, and thus ended the memorable seven days fight, in which the Baltimore Home Guards took such a conspicuous part. It answered to talk about for a long time and many was the hearty laugh we had over it for months after; on my return to the hotel I gave the rebel element that were boarding there to understand that the first one of them that said aught against me or the government, I would have them locked in the Fort. This had the effect to shut their mouths, as they hated the Fort worse than the devil ever hated holy water.

After my return from the war I became very popular with the men in our office, owing to the fact, that I was always ready to take the most extreme outer picket duty both day or night, and ready to go on a raid whenever desired, and always the foremost man; they all said I had good pluck. I told them that it had always been my motto to act and not talk, that I had never known a barking dog to bite.

There was one little matter that I omitted, while relating my campaign life in the army, which I will now relate. One night while I was on picket duty, on the extreme outpost, the officer of the day, in making his grand round about two o'clock at night, in company with two orderlies came riding up to where I stood; I hailed them in the proper way, ordering one to dismount, advance and give the countersign, which they refused to do and continued to advance, the officer in front, when I made one step forward and said halt, one step forward and you are a dead man. Dont you know me, said he, I am officer of the day, let me pass or I will have you arrested. If you are the General of the army, you can't pass me without the countersign, therefore don't advance another step or I shall fire. When he saw how resolute I was his orderly dismounted and gave the countersign, when I let them pass. He had made his brag, that he could frighten me into letting him pass without the countersign, for which he expected to have a good joke on me, but he soon found that he had made a grand mistake; I meant business, and he saw it. Had he advanced one step forward I should have most undoubtedly shot him. The next morning he sent for me and complimented me, for the manner in which I had discharged my duty, in not allowing him or any other man to pass me without the countersign.

I will now return to the Permit Department, where I was at work. I had a very pleasant time among the boys from that time, until the close of our connection in that office.

In the Spring of 1864 the Republicans held their National Convention in Baltimore. I had the luck to obtain a ticket of admission to it. Lincoln, as you know was unanimously nominated for his second term, and Andrew Johnson was unfortunately put in nomination by Parson Brownlow of Tennessee for Vice-President, (oh, what a misfortune it was) and under the excitement of the moment, a vote was taken, and he was declared the nominee. I turned to a delegate from Pennsylvania and said, that nomination I am afraid will prove a curse not only to our party, but to the whole nation, for no good, said I, can come out of Nazareth, neither can there any good come out of Andrew Johnson; I have known him for many years and have no confidence in his unionism or his professions of love to the Republican cause. My friend differed with me, and said that he believed, that he, Johnson, was a soundly converted man; I told him I hoped so, but had doubts, for I had known him too long and had never known him to entertain at any time one honorable principle; but at the same time, for the love of Lincoln, I should swallow the dose.

Very soon after the nomination we men in the Permit Department got up a set of meetings in various places in the counties, for me to speak at, one of which was at Westminster, Carroll county. It was a monster, we had all the bigbugs of both parties there, all anixous to hear the Buckeye. As soon as I arrived I was taken in charge of a committee, who wished to post me about what I should say. They told me to praise up Douglas, for he had many friends that would hear me, and the more I said in his favor, the better effect it would have. I told them all right, I know exactly how to treat that subject. When the hour arrived for the meeting to organize, they went about it with as much ceremony, as the Jews did, when they laid the foundation of the house of the Lord, in the days of Aaron. When I was introduced, I told them, that I had not come there to talk much about Mr. Lincoln, as he was as well known to them as he was to me, his public acts were before the country and it was their duty to endorse or respect them at the coming election, and from present indications I had no doubt, but they would endorse them from one end of the nation to the other.

Upon what platform do our opponents stand, and what doctrine do they ask you to endorse? Why they ask you to say by your votes, that the war for the Union is a failure; this they have boldly put forth in their platform, and this their press and speakers everywhere declare to be the case, but gentlemen has the war thus been a failure, if so, who made it a failure? Was it Mr. Lincoln or his friends, or was it "little Mack" and his friends, these are the questions that you are to decide; does any man doubt, that McClellan could have taken Richmond, when he first got in front of it, the enemy had but a small force there at that time, and what they had, were not prepared to make a very strong resistance, so there would have been no trouble with the large army, that he had to have marched in and captured the city, which would put an end to the war.

But instead of doing this he laid in front of that city some six weeks, continually sending out his bulletins "on to Richmond," until the enemy had time to concentrate all their forces there and fortify the place against him, then after one third of his army had died from deseases contracted in the swamps around Richmond, he finally spread out his army in a line, sixteen miles long, and made the attack; when the enemy found how he had weakened his strength, by the way he lengthened his lines, they with all ease broke his line, and he was compelled to retreat, and this they tell us he done in good order, and they might have added in quick order; he was able to fall back as far in one afternoon, as he had went forward in six weeks. So you see my friends that this was a grand failure. Further, while their candidate was doing all that he could toward making the war a failure in the field, what were his friends doing in Congress and the State Legislatures of the country? Were they not voting on all occasions against raising men and money, to put down the rebellion; can any gentleman before me, tell me the name of any man in or out of Congress, who ever voted for one man or one dollar to aid the Union? If you can, speak now or forever after hold your peace. Again, what were these friends of McClellan doing at Charleston in 1860, in their National Convention, the time they slaughtered Stephen A. Doug'as; did Douglas not go in that Convention with over twenty majority of the delegates? I say he did, then why was he not nominated? I will tell you; they were as near ready for a separation of the States, as they ever expected to be, and they knew that if they nominated him, that he would be elected. The Republicans had no party in the South and were divided in the North, so there would be no difficulty in electing Mr. Douglas, as he was very popular with the masses, but they had tried him in the Senate and found that he was not the man to be bought or made a tool of, or in other words, he was an honest man, and one that loved his country. Hence they slaughtered him in Charleston as also in Baltimore and nominated another, while the regular Convention nominated him, and then the bolters sent millions of dollars North to keep up a division in their ranks in order to elect a Republican President, so as to have an excuse to withdraw from the Union.

And now these same fellows I find all over the country have the impudence to look an honest Douglas Democrat in the face and ask him to vote for their candidate. I must confess gentlemen, that I am perfectly astonished at the amount of impudence these fellows have, for I had thought, that with their past record stareing them in the face, that they never would again have the hardihood to look any man in the eye, and ask him for his vote, let alone a friend of Mr. Douglas, the man above all others that they tried to destroy. This brought down the house with loud applause, especially the friends of Douglas; after a few more remarks I closed.

After the meeting was over I was surrounded by my friends and shaken nearly to pieces, many of them telling me that the course I had pursued would do the cause great good in that place, as there were a large number of the friends of Mr. Douglas there that night and were well pleased with my reference to him and said that I had told them the truth that night in a way that they would not forget.

I spoke at several other places in the counties around Baltimore, in a similar manner, with about the same effect and became very popular with the people whereever I went. After I had closed my appointments that I had made in Maryland, the Pennsylvania committee sent for me and I went there, where I met as usual a very warm reception. The committee sent me over my old stumping ground, where 1 had an opportunity of meeting my old friends as well as many of my old opponents; but here as well as in Maryland, I found that the great rallying cry of the Democracy was, the war was a failure; here they claimed to be Union men and to be better Union men than the Republicans were, they said that they were in favor of making peace with their erring brethren of the South, by calling home our troops and stop the shedding of any more blood, that we never could conquer them until we had killed the last man of them for they were to high minded to ever yield to Abe Lincoln or his hirelings; they further told the people that Lincoln had set the niggers free and that they could not live in the South after the war was over, but would come North and underwork the white laborers and be the means of starving them all out of the country, and fill the whole North with black laborers. These men had changed their plan of electioneering very materially in the last four years. Then they told the people that Lincoln and his party wanted to set the niggers free, and if they did, they were too lazy to work without a master and if free they all would come North, where they would steal and murder for a living, and that no man would be safe at night in his bed from them.

These and similar plans they resorted to, in order

to draw the people away from the true issue before them ; their war record they were not willing to talk about, but had a great deal to say about McClellan and he would have ended the rebellion if he had been let alone ; but they forget to tell the people that at the battle of Antietam when Lee was whipped and out of amunition and McClellan with twenty thousand reserve troops only two or three miles away, granted Lee an armistice just at night for twelve hours to bury his dead, which Lee took advantage of, and during the night in place of burying his dead made his escape with his army across the Potomac and got away. Why didn't McClellan capture him then? The answer is, he was not ready, he was to be the candidate for the Presidency in '64, he was to prolong the war, in order to build up a great National debt, to be chargeable to the Republican party, and this they intended as the rallying cry of the Democracy and through that cry they expected to elect little McClellan, and then he could make terms of peace to suit our erring brothers.

McClellan had been constantly making little speeches to the soldiers during the time he had command of the army, and always had a news paper reporter there to report his speeches, to send them to the North for publication. He had flattered his men into the belief that he was a great man, and indeed he had gained the good opinion of the people all over the country, and had he done his duty at Richmond or even at Antietam, nothing could have prevented him from being President. But as it was he had showed his intentions so clearly that the whole country lost confidence in him, not in his ability as a soldier but in his patriotism. Many of the best men of the country had serious doubts whether or not, that he had been the means of giving the enemy much valuable information, concerning many things that were transpiring within our lines; indeed the opinion became so prevalent that the department was compelled to suspend him from the command of the army of the Potomac.

These as well as many other of their short comings I made good use of. I challenged their leaders to meet me on the stump and discuss these great questions with me, but in most cases they declined to accept my challenge. At last however I found one fellow foolhardy enough to meet me; he had been a member of the Legislature in 1862, and was one of the fellows who voted against every measure brought before the House that session, that would give aid to the country in putting down the rebellion; indeed he went so far as to vote against allowing a man to make a union speech in the hall of the House of Representatives. I made the opening speech, and charged the Democrats with beginning the war, and furnishing fuel to keep up the flames, and showed by conclusive evidence that they were responsible for keeping it up. This I showed by producing the proceedings of their meetings and conventions, in which they had held out hope and encouragement to the rebels, as also their constant endeavors to prevent enlistments, and the raising of means to put down the rebellion. I charged them with prolonging it by their constant and even their present opposition to the Republican party who were trying to put it down; that the rebels looked upon it as in their favor, for I lived among them and knew what they said and thought.

I put the question to him, and demanded an answer if every man North of the Pennsylvania line had been a Republican, or in favor of putting down the rebellion at once, would Gen. Lee ever have come across the Potomac river, or would we ever have had to fight the battle of Gettysburg, Antietam, or the South Mountain? If you answer yes, I will tell you that the rebels say themselves, that they knew before they came over, that near half of the people on this

*10

side of the line were their friends. Then if that is so who were their friends? If it was not you Democrats, if it was not you, why do the rebels hurrah for McClellan since his nomination, why don't they hallo for Lincoln? Why can't you get a few cheers for old Abe from them, as well as for "little Mack."? Please answer some of these questions for me.

It was his turn to reply, but instead of replying to what I had said, he commenced on the negro, just as I expected; he proved by the opinion of some learned Democrat, that the negroes were not quite human beings as they had more bones in their feet than white men, and said we Democrats are better friends to the negroes than the Republicans are, for they desired to turn them loose on the world to take care of themselves, which they are not capable of doing, and we think they are better off with a good master to take care of them. Why even the clothes and shoes and the very hat that they wear, are provided by their masters turn the poor creatures loose upon the world when they will have to provide for themselves, you will then see what will become of them. (The poor fool forgot that the negro had to earn not only his own clothes, shoes and hats, but his masters and his families too, and if he could earn enough to support two families when he was a slave, he certainly could earn enough to support one, when he is free.) He then undertook to show by their love for the negro, and their undying support of Gen. Jackson, and the great love of the Union as it was before the war, that he was a better Union man than I was, and then closed and gave me the stand to make my reply.

I told him he reminded me of an old tanner in Ohio who had no sign to attract the attention of the people, his wife insisted that he ought to have one, so he went out and studied a while what kind of a sign he should have; at last the idea struck him, there was a knot hole in one of the boards of his shop, he took out his knife and cut the tail off an ox hide that laid there and stuck it in the knot hole, letting the huskey end of it hang out. Thinking it a good attraction he went to breakfast and when he returned he found an old traveller with his bundle on his back, looking at his sign. He said nothing to him, but got his horse and went away to plant some corn, and did not return for several hours, but when he did return he found the old traveller still standing there looking at his sign, and said, what are you doing ideling away your time looking at my sign; the old traveller turned and said, sir, I have travelled all over Europe and America and can very easily tell how the tide ebbs and flows, and how the sun rises and sets, in fact sir, I have never come across any thing in my life, but what I could investigate, unravel and make something out of it, but how in the devil that ox got his body through that knot hole, and has been all day trying to pull his tail through and can't do it, is more than I can tell; so I say, how in the devil after all your opposition to the Union, you can call yourselves Union men, is more than I can tell. This had the effect that I desired, for the crowd yelled and cheered until he got disgusted and left the meeting, and that was the last I ever heard of him. I continued my speech to a late hour, and closed amid the cheers of the crowd for old Abe and the Buckeye Blacksmith. Here I also paid a high compliment to Mr. Douglas, and wondered why the ghost of that great and good man did not rise and haunt the men that are asking his friends to vote the ticket that every rebel in the Southern army would vote, if they were allowed to. Mr. Douglas, I said was a loyal man to the flag, and his last words when dying, were, tell my boys who are absent, to be true to the flag of their country, and I was very certain that if he was living to day, that he would be a strong supporter of the war policy of the administration, for he did say a short time before his death, that "notwithstanding he and Mr. Lincoln had differed widely in politics in former days, yet he would stand by, and support him in putting down the rebellion, and to the honor of his friends who are living to day, the most of them do stand by the old flag, as their great leader would do was he still among us.

This course I found had a very good effect in harmonizing the Douglas Democrats, a very large number of whom were with us heart and hand in putting down the rebellion, as well as assisting us in re-electing Mr. Lincoln, as could plainly be seen by the manner in which they would cheer me whenever I made these favorable allusions to the memory of their great leader; also by their flocking around me after the speech was over, thanking me for the manner in which I had spoken of Mr. Douglas. I usually told them that it was my duty to speak as I had, for it was nothing but the truth that I had said.

I travelled from place to place and spoke for some eight weeks, making from six to ten speeches a week, many of them from fifty to a hundred miles apart, causing me to travel both day and night, and on most occasions speaking to large meetings in the open air, and at least one half of the time I had to speak twice a day, miles apart, so that when the campaign was over I was very much prostrated, so much so, that it took me several weeks to recruit my strength. I had spent in that campaign near three months hard labor and all the money that I had, but on the day of election had the glorious satisfaction of knowing that I had assisted in putting "little Mack" to bed and tucking the covers in around him, where he can quietly lay the balance of his life, dreaming about his future prospects for the Presidency.

The people in this election not only endoresed Mr. Lincoln's war policy, but his honesty and integrity as an executive, by giving him the largest electoral vote ever given to any man in this country. In doing that they not only condemned "little Mack's" war policy, but his loyalty to his country, by giving him the smallest vote ever given to any candidate who ever ran for the Presidency in a single fight in this country, and I would here say that their decision on this occasion was a very righteous one.

While I was speaking in Pennsylvania the papers said many fine things about me, which I took good care to send to our office, in order to let them know what I was doing, and how I was liked by the people up there. I sent them a glorious account of my debate with the Democratic Legislature man, and also sent them all the attacks made on me by the Copperheads, and they were not a few, for they piled it on me pretty heavy. This I liked, for the simple reason that if ever I loose confidence in my own integrity it will be when a Democratic paper speaks well of me. Their praise I never have had, nor never expect to court. I have always considered that their abuse was the best of proof that I was touching them in a tender spot, for I have always heard that a wounded pig would squeel, and the tree that bears the best fruit is clubbed the most. So I have found it in politics, the man that hurts the most will be abused the most, and if I was a agoing to make a dozen campaigns, I would be glad to have all the Copperhead papers in the country through which I expected to travel, to raise a howl against me, for it would be the means of bringing me into the favorable opinion of all decent men; and if ever I should make another tour I would get them to publish abusive articles against me, even if I had to pay for them as advertisements, so certain I would be that it would bring me into the good graces of the best men of all parties, which I have always tried to merit.

As soon as I had fully recovered my strength, I reported at Baltimore for duty and I was received with a hearty welcome from all hands, who I am satisfied were glad to have me back among them. They said that they were proud to have me as a companion, as there were few men who could kick up such a fuss among the Democrats as I had, and but few who could get as many complimentary things said about them, as I had while away from them. This of course was very pleasant to me to have their good opinion, and from that time until our connections as permit officers ceased we got along very pleasantly together.

About the close of the year of '64 there was a proposition made to present Mr. McJilton the head of our office, with a silver set, as a testimonial of our good feelings toward him for his kindness and impartiality in his intercourse with us, as subordinate officers. It was intended to be kept a secret until the moment of presentation, which was to take place at his house, on New Years morning. There had been nothing said about the manner in which it was to be presented until the day before its presentation. when I was called on by the committee who had it in charge and informed me that I had been selected as the speaker who was to make the presentation speech. I consented to do so, but told them as the time was short to prepare a speech in, they must not expect much of a one, but they said they would risk that, so the next morning we went in a body to Mr. McJilton's house, and there in the presence of his wife and daughter and all of the permit officers I made the presentation speech, for which I received great credit, not only from Mr. McJilton and his family, but all present. They requested me to furnish a copy of it for publication, which I did, and Mr. McJilton's reply, which I had published in a Philadelphia paper and a large number of copies sent to me for distribution.

Nothing occured between January and the first of April worthy of note, every thing went on smoothly, we had but little to do, business had fallen off greatly, and we were expecting that we were going to loose our places altogether, as Congress was talking about abolishing it during the session. About this time my health began to fail me considerably. I asked for, and obtained leave of absence for a month to recruit my health, and concluded to go out West for a short time, so about the 10th of April I packed up and started and went to Pittsburg, where I stayed a day or two, and from there I went to Beaver some thirty miles down the Ohio river, where I delivered a lecture; it was on the 14th of April, that memorable night that I never shall forget, nor shall I ever forget my dream of that night. I dreamt that I saw Mrs. Lincoln in the greatest agony that I ever beheld, dressed in white clothes, and seemed to be tearing her heart out of her bosom, and wailing in great distress. I was so much troubled about it that I could not sleep, but arose from bed and put on my clothes and went down stairs and at day break in place of going West, I concluded to go back to Pittsburg by an early train that passed there on its way East, and by the time we got half way to Pittsburg we met the train for the West, and received the sad news that Lincoln had been assassinated, and was probably dead, and by the time that we reached Pittsburg we got the news that he was dead. I went to the post office at once where I found more than five thousand people gathered together all bearing on their sad faces the truth of what I had just heard at the depot, Lincoln our Nations chieftain is dead.

As soon as I was recognised in the crowd, I was invited to say something to the people, as it was known that I was personally acquainted with him. I stepped on the post-office steps, took off my hat and said:

MY FELLOW COUNTRYMEN: I have a word to say if you will listen to me for a moment. I have traveled all over this continent as well as many parts of other countries; I have been rich and I have been poor. I have been on the topmost ladder of fame and I have been in the valley below, but I must confess that this is the darkest day of my life; our chieftain is slain and the nation mourns. I can say no more, my heart is too full for utterance. The best friend that this country ever had is this morning lying cold in the arms of death. God has permitted it to be so, therefore let us meekly bow to his will, for he doeth all things well.

With these remarks I left the stand, while there were thousands of watery eyes in the crowd. All seemed to realize the facts that I had just spoken. I had to wait a few hours for the train for the East and before I was ready to leave, one of the papers had published my short speech and complimented it very highly. I bought a number of copies of the paper and sent them to my friends in Baltimore and elsewhere. I went to Philadelphia where I still had my home (I had not gone to Baltimore to make it a permanent place of residence) and on my arrival I found almost every house in my part of the city draped in black. It looked very solemn—I could hardly realize the fact that he was dead, but alas, it was only too true. The house next to where I lived was not draped, I knew that they were cursed rebels, so I rang the bell and asked if they intended to drape their house, when I was told that they had nothing to drape it with. I told them that if it was not draped in one hour, I would not leave one brick on top of another, for, said I, your party has killed our President and you are glad of it, but you shall seem to mourn by draping your house, or I will have a posse of men here in one hour to tear it down, and then I walked away; but long before the hour was out they had it draped. I told my friends that I was the man to make a rebel understand his duty, and to do it to. That was the most sorrowful day that Philadelphia ever experienced; there was but one feeling there and that was a feeling of sorrow.

As soon as Mr. Lincoln's body had left Philadelphia, I returned to Baltimore with a sad heart, for I knew that my only true friend was gone, and now that the war was over, the Permit Department would cease and I had no friend to get me another place. On my return Mr. McJilton informed me that he had orders to dismiss all hands on the twentieth of the month, (it was now the first week in May.) He said he was sorry to part with us but there was no remedy for it. I put for Washington to see some of my friends to try for another place. Judge Sargent, the Commissioner of Customs, with whom I was well acquainted, told me that he would try and arrange it for me, so I went back in better spirits than those in which I had left. I said nothing about it to any of my colleagues, for fear they might interfere against me for themselves; neither did I tell any person where I had been, but waited patiently for the day to come when we were to be discharged. It came at last—it was on Monday, and about 10 o'clock I received my pay and got my discharge. I was about to walk out when to my surprise a messenger told me the Collector wanted to see me in his office. I immediately called on him, when he told me that he had appointed me at the request of some of my friends at Washington, an Inspector of Customs, at four dollars per day, and handed me the oath of office to sign, and then swore me in and sent my name to the Surveyor to enter on his books. As soon as Mr. McJilton received it he handed it to the clerk for the proper entry, and then took me by the hand and said, boys let us congratulate the Buckeye in his good luck in getting a better place than he has just left—he has been appointed an Inspector and I for one am very glad.

If a thunderbolt had struck them they could not have been more surprised. Here were all my old enemies just dismissed without any hope of another place, and I, who so many of them had so often treated with so much disrespect, promoted to a better one than I ever had before. The great trouble among them was, how I got it; who had got it for me; what influence could I possibly have brought to bear; they said the Collector would not have given me the place without some influence, more than my own. I told them that the Collector knew that I was an honest man and hence the appointment.

My dear young reader, you will here see another evidence, that by doing right, you must in the end succeed. I had always done my duty faithfully, and Providence was taking care of me now.

CHAPTER XI.

JOHNSON'S ADMINISTRATION. — HIS MOTIVES AND ASPIRATIONS. — HANGING MRS. SURRATT. — "A CAT IN THE MEAL TUB."—REFUSED TO SELL OUT TO JOHNSON. — RESIGNED MY OFFICE.

AS SOON as the excitement incident to the death of Mr. Lincoln had partially subsided, the eyes of the whole nation were turned to Andrew Johnson, who was now the legal head of the government. The South had reason to fear him, for they had said, and done many things against him while the war was going on, and now that he was at the head of the nation, they had reason to fear that he would retaliate upon them. The whole North seemed to have fears, that he would be more severe on traitors than was necessary. We conquered the rebellion, they had laid down their arms and had returned to their homes, and therefore the large majority of the northern people thought that we ought to be lenient towards them as long as they kept quiet and behaved themselves, but many had grave doubts whether Johnson would let them off without at least punishing their leaders, and after he had so promptly offered a large reward for the capture of Jeff Davis, we began to conclude that he intended to make short work with them. Also when Mrs. Surrat and her coleagues were tried and convicted his prompt action in their cases caused much alarm in the South, and considerable also in the North.

Many thought at the time and think so yet, that the ends of justice did not demand their executions so soon after conviction. The most hardened criminals that the world ever knew, are generally allowed thirty days in which to prepare for death, but here we have an old feeble woman, who is not charged with the crime of murder, but only with being accessory to the murder of Mr. Lincoln, brought before a court martial, at a time when calm reflection is almost impossible. Our great and good President has been murdered, and the whole nation cries for vengeance, it was scarcely in man to think, speak or act calmly on the subject at that time. There seemed to be no doubt but that Mrs. Surratt knew something about the murder, but suppose she did, was it necessary, to meet the ends of justice, to hang her the next day after she was convicted, or indeed was it necessary to hang her at all? Could we not have been lenient to her, and saved the disgrace of hanging an old woman, by sending her as we did others to prison for life. I think we might hove done so, and received the applause of the whole world for doing it.

But Andrew Johnson said no, she must die, and on to-morrow at that. The question very naturally arises, why was he in such a hurry, why not give her and her companions the usually allotted time? Was there any danger of her or them doing any harm when they were locked up in prison? Was he afraid that she would raise an army and be rescued from the hands of the government, or what was he afraid of. I have no doubts but that he thought the old proverb was true, that dead men and women tell no tales on the living.

It is very certain that he had some motive for acting so promptly in this case, and I have many doubts whether on the day of judgement, when he will stand before her at the bar of God, she wont accuse him of knowing as much about the murder of Mr. Lincoln as she did; there has always seemed something very dark and mysterious in that affair. Why did Booth and his companions untertake to kill Mr. Lincoln and all the leading members of his cabinet, and not try to kill Johnson the only man that could take Lincoln's place? None of the cabinet were eligible to his seat, then why try to kill them and not the man who was to fill his place. These are questions I fear will have to be answered in the last day.

It was in evidence at the trial of J. H. Surratt some time after the murder of Mr. Lincoln, that Booth was at the Kirkwood House on the afternoon before the murder, in conversation with Johnson. Why did he let him slip when he had such a good chance to put him out of the way. There must have been an understanding among them, that Johnson was to be let alone, as he was the only one of the heads of the government who was not attacked or an attempt made upon; yet notwithstanding they had spared his life, there is no doubt but that he intended to deal very harshly with the rank and file.

In 1841 after the death of Gen. Harrison, John Tyler began in good faith to carry out every measure that the Whig party had advocated and to all appearances bid fair to make as an acceptable a President to the Whig party as Harrison would have made. This of course he did, not as a principle, but for a motive. He expected to build himself up with the Whigs, so as to get the nomination in 1844 by them for re-election, but before six months had passed he saw plainly that the Whigs throughout the country were centered and fixed on Henry Clay, and nothing that he could do would be able to change that fixed determination. He therefore turned table not only to all his former principles and professions, but to the Whig party that had elected him Vice-President, and from that time until the end of his term used every power at his command not only to destroy the Whig party, but to build up the Democrats. The result was that when his time expired, he went out of office despised and hated by the good men of all parties.

So it was with Andrew Johnson, he intended not only to carry out every known principle began by Mr. Lincoln, but to go still further than he ever intended to go, for it was not Mr. Lincoln's intention to hang the leaders of the rebellion, but to deal leniently with them, but it was Johnsons fixed purpose to put his iron heel upon them and crush them to the earth as dogs. This he intended to do, not because the country demanded it, but as Tyler did to build up a Johnson party in the North, strong enough to nominate him in 1868, and had the Republicans throughout the country after he hung Mrs. Surratt have began to form Johnson clubs in every town and county as they did for Grant, he would have hanged Jeff. Davis and Lee as well as hundreds of others as high as Haman, but he saw very plainly that he was not the man. General Grant was in the hearts of the people; he had conquered the rebellion and saved the country from ruin, therefore they determined to place him at the head of the nation as a reward for his faithful services in the field, believing him as capable in the executive chair to serve his country as he was in the field of battle. Thus Andy saw that the thing was settled so far as his being able to get up a Johnson party was concerned so he, like his predecessor, John Tyler, concluded that if he could not rule, he would ruin, and at once turned the table to all his former professions and commenced an indiscriminate war upon the Republican party and all its known principles and politics, and at once commenced without the aid of Congress to reconstruct the rebellious States upon his own responsibilty, and in direct violation of the plans laid down by Mr. Lincoln.

It was his duty as soon as he was called to the chair of State, to have issued a call for an extra session of Congress, for the purpose of reconstructing those States in a manner that it might see proper. The South would have been satisfied with almost any terms that would have been proposed ; but in place of that, he undertook the job himself, and before Congress could meet in December following, he had so tampered with the leaders of these rebellious States by his appointments and reconstruction policy, that when they did meet they were not willing to accept any measure that Congress offered them, and from that day to the end of his term of office he never for one moment abated his opposition not only to every measure of the Republican party, but with every power at his command endeavored to crush and disgrace Gen. Grant, not that Grant had done any wrong, but to vent his spite on the Republican party for their great love for and confidence in him, and thus for near four years we as a party not only had the Democratic party in the North to fight but the whole South, with Andrew Johnson and all his officeholders to back them.

Early in the Summer after Johnson had become President, there were several applications for a change of officers in the Custom House at Baltimore, so I concluded, that as Mr. Hoffman the Collector had kindly given me a situation when I needed it, that it was my duty to assist in keeping him in his place, therefore with numbers of others I set to work to get signers to that effect, and in a few days succeeded in obtaining several thousand of the best citizens of Baltimore asking the President to retain him in office. When all was ready, a committee of the leading importing men of the city were appointed to take all the papers to Washington and present them to the President in person. I being a pretty good talker, they invited me to go along, (this committee was composed of both parties); when we arrived we were very cordially recieved by the President, and after shaking hands with him we presented our papers, each one making a short speech; none of us said anything about politics, only stated what the merchants wanted him to do. He during all our remarks stood calm and coldly, listened to us without a smile or a nod of his head, but when the last man, who had always been a rebel, came forward and said, Mr. President I do not come here as a Union man, but I come as a Democrat, I have not voted the Union ticket as I suppose these gentlemen have, indeed I have not voted at all since the war broke out, but I have come to you as one of the importers of foreign goods, to ask you to retain Mr. Hoffman, without regard to his political views. The moment that this gentleman said he had always been a Democrat, I saw Johnsons countenence brighten up with a smile, saying very pleasantly, I am glad to meet a good Democrat for I have always been one myself, and he appeared to take more interest in what he said, than all the rest put together.

From that moment I lost all the remaining confidence I had in him, and as soon as I could get to the cars I returned to Baltimore and went direct to Collector Hoffman's house and told him Johnson had gone back to the Democratic party and that he would be removed as certain as he lived, which he was in a few days.

As soon as Mr. Webster took his seat as Collector I put for Washington to try my luck again to keep my place, but this time I went to Montgomery Blair, he being very intimate with the President. I concluded that if I had any hope it was through him. Mr. Blair at once acknowleged my claims on the party and went with me to the President and then to the Secretary of the Treasury, where we had a very pleasant interview.

I returned home with bright hopes of success. A few days afterwards, Mr. Webster sent for me and told me that he had sent my name down for re-appointment, in due time it was announced in the papers that I had been re-appointed by Mr. Webster as an Inspector of Customs; this caused another flutter among my colleagues, all of them wondering where the influence came from, that held me in my place.

The situation that I now held was a more pleasant one than I had in the Permit Department, owing to the fact that the men composing the Inspectors Department were a better class of men and better Union men, than those that were in the Permit office; they were very kind and respectable to me which made our relations toward each other very agreeable.

About this time a friend of mine came to me one evening and asked me to go with him to a certain hall not far away, for a meeting. He said we have called a Johnson and Swann meeting and intend to form a club of that name, we have taken the start of the the other wards, so that if it comes to anything we will have the name of starting it. I told him that I would go along, but I could not take any part in it, for I had great fears that both, Johnson and Swann had or would soon desert our party, and I could not follow them. We went to the hall and found some seventy persons present. As soon as we entered some one proposed to organize the meeting by calling me to the chair, which I promptly declined; they soon found another to take the chair, who stated that the object of the meeting was to form a Johnson and Swann club of the sixth ward and proposed that a committee be appointed to recommend permanent officers for the club. I was named as one of them, but I again declined, when several present insisted on my reasons for declining to take any action in the proceedings. I told them that I had once read of a rat that went to the top of a meal barrel and looked down into, and saw plenty of good meal at the bottom, but at the same time saw a large lump in the centre of the pile of meal; he sat there looking at the meal, wishing for some of it, but what does that lump mean in the centre of the barrel, who knows but that is a cat covered up there, if it is, and I go down to get some meal, the cat will get me, so I think that I had better stay out. That is my case said I, it may all be right, but I think that I can see a cat in the meal tub and therefore think that I had better stay out.

What do you mean said the President by such talk. Oh nothing particular said I, but I don't like cats, this raised quite a laugh. When the business of the meeting was concluded, (every man in the house except myself signed the constitution) they took a collection to pay the rent of hall (which was one dollar and fifty cents). I told them that as I was the only officeholder in the house who had a good salary, I would pay their rent for them that night, and they could keep what they had raised by their collection for other expenses; this seemed to please them very much, but still they insisted on me to give them my reasons for not joining the club. The only reason that I would give them was, that I had concluded to wait a while to see whether it was all meal that I saw in the barrel or whether a cat was really there, as I had really suspected; if it should all prove to be meal that I saw in the barrel and no cat found among it, then I would take part with them, but not until then.

The next Thursday night they had another meeting when a number more joined the club. They called on me for a speech but I declined telling them that I had come there to listen and not to speak. Some of their new recruits I noticed were or had been rebels. They had some speaking that night by some of their local speakers, but none of any account; everything passed off very quietly, but I left with my mind fully made up that Johnson and Swan had forever left the Republican party and had sold out to the enemy.

The morning of the next meeting there were notices in all the papers that there was to be a grand rally of the sixth ward Johnson and Swann club, and that able speakers would address the meeting. I concluded to go and hear them, but to my surprise when I got there I found not only the hall and stairway full, but hundreds in the street. I thought this meant something; I therefore worked my way up stairs and into the room when I found it crowded with all the leading Democrats of the ward. They very soon proposed to organize the sixth ward Johnson and Swann club by electing a certain Democrat to be President. The regular President being in his chair declared the motion out of order as the club was already organized and the President in his chair; but they paid no attention to him and put the vote and elected their man. They ousted the rightful President and went to work. I turned to the old President and said dont you see the cat in the meal tub now? The most of the old members who had joined the club left as fast as they could get out of the hall, myself with them, and as far as I was concerned, that was the last Johnson and Swann meeting I ever attended.

Many of my friends thought it advisable for me as well as themselves to attend those meetings and appear to take some interest in them in order to keep our places, for if we were turned out some rebel would get our place. This I refused to do from the fact that I had never forsaken my first principles nor I never intended to do for the sake of a petty office under the government.

Things went on in the usual way until Thos. Swann appointed his registers who were to turn the State over into the hands of the rebels; this was done in the Summer of 1866. There was to be a Governor and

Congressmen elected that Fall and Judge Bond was to be the Republican candidate for Governor and John L. Thomas for Congress in my district. The Johnson men threw out the hint, that every man in the Custom House who voted the radical ticket would be turned out the next day. My friends advised me not to vote at all; many said that they would not go to the polls, but I was determined to die game, so on the morning of election I was the first man at the window ready to vote when the time arrived to receive votes. I found a man there to watch me, so in order that he might make no mistake, I opened my ticket and showed it to him, saying as I did so, you see that it is the genuine radical Republican ticket, go tell your master that I showed it to you, and without another word I walked away.

There was but one thing that saved me from being turned out, it was this : a few weeks before this, a ship arrived at quarantine with some fifty small-pox passengers on it; there was no law to compel an officer to board such a vessel, (although humanity did) and it was necessary for one to go, in order to separate the healthy from the sick ; they could not go ashore without an officer, and the question was, who would volunteer to go. There were ten men waiting orders but none of them were willing to risk their lives. I had a ship in charge at the time, but the Collector sent for me and asked me if I was willing to board that ship and discharge the passengers and their baggage. He said that it would be a humane act to do it. I agreed to go and did go and never left the ship until the passengers were all ashore at the hospital and the ship completely fumigated and hauled up to her dock. So when the demand was made for my removal a few days after the election the Collector sent for me and told me that for my humane act in boarding that ship at a time when no other officer could be induced to go, he should not trouble me about the way I had voted ; so

I slipped through that time, but several others were removed.

But still these villainous rebels were determined to follow me up and get me out, but found that they would have to change their programme. They next made their attack from Washington. They reported there that there were a number of officers unnescessarily employed in the Custom House and finally got one of Johnson's pimps sent over to investigate the matter; he of course was toasted and fed on the best, by the tools of Johnson in the Custom House, and without even calling to see if men were attentive to their business or not, he goes back to Washington and reported that myself and two or three others were of no account to the government, for when we had a ship in charge, we were never on it, but running about town drinking and neglecting our business. This charge they supposed we would be unprepared to meet, as there would be a peremptory order from the Secretary to the Collector to dismiss us without giving him a reason for it.—But in this they failed; Judge Sargent, the Commissioner of Customs had the case to investigate, he was my friend, and at once sent me a copy of the charges and gave me a chance to disprove them.

I went to the Collector and showed him the charges when he at once told me that I should have leave of absence to fight it out with them; he said that he was satisfied that it was false, and for me to go ahead until I proved it so. I went immediately to all the large shipping houses that I had unloaded vessels for, and showed them the charges against me, when every firm including the Baltimore & Ohio R. R. Company officers Spence & Reid, Kirkland, Chase & Co., F. W. Brune and Sons and many others signed a denial of all the charges brought against me, and also a remonstrance against my being removed, giving as a reason why they wanted me retained, that I was the most prompt and accommodating officer they ever had to transact business for them. When I had got through with my testimony I went to the Collector and showed him all my papers, which pleased him very much; he was glad I was so well fortified, and told me to take them direct to Washington, and give them to the Secretary in person, and I would find it all right. The next morning I put off with my bundle of documents, and in due time laid them before the Commissioner of Customs, who went with me to the Secretary, and laid my papers before him. The Secretary told us that they were unnecessary as he had just finished reading a letter from one of the largest importers of Baltimore, which satisfied him that the charges against me were false, but to accommodate me he would look over my papers, which he did, and then turned to me and said, go home and go to work, and as long as you perform your duties as you have done, you shant be put out of your place; I thanked him for his good opinion of me and left with flying colors.

On my return home I went to the Collector and told him all that had been said and done; he congratulated me on my success, and told me to attend well to my business, that I should not be disturbed. Mr. Webster the Collector was a true friend of mine, and although he had sold out body and breeches to Johnson and Swann, I shall ever feel grateful for his many kind acts to me, and at no period in my life will I prove ungrateful to him, should he need my services. He is a high toned gentleman, that would not stoop to an unmanly trick, at least I have always found him such.

After I had whipped them out at this last game of theirs, they concluded to let me alone for a while, but continued to work on the Collector to have me removed. The messenger at the Collector's door kept me posted about what was going on, I was therefore prepared at all times to meet all charges that might be brought against me. The Collector in order to get rid of their teazing him about me, told them that if they could catch me away from my vessel in working hours, sitting about a drinking saloon, he would turn me out. So that night they met at their club room and arranged a plan to trap me. Four of them were to come to my ship and pretend that two men from the country who had known me when a boy, were around the corner at an oyster saloon, and wished me to step around for a few moments and take a plate of oysters and a drink with them, and would be much disappointed if I did not come. But I had been posted by the messenger, who was present in the club room when the plot was laid. He had come to my house at midnight and notified me about their plan, so I was ready for them when they came, and told them that I always made it a rule after I unlocked my ship in the morning never to leave it until I locked it at night. If my friends wished to see me, they must come on board the ship, or wait about an hour, when it would be closing time, then I should be very happy to see them. They tried every plan they could think of, but it was no go. I knew what I was about, so they had to go away with a flea in their ear, and I had the satisfaction of knowing that I had beat them in this last effort to oust me.

Mr. Webster one day sent for me and told me it was his desire, that I should keep quiet and not abuse the President or Gov. Swann. Just let them alone and say nothing about them, that I could enjoy my own opinion without saying any thing about it, as the more I said the greater the opposition would be against me. I therefore concluded that it was best for me to take his advice, which I did, until Johnson and Swann undertook to send the United States troops here to forcibly eject the police commissioners out of office; this I saw was a high handed measure, one that was likely to bring on another bloody war, at least in Baltimore that might have spread all over the whole country. This I openly denounced, it was impossible for me to keep still, and I would here remark if it had not been for General Grant who was at the head of the army, coming to Baltimore and putting a stop to it when he did, God only knows how much blood they would have caused to be shed, but thanks to our noble General, he was the right man in the right place, came boldly forward and finished this job as he has done all others he ever undertook; promptly without saying much about it, as he don't talk much, but shows what he is by his acts. After this trouble quieted down things went on in their usual way, I said but little, kept very quiet and attended to my business, until about the first of January 1868, when they began to talk about assessing the men for political purposes. There was to be an election in New Hampshire in March, which would be the opening of the campaign of that year. Both parties were determined to carry it, and for this purpose we were to be assessed to help carry it for the Democratic party. I knew all about it in January but said nothing to any person but my true friends, but was determined not to pay a cent for that purpose. They had given out the word that whoever refused to pay their assessment would be turned out of office, the result was, all except myself, Ishmael Day and D. R. Mumma did pay it, and I am very sorry to say it, but it is true, that many of those who did pay their money to defeat Grant in '68, are holding good offices under him to day, while many who refused to pay are walking about, unable to get a place under the Government, but so the world goes, the greater the weather cock the better the luck.

They collected nearly all their assessments before they called on me, for they knew that I would refuse to pay, so they left me to the last, and when they did come they went away with a flea in their ear. I told them that I would give twenty dollars instead of ten, but I wanted it used my way, one dollar for a rope and the other nineteen to pay a man for hanging the traitorous villain Andrew Johnson. The young man who called on me said, that if I talked that way I would be kicked out of office before the next night, when I told him he had better keep quiet or I would kick him out of my office now, for I was a man of principle, and did not allow him nor the President or any other man to insult me in my office, and so far as paying money to aid the Democratic party was concerned I had been fighting them too long for that, and had lived before I got an office and could live after I got out.

As soon as the young man left I sat down to think the matter over, I had always been true to my principles, had never for one moment deviated from them and now should I pay tribute to such a scoundrel as Andrew Johnson, no never, my mind was made up in a minute. I would resign and in place of sending money to New Hampshire, I would go there and stump the State, so I sat down and wrote my resignation and handed it in, and bid farewell to Andy and his office and put for Washington and got some letters of introduction and left for New Hampshire.

CHAPTER XII.

STUMPING NEW HAMPSHIRE AND CONNECTICUT. — "HUNTING JOHN MCDANIELS BLACKSMITH SHOP." — GREAT ENTHUSIASM, HANDSHAKING, ETC.—"THE NEW HAVEN REGISTER."

IT WAS on the 6th day of February that I resigned and went to Washington, and that night at 9 o'clock I left for New York on my way to New Hampshire, although it was one of the coldest nights I ever felt, and I was going to a State that I had never visited before; I started as cheerful as if I was a boy, and had a gay ride that night to New York, and by six o'clock the next evening was in Nashua the first city in the State, just beyond the Massachusetts line. I inquired for a Republican Hotel, where I was saftely landed in a few minutes by the accomodating hackman of that house, which I found to be one the best kept hotels that I had ever visited; upon going to the office to register my name I inquired if there were any live Republicans in that place, when the landlord, who was behind the counter, said, I am a live Republican and there are plenty more of them at the tea table, walk in and take your tea, and I will introduce you to plenty of them when you are done your supper.

I went in, took my supper and when I returned to the sittingroom, I found a score of gentlemen waiting for an introduction to me; the landlord immediatly came forward and introduced me personally to each one of them, when we entered into a very pleasant conversation. They asked many questions about the people and their views in the South and what motives I had in coming to that country at that inclement season of the year, for it was about the coldest night that I had ever felt.

I told them all about the assessment to raise money to help carry their State for the Democratic ticket, and my refusing to pay for that purpose, which was the cause of my coming there, for the purpose, of undoing all that the money they were sending would do. I intended to go all over the State and talk to the people if they were disposed to hear me, which I had no doubt they would. They said they were going to have a little meeting that night, and I should go along with them to it which I did; they took me up into a room and told me this was a secret Grant club that they were attending, but that I should be admitted as a member, which I was in a few minutes afterwards. As soon as they were through their private business I was called on for a few remarks, when I arose and said: Mr. President, I have read in the good book that the whole need not a physican, only those who are sick; I presume sir, that not many of those present are in a very unhealthy condition at this time, particularly if they passed through the same ordeal that I did in getting in here; this raised a great laugh when the President said, that was speech enough for this night, we are satisfied that you can do it, we will give you a meeting to-morrow night, one that you will be satisfied with. The meeting was at once adjourned and I was received with a hearty welcome by all present.

The next morning I found the town filled with large

placards calling on all working men to rally at the City Hall that night, to hear the Baltimore Blacksmith, a loyal southern mechanic, make a speech; I was taken during the day all around the city to the leading workshops and introduced to all the workmen in them, so that by night I had become pretty well acquainted with the people. When night came I was escorted to the hall by a committee of Blacksmiths, and found the hall so packed with people that we had to get through the back window to get to the stand, and found it packed also. I found all of the elite of the city there, both ladies and gentlemen, so that there was scarcely room for me to stand. I was introduced, and began by saying, that this was one of the proudest nights of my life, coming as I did among them an entire stranger, to meet such an audience as I now saw before me, was very gratifying. But while I feel gratified at this very flattering reception that I meet here to-night, I fear that I shall not be able to meet your expectations, for as you perceive, I am a plain working man, raised in the South without the advantages of even a common school education, I therefore know but little about big words that some of our speakers use, in fact I only know four or five of those big words, and I hardly ever undertake to climb up them very high, for fear I might have some difficulty in getting down again, so I usually let what few I do know alone, (great laughter) and content myself with speaking in a plain matter-of-fact way.

What is it ladies and gentlemen which is dividing the two great political parties at this time; what are the principles laid down by the great Democratic party, do any of you know, can any gentleman in this house tell me, if there is, I will thank him to raise right up and tell us, for I am free to say that I have been for forty years trying to find out, and have never been able to find any other principle in them, but to love whiskey and hate niggers (loud applause). Hunting Democratic principles put me in mind of when I lived in Ohio; I wanted to find a certain Blacksmith to work for me, and started to hunt him up; after going some distance across the country, I came across a boy chopping wood by the road side and asked him if he could tell me the road to John McDaniels Blacksmith shop; he looked up and said certainly I can, keep down this road till you come to a fence on your left hand, take up that fence to the left until you come to the top of a hill, then take to the right down through the woods till you come to a small creek with a log laying across it, cross the creek and turn up to the right until you come to another fence, take the left hand end of the fence and follow it till you come to where three fences join together, you then follow the right hand fence until you come to the top of another hill, turn to the left and go down the hill until you come to another little creek with a pine slab laying across it, cross the slab and you will see three sycamore trees growing up out of one stump, there turn to the right and keep up the hill till you come to the top of it, and here he stopped as if studying the balance of the road, when I said, well which way then my boy? Oh, said he looking archly, I guess you will be lost about then, for that is as far as I know the road. And that would be the way with finding out what Democratic principles were; this raised a loud roar of laughter. I then commenced and showed them the great advantage the South had held over the North in the representation in Congress by counting a portion of their slaves as free citizens, and the great necessity there was to enfranchise the colored voters of the South in order to protect the North, for as the negroes were now free they would all be counted in the houses of representation, which would give the South over forty members in Congress after 1870, that they would not be entitled to, without enfranchising all the people. I then showed what the Republican party had done since they came into power, and how the Democratic party had tried every way they could to prevent us from raising men and means to put down the rebellion, and to prevent us from reconstructing the Southern States in a satisfactory manner, and now they have the hardihood to look an honest man in the face and ask him to put them in the control of this great country that they had used every power at their command to destroy. I as one individual beg leave to say no. Suppose ladies and gentlemen that you would find a man trying to destroy your house when you go home to night, and in conquering him you lost several of your family killed and wounded, and after you had succeeded in overcoming him you let him go without punishing him, would you be willing to employ him to watch your house for you after that, or would you not rather employ one of your friends who assisted you in saving your property? You will all say that you would employ your friend and not your enemy, that would seem natural. I will now put the question and I want some Democrat to answer it; was there one man in that rebellion who assisted in trying to destroy this country, or one man that fired a gun at a Union soldier or who ever dragged our flag in the dust, who was not at the time he did it a professed Democrat? I pause for an answer, come sing it out, if you know of even one that was not. There being no answer, I said how can they have the impudence then to ask you to trust them with the reigns of government, why give them the reigns of this great country in their hands, they would be like a beggar on horseback, they would ride it to the devil in a short time. This caused the wildest outbursts of laughter. I finally at the end of two hours closed my remarks by stating that if the people disired it, I would speak for them until the election. As soon as I closed the people crowded around me, shook hands with me, and introduced me to some ten committees who had come from various cities of the State to hear me. They had gotten up this meeting to try me, to see if I would suit the people of their country, hence these committees had been sent for. I had more than met their expectations so much so, that before I left the hall that night, they had made fourteen appointments for me in various parts of the State, and I commenced the next night to fill them. I spoke at Milford the next night and then went to Manchester, the largest city in the State, and the greatest manufacturing city also. There they had the largest hall in the State, it would hold six thousand people. The meeting was called for working men, but the hall was packed by all classes; we had a boss blacksmith for chairman, who introduced me in good style, and here I made a two hours speech but half of the people failed to get in and were determined to hear me, and as I had no meeting for the next night, I agreed to come back from the place I was to speak the next afternoon, and speak for them in their hall again at night. I had made my speech and had agreed to speak for them agina, but how to get out of that hall that night, was what bothered me, for everbody must shake hands with me, and I was afraid that they would kill me with kindness. Governor Smythe said, that no man had ever pleased their people as well as I had done, they seemed fairly wild, so much so that a large number of them went with me the next day, so as to be certain of getting me back that night. I went to my appointment where I met a large crowd and made them a very satisfactory speech and at the close of my speech a vote of thanks and a ten dollar bill to help pay my expenses was given to me, and after a little handshaking I returned with my friends to the city in time for tea, well pleased with my reception that day in a country place.

Our meeting was called for eight o'clock, but at six the Governor called at the hotel and told me that the hall was packed full of ladies, and I might just as well go over and begin then, as to keep the people waiting, for all was in the hall already that could get in. So I went over and found it true, there were not less than four thousand ladies seated; this hall had a private way leading to the stand, so that I had no trouble in getting to it. I was introduced that night by Ex-Governor Smythe, who done it in a fine style, making some happy allusions to the ladies. I began my speech by thanking the people for the many flattering receptions that I had met with since I had come among them, and said that I was at a loss to know what had caused my great popularity among the people, it was not my eloquence or fine speaking that caused it, for I was an uneducated man, and if it was not my good looks, I could not tell what it was. This of course started them roaring for several minutes, finally when order was restored I commenced to speak on the importance of the coming election; I told them that the eyes of every friend of Freedom and free Institutions was turned to New Hampshire, as she was the State that was to start the ball in the present campaign. I urged the necessity of standing by the party that saved the country, as the only party that had a right to rule it. I appealed to the ladies to give us their influence in this campaign as they had done during the war; I told them some pleasant things about female influence and then closed my speech.

The Governor came forward and said that it was the desire of the ladies that I should stand at the door as they passed out, to give them a chance to shake hands with me, and that many of them desired my photograph before I left. I told them that they should be gratified, for it had always been pleasing to me to take a handsome lady by the hand, and if they were not afraid to get in the hands of a Bear, I was not afraid to get into their hands; this caused a loud laugh.

I was taken around to the front door and stood in the centre, while the great mass of people passed on each side of me, each one as they passed, giving me a shake of the hand or arm, six or eight hold of each hand and arm at one time, so by the time that they had all passed I was nearly shaken to pieces. This was one of the most glorious nights I ever passed, and one that I never shall forget. The next morning I went to a photograph gallery and set for a card picture, and before I left the gallery there were over thirty applicants for a copy of it, and I was informed afterwards, that the firm had copied and sold over a thousand of them in ten days. I left Manchester with much regret, for a more pleasant or agreeable set of people I never met, nor shall I ever forget them.

I continued filling my appointments, until I arrived in Portsmouth, the only importing city in the State, here I met with a glorious reception ; here they had a navy yard which was pretty well filled with Johnson Democrats. I took occasion to pitch into them, charging them with treason and causing hundreds of murders that had been committed in the South since he had been President, winding up with Tom Moore's curse on a traitor, which is as follows :

Cursed be the slave, whose treason like a deadly blight,
Steals oe'r the councils of the brave and blasts them in their hour of might,
May life's unblessed cup for him be dregs with treacheries to the brim,
With hopes that but alure to fly,
And when from earth his spirit flies,
Just prophet let the doomed one dwell,
Full in the sight of paradise,
Beholding heaven, yet feeling hell.

This caused considerable shuffling in the crowd, the Republicans cheered and the other side looked daggers at me but kept pretty quiet. I left with flying colors for my next meeting, with the best wishes of all of the friends of Grant and the Republican party. I continued to speak from place to place, with unbounded popularity until Monday the day before the election, when I was to close the campaign in Nashua, the place where I began to speak. I was received with open arms by my friends and had a monster meeting. I made a long speech and closed by thanking the people for the kind treatment that I met with, while sojourning among them. I had made forty-two long speeches in twenty four days and was about to leave them, possibly never to meet again, but I shall never forget New Hampshire.

As soon as the meeting was over I was met by a committee of ladies and gentlemen, who presented me with several nice presents, and a nice little roll of greenbacks, and after a general round of hand shaking and parting good byes, we parted, hoping to meet again in Washington a year from that. The next morning I left for Connecticut, where I was to begin a campaign, and arrived at West Meridan about eight o'clock that night.

When I arrived at the hotel, I found no person there except the landlady, who told me that all the gentlemen about the house had gone over to the hall to hear the great Blacksmith speak, but she feared he was not there, as he had not come in the Boston train. I asked her where the hall was, when she pointed it out to me; I went over and found it crowded, but worked my way to the stand, where I found Hon. Henry Wilson speaking; as soon as he saw me he said, here comes the Blacksmith, who you all want to hear.

I had made arrangements with the committee at Nashua to send me the result of the vote of their State at nine o'clock by telegraph. Mr. Wilson had just closed, and I had been introduced to the meeting, when some man cried out, here is a dispatch for the Blacksmith; it was handed up to me, I opened it and after looking over it a moment, I turned to the audience and bowed very politely, saying how are you Mrs. New

Hampshire, twenty-five hundred Republican majority and no mistake. This caused the wildest outburst of applause I ever witnessed, it was full five minutes before order was restored; I had to read the dispatch over several times to satisfy the crowd, after which I made them one of my best speeches, which seemed to give entire satisfaction.

After the meeting was over a number of the leading men of the State, who were there attending a State convention with Mr. Wilson and myself, returned to the hotel where I had put up, when a handsome supper was prepared; we did ample justice to our appetites and then went to business. They proposed that I should take the hardest Democratic county in the State as my field of labor, promising to give me a good speaker to assist me, which they did. We had two days to rest in, to give the town committee time for to get our meetings ready for us. I went to New Haven to make a speech before starting up to my mountain district; here I met the dirtiest little paper that I had run against in the New England States, called the *New Haven Register*. He began his dirty slang at me before I came to the State, and continued it all the time I was there. I went in due time to my appointments where I stayed some three weeks, speaking day and night in my usual way, leaving each place with the good feelings of all good people.

The chairman of the State Committee had written to me that I was to close the campaign on Saturday before the election, at New Haven; he said it would be the largest meeting that ever was convened inside of a house in the State, for every body wanted to hear me speak, so I must prepare myself for it. I went at the proper time and found one of the largest meetings that I had ever seen inside of a house; the fashion and beauty of the city were there, every spot that a human being could stand in was full. I was introduced to the meeting by Governor Buckingham, who told me that the editor of the *Register* was there to take notes, in company with several others. I concluded to quit even with him that night, so after speaking on various subjects for a while, I remarked that the Democrats were terribly frightened about negro equality, they had great fears that the two races would inter marry with each other, but I thought they were frightened without a cause. It was a matter of taste who we married; if a Democrat wished to marry a colored lady he could do so, if he could get one, but I would advise them not to come to Maryland for one, as our colored women were to sharp there to marry a Copperhead, but in order to quiet their fears on that subject if I were in your next Legislature I would introduce a bill like this, that if any colored lady shall hereafter marry a white Copperhead, knowing him to be such at the time, she shall be deemed guilty of a misdemeanor, and upon conviction before any court having jurisdiction of the same, shall be sentenced to read the *New Haven Register* through every morning before breakfast for one week, and I will bet my life that she never will be caught in such a scrape again.

This almost tore the house down; they shouted with laughter; there were some dozen or more colored ladies sitting just to my left, in one seat, I turned to them and said, do any of you desire to marry the editor of the *New Haven Register*, if you do I suppose you can get him They all sung out we don't want him; this raised another great shout, which was too much for the editor, he raised up and left, and as he went I sung out, you have frightened him off ladies, he is going to try his luck in some other quarter, he sees that he has no chance here. There was but little more speaking done that night, the people all rushed around me with their congratulations in so putting down the *Register* man, that I hardly had time to get ready for the train that left at twelve o'clock that night, in which I was going home. I got off however and arrived in New York the next morning, spent the day there in company with Governor Curtin and other speakers who had been speaking in Connecticut, On that night I left for Baltimore, where I arrived in safety on Monday morning.

CHAPTER XIII.

CHICAGO CONVENTION—SPEAKING IN INDIANA—I'LL BET FIFTY DOLLARS HE IS THE BUCKEYE BLACKSMITH—TOOK DOWN THE COPPERHEAD MILLIGAN OF MORGAN'S RAID NOTORETY—SPEAKING IN MAINE PENNSYLVANIA AND NEW JERSEY.

I SPENT a few days at home and then started to make my way to Chicago, to attend the National Convention in May, that was to nominate General Grant for President. I went direct to Indiana and commenced speaking throughout the State, whenever I could get up a meeting. I had never been in that State before as a speaker, and it was more difficult to get up a meeting on that account, but I had too much experience in politics, to be beat when I undertook to get up a good meeting. I took a new plan with the Indiana boys, I secured a place in which to speak, then got my own bills printed, heading them with War! War! War! one thousand volunteers wanted immediately, not to fight Jeff. Davis, but to hear a genuine live Southern Republican make a speech to-night, at (naming the place of meeting.)

This being a novel plan of advertising, it took well every body was wondering who and where the man was, none of them suspected me, for I looked too common. When night came I waited until the crowd gathered and it was a big one, all looking anxiously for the speaker, there being no name attached to the bills they did not know who to call for. At last I stepped on the stand and said: gentlemen you seem to be waiting for your speaker, did any of you ever see an orange that grew in Ireland, if you never have you never will, for there never was one that growed there, this raised a big laugh; let me ask you another question, did you ever see a real live Southern Republican, if you have not, look at me, for I am one dyed in the wool, here was another laugh. I told you so, said one to another, I thought he was the man.

I then took my coat off and commenced rolling up my sleeves, when an old fellow sung out "I'll bet fifty dollars that's the Buckeye Blacksmith, I saw him do that same thing thirty years ago." Not so fast my friend said I, you are making me too old, remember there are ladies here, and they don't like old men, this caused another laugh. By this time I was ready to speak, and commenced and spoke for near two hours, in my most happy style, causing the wildest outbursts of applause; when I closed I found many warm friends around me. I had pleased them so well that they not only paid my bill at the hotel and refunded me what I had paid for my bills, but telegraphed to several other towns for meetings for me and took me in a carriage to my next meeting, sending two of their best citizens along to introduce me to the people where I was to speak.

I had no more difficulty in getting up meetings after that, but had more invitations than I could attend to. I met many very bitter Copperheads in that region; at a town called Anderson, I came across that celebrated Milligan who was sentenced to be hung for being accessory to the murder of several citizens who were killed by John Morgan while making his great raid through that country, but was pardoned by Mr. Lincoln through the intercession of Gov. Morton. This Milligan sneered at some favorable remark that I made about Gov. Morton, when I told him he was the last man on earth that ought to sneer, for said I if it had not have been for that good kind hearted man, you would be rotten in your grave to-night with six foot of hemp around your neck; he jumped up and said he would thank me to tell him who had given me so much information. I got it from the records of the war department, said I, and was mad enough when I saw it, at Lincoln and Morton to have cursed them for interfering in the case. They ought to have hung every man that had any hand in pioneering Morgan and his men through the country. I lived in the South and know what I say is true, that you and such men as you prolonged that war for more than two years, and there are more than three hundred thousand men now in their graves useless to themselves and the country, that would to-night be at home with their families, if such men as you had been hung when you ought to have been.

Yet you have the hardihood in the face of all these facts to set up and sneer when a great and good man's name is mentioned. You ought to thank God three times a day for the balance of your life, that I was not President at that time, for had I been, I would have made hemp command a better price than it does now, I would have hung as high as Haman, every man North or South that ever raised his arm or voice against the flag of my country. God bless that old flag, I love it dearly, and she still floats over the land of the free and the home of the brave in spite of you and John Morgan and all your hellish crew. This was more than he could stand, so he left amidst the roars and laughter of nearly all present; this was a gay old night for me, and I left there a very popular man.

I continued to speak until I got to Logansport, where I made my last speech before going to the convention, which was on Saturday night, after which I took the train for Chicago, arriving there the next morning. I stayed in Chicago until the nominations were made and then left for home to rest awhile. After I had rested a week or two, I started for the Northern tier of counties in Pennsylvania, where I travelled from town to town laboring day and night, until July, and was then taken sick and had to come home; many days while up in that mountain country I had but one meal to eat a day, for the want of money to buy more. I hated to make my situation known, the people being strangers to me, at last I worked my way to where I was known, when I fared better. Had I told the people my situation they no doubt would have provided well for me; as it was I felt satisfied that I was doing my duty to my party and also the country, it was not money that I had in view, but a fixed desire to aid Grant's election. I arrived home about the middle of July, quite sick, and remained there until the first of August, when I got well again, and concluded to go to the State of Maine, where they had just opened up a very lively campaign.

I left Baltimore on the night of the first of August and went direct through to Portland, Maine, without stopping, arriving there the second day after. I left the cars, carpet bag in hand, for the City Hotel, but had not gone far when I met a man who said, aint this Mr. Bear of Baltimore? I looked at him and at once recognised him as the master of a ship, that I had discharged some years before. He asked me where I was going, and I told him my business, when he said that I had come at the right time, for they were going to have a great meeting there that night, and wanted all the speakers they could get. I am a Democrat said he, but that don't make any difference, you must go home with me and stay at my house, and I will go with you and introduce you to some of the leading men of your party. I went with him and made his house my home while I remained in that part of the State, and made a good Republican out of him at that.

The captain took me around that afternoon and introduced me to the leading men of our party, they having heard of me while in New Hampshire the winter before were much pleased to have me visit their State, and said that they had plenty of work for me, that they needed me very much that night. I went to their great City Hall, and found as many outside as there were inside, all clamoring for a speech. I went in and found a gentleman speaking to a packed house. In a few minutes a committee came to me and asked me if I could speak in the open air, if I could there were more people outside than inside, and I had better be sent out there. I went and in five minutes I had them roaring, they cheered so loud and often that the crowd in the house heard it and began to leave by hundreds, and the committee had to stop me, until the other gentleman was through, when the meeting was adjourned to the street where all could hear me, when I finished my speech, (and if I ever made a good one I made it that night. I told all my good anecdotes with good offect, and after we were through I was made the Lion, in the place of the Bear, that night. The committee made a series of appointments for me, through the mountain regions of the first congressional district, where I went after speaking a few days in the neighborhood of Portland. I had a pretty tough time of it while travelling among the mountains, owing to more ignorance among the people than I had found in the Eastern States. I had a fine young speaker with me, he done the smooth talking and I done the rough, but we got through all safe, without the loss of a man, or a drop of blood, we returned to Portland to make the closing speech of the compaign, which was on Saturday before the election on Monday. I spoke to two very large meetings where I bid them a final farewell, and left for Pennsylvania on Monday morning, arriving in Philadelphia on Tuesday afternoon just in time to attend their great mass meeting that night. I went to the telegraph office, where I expected a dispatch, giving me the result of my labors; I found one awaiting me with the glorious news that we had crrried, not only the first, but every district in the State, this was glory enough for one day.

I went to the great meeting on Broad street, where they had several stands erected; it was arranged for me to speak on the main stand first, in order to draw the crowd together. I commenced by telling them that as I came there I passed a crowd of Democrats who had just heard the news from Maine, singing that good old hymn, "Hark from the tombs a doleful sound," but they had altered it, they sang:

"Hark foom Maine a doleful sound,
Mine ears attend the cry,
Ye Democrats come view the ground,
Where you must shortly lie."

This raised a great roar of laughter, and as they finished that verse a sound came up from Maine to the Pennsylvania Democrats in answer to their song:

Rebels this clay must be your bed,
In spite of all your towers,
The Copperheads throughout the land
Must lay as low as ours.

this was all that it was necessary for me to say, I had filed the crowd as full as they could hold, and then left the stand, but remarked as I done so, gentlemen if we do our duty in Pennsylvania this Fall, you will hear our Copperheads singing about the fourth of November next,

Plunged in a gulf of deep despair,
We wretched sinners lay.

I then bowed and left for the next stand, amid the shouts and laughter of ten thousand people. I mountthe next stand and went over the same thing, and in five minutes had another crowd roaring; I then passed to the next stand, and done the same thing over again, and so on, until I had gotten up a good meetat all the stands. I received great credit from many of the leading Republicans of the State, for the manner in which I drew the people together at the various stands that night, all declared that the "Buckeye' was ahead in getting up a crowd.

I rested the next day, and then made arrangements with the State committee to canvass the State for them; they knew that I was coming and made a number of appointments for me, the first one, at Chambersburg in Franklin County, near two hundred miles West of Philadelphia. I was to stay in that county a week, when they would have other appointments ready for me. I left Philadelphia on Monday morning and arrived in Chambersburg that afternoon in time to speak to a very large meeting. I had to do all the speaking myself, as the other speaker who was to assist me failed to get there. As soon as I was done speaking the chairman of the County committee handed me a dispatch directing me in place of filling five other appointments in Franklin county, to report to him in person at all hazzards the next day by two o'clock, which I did by starting at two o'clock that night. It appeared that the State committee had made a mistake in sending me to Franklin county, they having promised me to other meetings in a different part of the State, and for that reason I was recalled as above stated.

Some ten days prior to the great mass meeting at Philadelphia, the Democrats of Montgomery county, called a meeting at a place called the Trappe one of their strong holds in the county, the Republicans called one in the same place on the following Tuesday; the two committees made a bet of an oyster supper for a hundred men, upon which party would have the largest meeting. I was very popular with the people through that region of country, it being the place where I had made so many Lincoln votes eight years before. The Republicans took advantage of my popularity, and sent bills all over three counties assuring the people that the Buckeye would certainly be there; the Democrats denied, saying that I was not in the county but the Republicans sent out riders all over the country to tell the people that I was in Philadelphia and would certainly be there.

When I arrived in Philadelphia the day of their meeting, I met their committee, who were greatly rejoiced that they would be able to fulfil their promise to have me there in time for their meeting. They said that they would have lost a hundred votes had I failed to be there. We took the cars and in due time arrived at the Trappe, where I was met by several hundred men and women who had already commenced pouring in by hundreds from distant sections of the country. I was nearly shaken to pieces by them, they being so glad to see me.

By eight o'clock that night no person estimated the crowd to be less than from six to eight thousand people, the Democrats had given it up long before we began to speak. I was the first speaker and spoke one hour, telling the people as I closed that I had just been informed, that several large delegations were still coming, and that I would speak again, after two other speakers were done, so that all might hear me. This pleased them very much and I retired to take a little rest.

At the close of the speech of the last gentleman that was to follow me, I was again introduced, this time to more than eight thousand up turned faces, all anxious to see and hear the "Buckeye" I told them that I had reasons to feel proud to stand where I now stood, looking as I now did into so many smiling faces. Many years ago I came among you as a mechanic, you placed confidence in me then as an honest man, and I feel proud tonight my fellow countrymen, that I can see in your smiling faces that I still have that confidence. What is it my friends that has brought so many of you here tonight from your quiet homes, many of you from a distance, it was not to see and hear me talk. No my friends you had a higher motive in view than that; God has given you a great and glorious country for your inheritence, you have come here to show your devotion to that country.

It is only a little over three years since the last enemy of this glorious country was compelled to lay down his arms and cease fighting to destroy it, and I have no doubt but that many of you were there under that sour apple tree, to witness their surrender, and now the question is to be decided in a few weeks, who shall govern this glorious country of yours, the men that fought more than four years to destroy it, or the men that spent three thousand million of dollars, and three hundred thousand lives to save it. This is what has brought you here my friends, and I see very plainly by your looks to night which side you are on. Have patience my friends until the third of November, and you will have the glorious satisfaction of seeing this rebel Democracy not only surrendering their rebel heards to General Grant again, but you will see them buried so deep that it will take the resurection gun to awaken them again; this caused long and loud applause, and finally at twelve o'clock I closed, never to forget that nights proceedings.

It was one o'clock before the crowd got away, and I had to get a wagon to take me across the country, some twenty miles to intersect the Pennsylvania rail road, in order to reach my appointment the next night two hundred miles up the Susquehanna river; I had not slept a moment for two nights, but I was determined to make it, and did do it, arriving just as the people began to gather at the stand; I was taken to a hotel and got a harty supper and was already to speak, by the time the crowd had gathered. This was another monster meeting; no other speaker being there I had to speak over two hours, which pretty nearly used me up, but I stood it. My speech that night had a good effect, as the election afterwards showed.

I got a good nights sleep which refreshed me very much, and left next morning for Bloomsburg in Columbia county, where I was to speak at a mass meeting in the afternoon. Here I met Senator Cragan of New Hampshire, who was to speak with me; this was Senator Buckalew's home and we had him to hear us. This was the place where seven hundred Democrats organized and equipped themselves to resist the draft in time of the war; it was known as the fishing creek confederacy, which cost the government eighty thousand dollars to put it down, this was a good text for me. I was very popular in that county as a speaker, having often spoken there. I charged the Democrats with being the anti-war-party, which they could not deny in that county. I laid it on thick and hard that day, which pleased my friends very much. After the meeting was over I had to shake hands with thousands of the people; one lady said I must sit down and take her daughter, a girl fifteen years old on my lap; I done so, when she said, just here in this woods you took me on your lap when I was a little girl, and I hope you may live to come back and take my grand daughter on your lap when I get one. This pleased Messrs. Cragan and Buckalew who remarked that they never saw a more popular man among the people than I was. The reason why I was so popular with the people, I always after speaking went down among them in a friendly way, shaking hands with them in place of shutting myself up in a hotel parlor as most speakers do.

That night I had to speak to a mass meeting at Northumberland where I arrived in time to get my supper and be the second speaker. Here I found another very large meeting; all the old residents who had heard me speak in 1840 of both parties were there, and the chairman of the meeting told me that he wanted me to make the best speech that night that I ever made, as I had all of the best men of the county there to hear me. When I was introduced I said that when I last had the pleasure of speaking in that place, my opponents stoned me, because I held an honest difference of opinion with them, but times have changed since then, we were at that time fighting for a principle, now we are fighting for our country, and I hope all of this vast crowd which I see before me are in favor of a united country, if they are, there would be none left to throw stones; this took well with the crowd. I then went on to show that the Republicans while fighting the rebels in the front with the bayonet that they had to fight the Democratic party in the North, both in Congress and every State Legislature to raise men and means to put down the rebellion, winding up my speech with these words: In conclusion gentlemen let me say, if any man here to night can show me where one Democrat in Congress or any State Legislature in this Nation during the entire war ever cast one vote to aid in putting it down, I will stop speaking and agree that they have a right to rule the country. This had a good effect, for they were like the man in the scripture, dumb and not able to open their mouth.

The next day Senator Cragan and I had another monster meeting in Danville, Montour county, here also I was very popular, having at one time worked there taking pictures. The great Montour Iron works are located here and employ a large number of hands who were all anxious to hear a mechanic speak ; here I took protection as my theme to speak upon, which the leaders of our party thought the best subject to agitate before the crowd that would hear me. I was at home on that subject, and gave entire satisfaction to all present and left the stand amidst the cheers of the people.

As soon as I was done, a carriage stood waiting to convey me to another mass meeting that night, some twelve miles from Danville. Senator Cragan was unable to speak twice a day, therefore did not accompany me. That night after speaking over an hour and a half my voice failed me and for the first time in my life I broke down before I was through my speech, but my friends rallied around me, and by the aid of a good sweat and a warm room, I rallied sufficently by morning to resume my travels.

My next place was a large county meeting in Union county where I met the Hon. J. B. Packer the member of Congress from that district; we had a fine time of it, many of the old farmers that had heard me years before were there, with their whole families to see the old "Buckeye", and to hear him make another speech, and many of them shed tears, when I made an allusion to the sacrifices that they had made to save the Union, as some had lost a son, a brother or some near friend in the war; I never met a warmer reception in any place than I did there.

I went the next day to Sealings grove, where I was to speak that night, and put up at a Democratic hotel there being no other in the place. I was soon told that I would have opposition that night, by a man who boarded at my hotel; alright said I, that is just what I want, who is he, I should like to take a look at the fellow. He was pointed out to me by one of his friends; is that him said I, well it wont take me ten minutes to set the whole crowd laughing when I

*12

begin on him, but don't say anything about it, or he will back out; let us have a little fun at his expense, said I. He promised to say nothing, but I knew he would, as he was a Democrat and a friend of the man who was to reply to me.

At the supper table a very important stuck-up-looking young fellow sitting opposite me said, Mr. Bear do you not have opposition sometimes in your meetings, dont some of the Democrats want to reply to you? Sometimes said I, but not very often, those of them that can speak have more sense than to undertake it; I sometimes meet with one that is green enough to undertake it, but he dont generally stay long in the town after he is done with me, particularly if there are many boys about, for you know that boys like to laugh at and tease people who are not very sharp.

Night came on and with it a large crowd; they had a fine stand fixed up for me, and I was introduced and spoke for near two hours, winding up by saying, why don't the Democracy meet and tell us what claims they have upon the people for their votes? Our leaders have tried to force them out, but they refuse to come, preferring to stick to their old song that we are in favor of negro equality; I will meet the best man that you can raise in the county to-morrow, or any other day and discuss living issues with him, but I will hold him to the questions at issue, but my man failed to put in an appearance and I had the field all to myself. After the meeting a number of my friends walked with me to the hotel and we had a hearty laugh over what had occurred at the tea-table, the landlord among us; he was a Democrat, but a very clever fellow; he said that I had scared that fellow out of the notion of replying to me, by what I said at supper he being at the table at the time I said what I did.

I went next to Sunbury where I had one of the most genteel meetings that I ever addressed; a number of the first ladies of the place were there to hear me who were not in the habit of attending political meetings; I took advantage of their presence and devoted half of my speech to female influence, giving a full history of their toil and labor in behalf of the patriots, cause not only in the revolutionary war, but in our late struggle for the Union, and wound up by appealing to them for their influence in the election of Gen. Grant. This highly pleased them and many of them came forward after the meeting and thanked me for my very complimentary allusions to them. I left Sunbury that night at twelve o'clock as popular as any man ever left a place.

After leaving Sunbury I made a tour up the Juniata river, speaking at Mifflin to a large meeting, the next day, then at Lewistown, Huntington, Tyrone, Altona and Hollidaysburg, having large and successful meetings at each place. From Hollidaysburg I returned to Philadelphia, where I spoke two or three times, closing the night before the State election. On my arrival back to Philadelphia, I found a letter from the New Jersey committee inviting me to speak for them until the Presidential election, provided they were done with me in Pennsylvania; they were done with me there, and I therefore accepted the New Jersey invitation and spoke in Camden the next night.

The committee that engaged me made an appointment for me every day or night until the election. One of the first places that I went to was Tuckerton, a small town on the bank of the ocean in Burlington county; I did not expect to meet many people there, but to my surprise when night came, the people came flocking in by hundreds until we had a mass meeting, that would have done credit to a city, and in all my travels through life I never met a more pleasant reception than I did at that place. I was taken to Dr. Pages private residence, where I was toasted, feasted and flattered, as though I had been a king; the people were not rich in this region, but they were the most hospitable people I ever met.

I had another fine meeting in Vincentown, a place where I had spoken before, where the people tried how much fuss they could make over me; I left there more popular than I ever was. I went from there to Melville, one of the largest manufacturing towns in West Jersey, where I had a monster meeting; here I took up the tariff question, which suited them in that place. The Democrats got up a procession at the same hour that our meeting was called, and formed their procession directly in front of the wigwam, where we held our meeting; this was done in order to keep their party from hearing me, but it was no go. As soon as our band struck up a tune, the people crowded into the wigwam until every available spot in it was full; I commenced and spoke until their parade was over and dismissed, when their leaders acknowleged that half of their men stayed to hear me speak.

My next appointment was at Haddenfield, Camden county, where I was to meet Ex-Senator Frelinghuysen; here we had another great crowd, it was an afternoon meeting, to be held in a large hall. Haddenfield is an old fashion town, settled mostly by business men and retired merchants from Philadelphia. Just as the meeting organized a gentleman came forward and said that the committee had sent another speaker for the meeting, (a gentleman from Ohio); he was introduced to the chairman of the meeting and it was arranged that I should speak first a few minutes to draw the crowd together, then the stranger a short speech, and Mr. Frelinghuysen make the main speech of the day, and I to close up the meeting with a few good stories. But in this arrangement we were doomed to disappointment, for when this Ohio man got the floor, he spoke nearly three hours, talking about nothing that had any bearing upon the subject before the meeting (what a great pity it is, that speakers don't know when to quit). Mr. Frelinghuysen was so disgusted at the manner in which he was treated that he only spoke ten minutes, and I closed up with a few anecdotes. One of the wealthy citizens made a big party that night, Mr. Frelinghuysen and I were the invited guests and were serenaded in a splendid manner, but the Ohio man had so offended the people by the way that he had treated us speakers, that he was not invited, which gave him great offence. The greatest fault that a speaker can commit, is to speak the same thing over to the same audience in order to make a long speech, particularly when there are others to speak. This speaking to kill time has rendered many good speakers unpopular. My plan has even been to quit when I was done, and for that reason have never driven my audience away while I was speaking, and could always get a larger audience to hear me, where I was best known than I could among strangers.

I went from this place down among the glass blowers and wood choppers, here I met some pretty hard customers, some of them very ignorant, as much so, as any I ever met, but the name of the "Buckeye" would bring them out to our meetings and if they were not to full of Jersey whisky they would listen to me very attentively, but generally the Democrats will get them too full to understand much that is said, after staying a few days in that part of the State. I went to Salem county, where we had a large mass meeting at a place called the Pole Tavern, a very noted place; here I met Senator Cattell, who I found to be one of the most glorious men I ever met, and a very fine speaker, and I met many of my old friends of former years; they gave me a very warm greeting.

I stayed a few days in Salem county, spoke at several of the most public places in the county, and then left for Bridgeton one of the prettiest little cities in the State; here we had a monster meeting and procession. Senator Cattell and I spoke, after which we had a grand supper, gotten up by ladies of the place. While the Senator was speaking some drunken shoemaker called him a liar, I at once took it up and went down to thrash him, but before I got there the boys in blue had sent him flying from the crowd; my resentment of the insult to their Senator made me very popular not only with him, but all his friends. I spoke in that county several times, winding up in that part of the State at a small town called Newport; our meeting was not large, but it was about the gayest meeting I ever attended; one half of the audience were young ladies and a prettier set I never saw, they sung songs after I was done speaking until midnight, when we adjourned to the hotel and partook of a hearty supper, after wich I left in company with Sheriff Peacock who had taken me to all my meetings in the county, and with whom I stayed while in Bridgeton; he is a tiptop man, and has as fine a family as the county can produce.

On my way back to Camden I learned that Professor Lovejoy of Maryland was to hold a debate with one of the Camden Democrats at a small town on my road up. I concluded to stop and take a hand in it, therefore when within a mile or so of the place I got off the cars and stayed with a friend until the time for the meeting, when I quietly went in and took a seat in a back corner. As soon as they had made their speeches, a motion was made to adjourn, when J. W. Hazleton who knew I was there, raised up and moved that they now organize a mass meeting to hear the Buckeye Blacksmith, who was now in the room, make a speech; this took the whole crowd by surprise, as but a few knew I was there. The motion carried and I walked forward and was introduced, the whole Democratic party of the neighborhood was there to hear the debate, which was lucky for me, to have a chance to give them my views on the subject. This Democrat had alluded to me several times in his speech, as though he would like to have a chance at me in a debate, so when I commenced, I told the audience that I had accidently dropped into their meeting and had been very much amused at the remarks of the very learned gentleman who had last spoken, particularly when he said he would like to get hold of me, and now that I was here he had a chance to get into the Bears hands, and if he chose to attempt it, his mother would'nt know he was out, when he got through with me; why said I, his whole theme has been the nigger, it was nigger when he began, and nigger when he closed, he seems to have a bad opinion of the nigger, as he calls him; possibly he has a right to have, possibly some colored lady has given him the cold shoulder at some time, if so, he is excuseable for his opposition to them; and turning to him, said, was you ever sacked by a colored girl? He sung out no sir. This brought the house down with thunders of applause, and as soon as it subsided, I turned to him again and said, do you still want to get hold of the "Buckeye"? This brought down the house again, and thus I went on until there was not greese enough left of him to fry a mosquito, when the meeting adjourned with loud and long cheers for the "Buckeye", and I'll bet my head that he will never tell another audience, that he would like to get hold of the "Buckeye Blacksmith", that will be a night long to be remembered by those that were present.

I left the next morning and spoke in Camden county some three times, closing the night before the election, at a place called the Flat Iron, in the surburbs of the city of Camden, where I met a drunken Democratic crowd, who had collected there to break up our meeting as they had done many others; but I pitched into them, I told them that by that time the next night they would be howling out of the other side of their mouths, that we would bury them so deep the next day, that even whisky would not be able to resurrect them. I made my speech in spite of them, and in closing told them that I could thrash the best man they had among their cowardly crew, if they dared to come forward to the light, but it was no go.

I finished my speech and came away with flying colors, crossed over to Philadelphia and the next morning took the cars and arrived home in Baltimore at one o'clock, in time to vote for Grant and Colfax, and thus ended that campaign.

CHAPTER XIV.

APPOINTED A SPECIAL AGENT IN TREASURY DEPARTMENT.—GUBERNATORIAL CAMPAIGN IN PENNSYLVANIA.—CONGRESSIONAL CAMPAIGN IN MARYLAND.—THE PREACHER AND THE WASPS.—STRIKE A LIGHT OLD WOMAN, I'M ALL UNRAVELLING.

THE ELECTION was over, Grant was elected, but I was very much broken down in health, after eight months hard labor. I had but little money, out of employment and surrounded by Democrats that only pointed the finger of scorn at me. Whenever they met me, I tried various plans to get something to do, but tried in vain; I got up a small useful article, that every family needed, and tried to sell that, but they would tell me that I was too black for them, and refused to buy of me, and some of the very men that pointed me out as a nigger worshipper at that time and kept many persons from buying from me, are this day holding office in the Baltimore Custom house. This shows the principles of designing politicians, use you when they want you and kick you after they are done with you, this has been my experience through life.

As soon as Congress assembled in December, I went to Washington and got all the leading Republican members of both houses to sign a petition to Mr. Webster, to put me back in my old place. I had thirty Senators and fifty members of the house to ask him to put me back, but he refused to do so, giving as a reason, that it would be a bid for Grant to keep him in his office, and thus I was left to work my way through the winter, the best I could. The 4th of March came at last and although I had worked eight long months, and went through as many hardships as any man ever did, I could not raise money to go and see him take his seat. But my organ of hope was large, and I looked forward to better days. I intended to apply for a special agency in the Treasury Department, as soon as Grant had his cabinet made up and concluded that I must do something to show the department that I had a capacity for that branch of business. There were rumors of fraud in one of the internal revenue districts of Baltimore, that the Assesor was playing in the hands of the whisky ring, so in connection with another gentleman, I went to work and made out a very strong case against him. I took the proofs to Washington and laid them before Commissioner Delano, whose solicitor pronounced them strong enough to remove any man. Mr. Boutwell at once removed him, but lo and behold, that same man has lately been appointed to office again in the Custom house; this is the way politicians do business; as soon as I made out a case out against him, I went to see President Grant and made my wants known to him, he at once sent me to the Treasury Department and in two hours after I was appointed one of the special agents of that department at five dollars a day, and went home with flying colors, but by some hook or crook in sixty two days after I was discharged. I went to Washington and could get no reason for it, neither could I find out by whom it was done.

Mr. O. D. Madge, the head of my department went to work and raised some money, to pay my expences in Pennsylvania to stump the State for Gov. Geary, who was runing for his second term.

I started and went to Philadelphia, where I made a few speeches around the suburbs of the city, and then left for the western part of the State; my first appointment was in Waynesburg, the county town of Greene county, one of the most rabid Democratic counties of the State; indeed this county bordering as it did on Virginia, gave the government more trouble during the war to keep them in subjection than any county in the State. It was court week, and the day of court when the the most of the people of the county were in town, I consequently had a very large meeting; I had all the leading Copperheads of the county at my meeting, as well as all the leading Republicans, including Hon. J. B. Donley the member of Congress of that district, who I found to be a live and active Republican, one of the best in the county. My meeting was at one o'clock and as I had never spoken there before, all were very anxious to hear me. I had all the Democratic speakers and principal men in the county to hear me, I therefore expected a pretty lively time of it, but had no fears but that I would come out all right.

I was introduced and commenced by referring to myself as being a plain, uneducated man and therefore should not attempt to make anything but a plain speech. I then told them, that from my long experience in politics I had become fully satisfied that the masses of the people, without regard to their political views, were honest, that what the people wanted is truth, this they could not get from the Democratic leaders; I told them there was not a Democratic speaker, from his honor the judge of the court, down to their commonest speaker in the county, who would meet me on the issues which divided the two parties, and stick to the question. They are going to have a meeting to-night, said I, and they will tell you all about a nigger; they even know how many bones he has in his feet; they will tell you that his nose is flat, his lips thick, his heel long, and all that kind of talk, but this is not the issue that we have to meet; the true issue before the people to day is; shall those who sacrificed their blood and treasure to save the Union rule it, or those who did all they could to destroy it? Now the question is this: how many of you Greene county Democrats aided in putting down the rebellion, and how many of you aided in furnishing the fuel to keep up the flames of rebellion! You who assisted in putting it down have a right to say in this matter, and you who did not, I would advise to take a back seat and keep your mouths shut.

I went on in this way pitching into them for at least two hours, they looking daggers at me all the time, but I cared nothing for that, for I had friends enough to sustain me. What few Republicans there are in the county are made of the right material, they know their rights and have manhood enough to maintain them.

That night the unterrified held their meeting; they had two speakers, the first one was a Doctor Patton, a very intelligent man, but not a very good speaker.— He raved and foamed about what I had said, misquoted much of my speech and seemed to be angry at me for telling beforehand what he wanted to say about the nigger; but he pitched into the nigger and dissected him pretty well. He proved at least to the satisfaction of some of his hearers that the nigger was not exactly a human being.

The next speaker was a man by the name of Crawford, he was a much better orator than the doctor. He pitched into me rough shod, but did it in such nice style that I could not help but admire his tact in getting a laugh on me. (I always liked a good joke if it did turn the laugh on myself.) This speaker also gave the nigger more attention than he gave any other subject. (I would here remark that I defy any Democratic speaker in this nation to make a speech thirty minutes long, without naming the word nigger, it can't be done. What! a democratic speech without the nigger, that would be ridiculous.)

I left the next morning for Carmichaels, a small town in the same county. Here I met some very good men of both parties; here I found the greatest opposition against Gov. Geary that I had yet found. He had made a speech there the year before in the Grant campaign, which had given some offense, and I had hard work to heal up the sore that he had made, but I did it by appealing to their love of Republicanism, to vote the party ticket.

From here I went to Brownsville in Fayette county. It was the week of their Fair; the town was full of people, which enabled us to get up a monster out-door meeting. Here also I met plenty of the unterrified, many of them being full of Democratic argument, (whisky) were quite noisy, but there were too many of the boys in blue present to permit any trouble from them, and after two or three of their most noisy ones got knocked down for their insults, the rest took the hint and behaved themselves.

The next night I had a meeting in West Brownsville, a small place on the west side of the river, in Washington county. Here I met the most degraded drunken crew that I ever saw; they were determined that I should not speak that night, and some of my friends advised me not to attempt it, for fear of an outbreak, but the Brownsville boys knew what kind of a place it was, and came over in full strength to sustain me while I made my speech. From there I went to Bellville and spoke to a large out-door meeting and walked nine miles next morning before breakfast, in order to take the boat to Pittsburg, having received orders from the State Committee to return to the eastern counties to speak.

When I returned to Philadelphia I found that the Delaware county committee had engaged my services for that county as the only person who could reconcile the disaffection that existed in that county among our own party. Geary had become so unpopular with the best men, owing to the unwise use he had made of the pardoning power, that there were great fears that we would lose the county, and in addition to this, the oldest paper we had in the county was out against not only Geary, but two of the county nominees.

I went there and filled a series of appointments from that until the election. Our plan was to take a horse and wagon and ride around all day among the people, invite them personally to come and hear me speak, and in that way got them out to our meeting through friendship to me, when nothing else could have gotten them out, then through my earnest appeals to their party prejudice and my good humored way of coaxing them we were able to carry the county by nearly its usual majority.

My plan was to get them to our meetings, tell them a few good stories, and then make an appeal to their patriotism, speak of how they had stood by the party and our country in our darkest hours, and now because one man had made a mistake and committed an error, no doubt of the head and not of the heart, we must not forsake the old ship, and let her fall into the hands of the very piratical crew that we had spent so much money and sacrificed so much blood to overpower, and keep from sinking the very ship that we are about to surrender into their hands, by refusing to support the ticket that the party had given us.

By my earnest appeals and constant labor both day and night for several weeks we were able as above stated to save the county. On the night before the election I spoke at Marcus Hook at eight o'clock and then rode in a buggy nine miles, (the horse ran away and upset us once) and made another long speech, and then back nine miles more the same night. This my dear reader is the way that I have worked for my party, and that without pay or any other reward than their thanks. The morning of election I took leave of all my Delaware county friends and these were not a few, and returned home crowned with laurels, but had no money. I went to Washington again to try for something to do, when Mr. Madge my former head officer had me reappointed back in my old place, and where through his influence, as one of the best friends I ever had, I have ever since remained. I went to work as an assistant to special agent, J. B. Morris, who was located at Baltimore, and who was a good Pennsylvania Republican and have had a very pleasant time with him since we have been together.

As I was now in a situation which I expected to keep, I again made up my mind to let politics alone, but one of my greatest faults through life has always been whenever I took sides for any man, I would stop at nothing that was fair to aid in electing him. Accordingly in 1870 I had a friend, Wm. M. Marine, an enterprising young lawyer who I had known as a friend and advocate of human liberty. I knew him to be sound on all of the great questions of reform and progress of the present day. He was a candidate for the nomination for Congress in my district; I felt that he deserved it. He being an excellent speaker, I concluded to stump the district with him in favor of his nomination. We did so, and had a very fine time of it; we had large and respectable audiences wherever we went, we carried every election district we spoke in.— The result was, that my friend was nominated but the district being six thousand against him he was not elected. Mr. James A. Gary was the nominee in the fifth district, and there being a large colored vote in that district it was supposed that we could carry it for him

The colored people having heard of my speaking, in the second district for my friend Marine, insisted on my being sent among them. I therefore concluded to go through the lower counties of this district and speak for him. Mr. J. H. Butler a very prominent speaker of Baltimore agreed to accompany me, so we got a first class horse and carriage and started, this was the gayest campaign I had ever had. The whites were generally bitterly opposed to me, they thought it terrible for a white man to ride around speaking with a negro. We had to eat and sleep with the colored people in most places, as the whites would not keep us, but that was only fun for me, for I have always thought that a colored patriot was a better man than a white rebel, so I preferred staying with them.

The first place we went to was Calvert county, where we had a very large meeting, we had all the white rebels of the neighborhood there looking as mad as the devil at me, but I cared nothing for that, I pitched into them, I told the colored people that their getting a vote had rather upset the Democrats, they reminded me of an old preacher who had a pair of buckskin breeches that he always wore over his pants in the Winter to keep the cold out, and during the Summer they were hung in the garret out of the way. In the Fall a number of wasps crawled into them to avoid the cold, and finally froze there. One cold morning the old man told his daughter Betsy to get his leather breeches for him, she got them, he put them on with the legs full of frozen wasps, he went to the church and found a warm stove, and soon after he began to preach the heat of the room soon thawed the wasps into life, and just in the midst of the sermon one of them stung him on the leg; he slapped down his hand and began to rub, which set several others to stinging, and him to rubbing worse than ever, until the whole audience became interested in knowing what was wrong, when the man looked up and said, "brethren the spirit of the Lord is in my heart, but the devil is in my breeches;" so it is, said I, with these white gentlemen, (pointing to them.) The spirit of Democracy is in their hearts, but your voting has put the devil in their breeches. This raised a great laugh among the colored people.

I then asked the colored people if these white gentlemen were not trying to get their votes, they sung out "yes." Why that is funny said I, they used to call you damned niggers, did'nt they? "Yes they did," cried out an old man; they used to say you had flat noses and thick lips, and long heels, and crooked shins, and curley hair, did'nt they? "Yes bless the lord they did," cried a dozen voices; yes said I, and they said more than that, they said you stunk like the devil; "that's the god's truth," cried out an old black woman; "hear him men," said she, "every word the man says is true, bless the Lord I know it." I told them that their duty was a plain one, they must stand by the party that gave them their manhood, they must stand by themselves, and see that their rights were not taken away from them. And their votes since show that they not only know their rights but are determined to take care of them.

We had a monster meeting at Port Tobacco, in Charles county, there were a large crowd of rebels at it. I told the colored people that their getting a vote had put the Democrats in a bad way. I told them it reminded me of a man in Ohio, who was in the habit of coming home drunk every few nights, (he was a Democrat of course, said I,) and his wife always set a bowl of bread and milk on the table for him to have a lunch when he came home. So one night one of the children dropped a small ball of silk thread from her work basket into the bowl of bread and milk, the mother not noticing it went to bed. John came home, got his milk and bread and went to work eating it, while doing so he swallowed the ball of thread the loose end of it sticking between his teeth; he felt something tickling him in the throat, he said what in the devil does all this mean, and began pulling it out, but before he had got more than a yard or two out, he got frightened and sung out Peggy, Peggy. She jumped out of bed and said, John don't make such a noise, you will waken the whole neighborhood. I don't care a durn, strike a light woman, strike a light, I am all unravelling. That is the way with these white gentlemen, (pointing to them,) your right to vote has unravelled them, they don't hardly know what to do, and I would not be surprised to see them before the election, picking up your little colored children in the streets and kissing them, and swearing they are the prettiest children they ever seen, that they look like their father, all for the sake of getting the father's vote. You are not a damned nigger now, you are our colored fellow citizen now aint you, said I? "Hallelujah to de lamb, every word de man is saying is the God's truth," said an old man.

Then if this is true, stand by your manhood, since you are men, and don't suffer these men to mislead you on the day of election, and if they can buy poor white men's votes for whisky, teach them that the black man has more self-respect than to suffer himself to be bought with a glass of whisky or at any other price.

Gen. A. E. King one of the finest and most popular speakers in the State, in company with Mr. Gary and other able speakers, met Butler and I at all the mass meetings that were held in the district. In the interval between these meetings Butler and I would hold one or two small meetings every day. We had a large barbecue in St. Mary's county, where I think there are about as many conceited Democratic lawyers as I ever met; they challenged me for a debate, I accepted it, both parties were to be there, (these white Democrats had no objection to eat the niggers bread and meat when they could get it, but were above voting with them.)

Well these lawyers had a speech written out, and it mattered not who made the speech, they all made the same one. I got hold of it, and when we met to have the debate, I spoke first and made his speech and replied to it in advance of him; this of course took the wind out of his sails and left him unprepared to answer me, he got very angry, charging me with unfairness, but I contended that I had a right to suppose that he was going to say just what I had told the people he would, for said I there are fourteen speakers of your party in the county, and every one of you make the same speech, you have but one and can make no other. This raised a great laugh, and one old Democrat said that he was ashamed of his party for letting a Blacksmith beat them out as I had. This lawyer had an arm full of books with him, but I told the people what he would read out of them, so when he would read from a book the whole crowd would laugh, I having read the same from a piece of paper. Butler made the closing speech, and I don't think that lawyer will want to meet us again in a debate.

We had a very large meeting at Bryantown, the home of Dr. Mudd of Dry Tortugus notoriety, As soon as I was done speaking the doctor demanded a right to reply to me, he said they never allowed a man to speak there without a reply, I told him all right, and he mabe a reply, but not being a very good speaker, made but a very poor attempt. Butler followed him and before he was done with him, he had even the doctors white friends laughing at him.

Thus butler and I travelled from place to place, for nearly six weeks, eating and drinking, sleeping and speaking together, and I must say that I never had a more pleasant companion in all my travels. Butler is a glorious good fellow, if he is a colored man.

Although we returned home without accomplishing

our object, viz; the election of Mr. Gary, we felt satisfied that we had not only discharged our duty to him, but to the Republican cause.

I received much praise for the manner in which I conducted that campaign, by some of the leading men of the party, particularly the Hon. J. L. Thomas the collector of the port of Baltimore, who I consider one of the best Republicans in the State; and who I am certain was one of the best collectors Baltimore ever had, my official relations with him for four years satisfied me that he is an honest man, and I challenge any Port in the United States to produce a more honest or faithful set of men than his subordinate officers were the day he left the Custom House.

It was my duty as an officer, to look after his men, and see that they attend well to their business, and I am proud to say that with few exceptions I always found them prompt to duty.

CHAPTER XV.

SETTLED DOWN TO BUSINESS.—STUMPING IN PENNSYLVANIA.—"PEGGY WHEN DID I SWALLOW THOSE GOSLINGS."—GREELY BROKE UP THE DEMOCRATIC PARTY.—SPEAKING IN NEW JERSEY.—ADVICE TO YOUNG MEN.

ON MY return from my tour with Butler, I settled down to business again and although very much broken down by constant travelling and speaking both day and night. I soon rallied again to my usual health and strength, and from that time until July 1872 mingled but very little in politics, but continued to assist special agent Morris in the business of our office, with whom I get along on the most friendly terms, nothing occurring to mar our happiness, and I am very certain, that the last four years have been the happiest years of my life, and I sincerely hope that we may be spared to pass four more years as pleasantly together as we have the former, having devoted the best part of my life to the service of my party I think it nothing but fair, now that I am old, that the party should take care of me, which I have no doubt they will so long as I conduct myself in a proper manner.

General Grant having received the nomination for his second term, with that great and good man, Henry Wilson for Vice President, I concluded to take the stump in Pennsylvania, in support of them, and about the first of July started for that field of labor. I had not been there many days before I found that Grant would gain an easy victory, the old dyed-in-the-wool Democrats would not swallow Greely, he had said too many hard things about them in former years for them to bite at the bait, we had however a hard fight before us. General Hartranft was our candidate for Governor, and Buckalew his competitor was very popular and hard to beat. In addition to that Hartranft was unpopular owing to the many falsehoods that the Democracy had trumped up against him, and instead of the fight being between Grant and Greely it was pretty much entirely between Hartranft and Buckalew. I was not long in finding out Buckalew's weak points, one of which was his speech and vote in the Senate of Pennsylvania the winter before, on what was known as the Screen Bill; this speech and vote were very unpopular among the miners throughout the State. I prepared myself with the official journals of the Senate and went down to the mining regions of the State, and pitched into him, with my documents to prove what I said, and I have no doubt but these journals had very much to do with his defeat, as it was impossible for him or his friends to get around them.

I had considerable fun with the Democrats about Greely; I asked them if they thought he was an honest man, some one would sing out yes, when I would reply, well let us see what he says about you and your party, and then read an article from his paper calling them thieves and drunkards and every other vile name he could think of, and then ask them what they thought of that, if he is honest he wont lie, and if he don't lie you are a thundering hard party, at least your own candidate says so. I had a large meeting at Shamokin, one of the strongholds of the Democracy, when I asked them why they had taken Greely as their candidate, or had he been forced on them by their leaders? I know you hate him, I feel sorry for you, it is a pill you hate to swallow, but you can't help it, bitter as it is you have to take it.

I told them it put me in mind of a fellow who came home very tight, (he was a Democrat of course,) and felt sick, and called his wife to get him a bucket for he must throw up. She took the light and went to the kitchen for one, but he was too sick to wait for her and seeing something behind the stove that looked like a bucket, he emptied the whisky out of his stomach into that, but instead of it being a bucket it was a basket full of young goslings, that she had put there to keep them warm. The goslings began to squirm around not liking the smell of his whisky, when she came with the light and he saw the goslings he turned to his wife and said: in the name of God Peggy, when did I swallow all these goslings? So in the name of God how could the Democratic party swallow Horace Greely? This created a loud and long laugh, many of the old Democrats joining in it heartily.

I had a large meeting in Lock Haven, another stronghold of Democracy and had plenty of them at my meeting. I told the people that I had not one word to say against Mr. Greeley, for I considered him one of the best men that ever lived; he had done more for the benefit of this country than any man living, and indeed I consider that he has done more than all the men put together that ever did live in the country. Henry Clay, Daniel Webster and all the leading men of the nation labored and died without accomplishing the object they had in view. The great Whig party existed fifty years and failed to do the job. Mr. Lincoln in the Presidential chair, with Grant at the head of the army could not do it. But Horace Greeley stepped in and has done the job without charging a cent for his labor, for which he deserves the thanks of this Nation. That is he has broken up the Democratic party, and if that does not entitle him to the thanks of the country, I should like to know what would; this created considerable skuffling among the unterrified, and laughter among the Republicans.

I spoke at several other meetings on my way out to Lawrence county, where I intended to pass some time, in order to fight the Democratic candidate for Congress; he had been elected two years before by a split in the Republican party of that county, he having beaten a bosom friend of mine by that means. I felt determined to beat him this time if possible, I went to Lawrence and commenced speaking, charging him with certain votes in Congress the winter before, which he and his friends denied, charging me with falsehoods and demanding the proof; I had no proof further than newspaper proof, which they denied. I was determined not to be beat, so I left some of my appointments to be filled by other speakers and left for Washington city in order to get the journals of Congress to prove the truth of what I had said.

As soon as I had left they said that I would never return, that I had taken that method of getting away, but they had missed their mark, for I went as fast as the cars would carry me, and drew a half months salary, and bought out of my own money the whole set of journals of the winter before and the same night took the cars back, and in three days from the time I started I was back among them fully armed and equipped to make good every word that I had said about his votes, and then made appointments through three of the counties composing his district. My journals struck them like a bombshell, wherever I went, his friends would deny what I said and challenge me for the proof, when I would open my big book and ask them to step forward and read it for themselves, this was a settler. They were unable to answer it and

I have no doubt but that those journals were the means of uniting the Republicans in Lawrence and Beaver counties and of his defeat; I spoke in all the principal places in three counties, producing my documents on all occasions and inviting the people to examine them for themselves.

The Pittsburg and other papers through the district gave me great praise for my energy in procuring the proofs of the charges that I made and the labor I performed in laying them before the people; I certainly labored as hard in these three counties as ever I did in my life, and think that I am entitled to some credit for what I did. There are but few as poor as I was, that would have taken their own means and went four hundred miles and bought documents, to carry one congressional district. But I was determind to beat him and I did beat him, this has always been a great fault of mine, to spend all I ever made in trying to promote my party. If I had have been a little more selfish and looked after my own interest as well as I did the interest of my party, it would have been better for me; but I never think of myself when my country or party need my services, neither have I ever counted the cost, but go ahead at all hazards, believing in the old proverb, that duty before pleasure is the best motto.

I closed the campaign in Pennsylvania on Saturday before the election and returned home to wait the result. It was generally conceded, that if Hartranft carried the State, that there would be no more meetings held, as all knew that Buckalew would get more votes than Greeley, as there were thousands of Democrats that would not vote for Greeley that would for him, therefore the fight was entirely on the Governor and Congressional vote, the most crazy Democrat in the State had no hope of electing Greeley.

When I got home, every person I met wanted to know how Pennsylvania was going for Governor. I told them that Hartranft would be elected by at least twenty five thousand majority. They would look at each other and laugh, and some said I had gone crazy, they had been led to believe that Buckalew would certainly be elected, and I think he would have been, if the election had taken place six weeks before it did, as Hartranft's friends had not at that time prooved the charges brought against him by the opposition to be false, which we did during the last six weeks of the campaign to the entire satisfaction of all honorable and thinking men of both parties; a deeper or more villainous scheme was never invented, than the one they got up to defeat the wishes of the people and them into support of Buckalew their candidate, but it failed.

The day of the election I left for New Jersey, to speak in the first congressional district in favor of my old friend, J. W. Hazleton, who was running for his second term. The Democrats had taken up a liberal Republican, a great friend of Mr. Greeley, against him and were expecting to carry enough Republican votes to elect him easy. They were very bitter against Hazleton, he was and had been for many years a leading temperance man, and that was enough for them, for everybody knows, that bad whisky has ever been a leading commodity in their stock of trade. This liberal Republican candidate of theirs lived in Vineland City, where Mr. Greeley owned property, and where he oftened visited and lectured, and consequently had a number of warm Republican friends, who would vote for him, this they thought would enable them to beat Hazleton. As soon as I got there and began speaking they met me and challenged me to debate with their candidate, I of course accepted, and a meeting was arranged, but when the time arrived my opponent failed to put in an appearance, but sent a substitute in his place. He was a very clever fellow, but knew but little about politics, so it was not much trouble to put him to flight.

I commenced my debate by stating that the only principles that the opposition had yet advanced, that I had heard of, was anything to beat Grant. Now I will ask the gentleman who is to follow me to tell us why they have such a desire to beat Grant. Is it because the day he was elected four years ago, that our bonds were worth but seventy two cents on the dollar, in the bank of England, while their own bonds were worth ninety three, and to-day our bonds are worth ninety three and a half, and theirs are worth but ninety two and a half, or is it because that our bonds were only worth in Frankfort the great money centre of Germany, sixty nince cents on the dollar, while theirs were worth ninety six four years ago, and to-day our's are ninety six cents while theirs are worth but ninety five. Or is it because the day Grant was elected that gold was worth one dollar and thirty seven cents, and to-day it is worth but one dollar and fourteen; or is it because the day Grant was elected you could buy a hundred dollar bond for seventeen dollars less than you could a hundred dollars of gold, and to-day you can get a hundred dollars of gold for four dollars less than you can get a hundred dollar bond.

Now I submit it not only to the gentleman who is to follow me, but to every candid man present, if they have ever known or heard of any Government, whose paper bonds were worth more than their par value at home, except ours, and if ever ours were until now, these statements that I dave made are facts known to every man who now hears me, and of which every man is proud.

I would here ask the gentleman to tell us what has brought about all these happy results, and for fear he will fail to inform us, I will give you some of the reasons which produced them.

When the war was over, and Andrew Johnson became the President, he undertook to control the Government independent of Congress, thereby bringing himself in direct conflict with the legislative branch of the same; the result was not only the people of our own country, but the Government of the whole world lost confidence in our ability to meet our obligations, the result was we had no credit at home or abroad, but as soon as General Grant took charge of the helm of State, in unison with the great Republican party who had achieved so much, confidence became at once restored and the result was brought about, our credit began to improve abroad as well as at home; gold began to fall, and our bonds to increase in value and demand, until to-day there is no Government on earth whose credit either at home or abroad, stands as high as ours, then why change it, why not let good enough alone.

Suppose you elect Mr. Greeley, what could he do with both branches of Congress against him? Do you want another dead lock between Congress and the President for four years more, as we had under Johnson? I say God forbid it, rather let us go on under our gallant leader General Grant, who is in full sympathy with Congress on all questions that pertain to the welfare of our country. This argument had the effect that I desired, it pretty nearly shut the mouth of my opponent as he was unable to answer it.

In his reply he had considerable to say about the great principles of the Democratic party, saying that it was principles and not men that his party advocated, but failed to tell us what those principles were, making as all who heard him acknowledged, a very poor attempt at a speech. In my reply to him, I asked what those principles were that the gentleman had been talking about, he certainly having failed to tell us, and I had many doubts whether he or any other man present could give us the information, it would be a pretty hard thing to perform. I once heard an anecdote related on that subject, which ran thus:

An old minister dreamed that as he went to church

on Sunday, he met the devil on the road, who accused him of being selfish in denying that he (the devil) had any power on earth. Well I don't believe that you have, said the minister; the devil replied I will prove that I have, provided you will give me credit for it publicly, after I have done so. The minister not believing that he could do anything, agreed to it. Now said the devil I will do any three things that you propose or I will give it up. Well said the minister pull up that big white oak tree that stands there; he thought in his dream that the devil took hold of it and pulled it up as though it had been a straw, and laughed at the old man. Now for your next job. Well said the minister, level down this rocky mountain into the valley and make it smoothe; the devil he thought put his arms around it and drew it down into the valley making it level. This frightened the old man somewhat, the devil only laughed at him and said come on, you have one chance more; the old man studied a moment to think of what he should tell him to do, all at once the idea struck him, handing the devil a pencil and piece of paper told him to sit down and write out the principles of the Democratic party in New Jersey. The devil looked him in the eye for a few minutes and then began to cry, saying you have got me there Parson that is more than I bargained for, and bidding the old deacon good morning, he walked away; this raised a good laugh, and concluded my reply by saying that I supposed that it would puzzle even the devil to tell what their principles were.

That one debate satisfied them, for they found that they had no child to deal with when they got hold of me, I was too well posted on all the political questions of the day for them to attempt and argue the issues that were before the people, with me. A few days after my debate, Mr. Hazelton sent a gentleman to assist me in Salem county, by the name of Peck, who I found to be not only a very intelligent gentleman, but a first class speaker. His manner of speaking was somewhat different from mine, he made very strong appeals to the finer feelings of the people, showing strong reason why they should stand by Grant and the party, while I used my documents and pitched into the Democrats, using many of my anecdotes to make the people laugh.

Mr. Peck being a writer of some note in the Washington papers, as well as an employee of the Treasury department, he was well posted on all of the live issues of the day, which made him a very agreeable companion as well as a very suitable speaker to travel with me. Mr. Hazleton knowing this arranged it for him and I to travel together, which we did for some two weeks, speaking every day and some days twice. The people of Salem county as well as through West Jersey are generally a very sociable as well as hospitable class of people, the result was Mr. Peck and I had a very pleasent time while among them, they fed us on the best and gave us a hearty welcome wherever we went.

I was so much pleased with Mr. Hazleton's treatment while in his district that I hope his constituents will have the good sense to nominate him next year for a third term, for I am very certain they could not get a better man, if they do Mr. Peck and I will stump his district for him if we live.

I left New Jersey a few days before the election fully satisfied that our labors would be crowned with success.

The result of my labors in that district were crowned with glorious success, instead of Hazelton having two thousand majority as he had two years before, he had near seven thousand this time, and his opponent left the district a few days after in perfect disgust, to seek retirement in some more congenial latitude. I returned home in time to vote, pretty much worn down by my arduous labors for near four months. I have become old and can't stand the hardships I once could, and I often wonder how I have been able to undergo what I have. Neither will it ever be known in the world what I have endured for my party and its principles, and now when I am old and not able to work after having devoted all the best part of my life to the service of my party, many of those who now hold an office and are enjoying the fruits of my labor, have tried to deprive me of the small place that I have and thus deprive me in my old days of a means of getting a living.

Thus it is and always has been with politicians, you are everything when they want you and nothing when they are done with you. If it was the last advice that ever I expected to give to a young man, I would tell him to beware of a tricky politician, for they are not to be trusted, and I do assure you, that had I my life to live over again that I would never be one, but as it is I expect to devote the few remaining days of my life to the service of my party. Being too old to commence a different calling, and having made politics the study of my life, I am now unfit for any other business.

And although I have devoted the best part of a long and eventful life, to the interests of my party and its principles, without saving a dollar to support me in my declining years, yet I have the glorious satisfaction of knowing that I have lived to see, and to aid in the overthrow of the two greatest evils that ever cursed our glorious country, viz: the destruction of slavery and the Democratic party. I was fully satisfied for more than thirty years past, that in order to destroy that party, that it was necessary to take from it the props that held it up, slavery being one of its main pillars, hence destroy it and the party must fall for the want of support.

The Democratis party never had but two pillars upon which to stand, or upon which it has stood for fifty years, they were slavery and whisky, destroy them and you will hear but little more of the Democratic party. I have lived to see the one destroyed and have spent half of my life in helping to do it, and sincerely hope that I may live to see the day when their last prop will be knocked from under them.

And now before closing this little narative of my life and travels, I wish to say that no doubt but that I have made many grammatical errors, and many very pleasing incidents have been omitted, having written this work entirely from memory and it embracing a period of over sixty years, it could not be expected that I could recollect every thing that should have been mentioned in a work like this. And if it had not been that I have the greatest memory of places, times and occurrances, of any man living, I could not have possibly written this book. Being as I was deprived in early life of an education, I was compelled to depend upon my memory for all business purposes, it became very sharp, and old as I am I could describe almost every place that I ever spoke at in the last forty years; but not being a writer I have left out of their place very many of my best anecdotes as well as many pleasing incidents that have occured during my travels. Many of the anecdotes that I have used in this book, were original with me, I having used the most of them thirty years ago, and therefore they may appear stale to you, having heard them before, but still I was the author of most of them.

My dear reader I have given you in my own plain way, some of my political experience, travels and labor in politics, as well as many of the incidents which have occurred during my eventful life, hoping that it may not only prove interesting to many of my friends who may read it, but also be instructive in a political point of view. It has been my aim and desire in presenting what I have written, to introduce nothing but the truth in as plain and condensed manner as my limited education would admit of, and I feel very certain that all who are personally acquainted with me, and have a knowledge of my labor for and devotion to my party, will fully appreciate not only my little book, but my energy and labor, as well as my motive in placing this history before the public; for I do most positively assure them that at my age of life, I never should have undertaken such a task, if it had not been that I was poor and although holding a small office, which at the best is an uncertain means of a living not knowing what hour I may be dismissed, and supposing that with this little history, I could make a living the the balance of my life, I was advised by my friend, Special Agent Morris to attempt the task of placing this volume before the public, hoping that it may be as acceptable to them as my speeches have always appeared to be.

And I will here take occasion to assure my friends that let my days be many or few, whenever the party needs my services and I am able to obey their call, that they will always find me ready and willing, as I ever have been to assist in the great cause of republicanism, no matter in what circumstances I may be placed.

But before closing this history I have a few thoughts to give to my young readers, hoping they may receive it kindly as coming from a friend, for I mean it in no other than a kind spirit, my first advice is, under all circumstances and in whatever position you may be placed, obey and respect your parents, for in doing this, you not only have the promise of the life that now is, but of that which is to come. It has been my experience through life, that whenever I found a young man who obeyed and respected his parents, he always succeeded well, and was universally respected, but on the other hand, I scarcely ever knew one who disobeyed and maltreated his parents but turned out to be a poor miserable wretch, unfit for any other society than the lowest dregs, and nearly always came to some bad end.

The best thing for a young man to do, is to learn a trade and be content with making an honest living, and be sure to let politics alone, for it has ruined a hundred where it has ever benefited one, for I do assure you that but few men ever made much money out of politics honestly, therefore if you wish to lead an honest and virtuous life, you had better stick to your trade and let politics take care of itself; it will lead you to the drinking saloons, where you will contract the habit of indulging in those drunken brawls that so often occur in those places, I therefore advise you to make this the rule of your life, never to touch or taste intoxicating drinks of any kind, for I do most positively assure you that you cannot receive any real benefit from it. Alcohol, according to the opinion of the most learned men that ever lived, in all its various forms and degrees of strength is a poison, and forever at war with man's nature. It is indigestable and cannot be converted into a nourishment, but is a highly inflamable stimulant, it is calculated to irritate the stomach, corrupt your blood, inflame your liver and weaken the brain, it is a witch to your senses, a devil to your soul, a beggar's companion, a wife's woe and children's sorrow, and I am very certain that the corner stone of the first still house that was ever built, was manufactured in hell. Its first production was a liquid fire, a material devil that has blasted not only the beauty of many of the fair women of our land, but the prospects of thousands of the best men the world ever knew. I therefore advise all young men to shun it as you would a viper.

I advise you to not only let politics and strong drink alone, but to make up your minds never to play any game or games of chance, for it is calculated to lead you into bad company and bad associations, that may finally lead you to ruin. I have known hundreds of young men with a fair start in life, with a brilliant career before them entirely ruined by allowing themselves led into gambling and drinking by beginning in a small and apparently innocent way. It is the temperate use of liquor that leads to drunkeness and innocent gambling that leads to greater crimes. I once knew a man of eminence, who was a brilliant member of Congress, and stood high before the American people as one of the leading men of the nation, but in an evil hour was led astray, and in less than five years from the time that he stood high in Congress, he became a poor, miserable, degraded drunkard, and finally died in one of the Southern cities, far from home and friends, a beggar. Thus my young friends you will see that gambling and drinking, (for they are twin brothers,) will not only ruin the poor mechanic and laboring man, but it has ruined many of the brightest intellects that our country or the world ever produced.

Don't let the example of some friend or neighbor of yours, who has always been a moderate drinker and never a drunkard, be the means of misleading you, although he has escaped the drunkards fate, you may not be as lucky as him, and before you are aware of it may fall a prey to its bewitching influences, I therefore advise you to let them alone. With these few lines of advice to my young friends, I bid you farewell.

www.ingramcontent.com/pod-product-compliance
Lightning Source LLC
Chambersburg PA
CBHW032056220426
43664CB00008B/1024